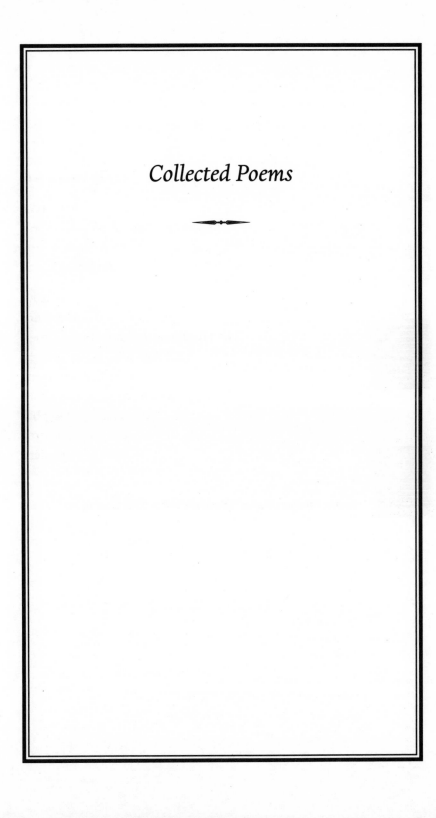

Collected Poems

Collected Poems

Vikram Seth

WEIDENFELD & NICOLSON

First published in Great Britain in 2015 by Weidenfeld & Nicolson

An imprint of the Orion Publishing Group Ltd Carmelite House, 50 Victoria Embankment, London EC4Y 0DZ, An Hachette UK Company

10 9 8 7 6 5 4 3 2 1

Mappings first published by Writers Workshop, Calcutta 1981

Some of the poems in *Mappings* have been published by *The Threepenny Review*, *London Magazine*, Sequoia Press and *Blue Unicorn*.

The Humble Administrator's Garden first published by Carcanet Press Ltd 1985

All You Who Sleep Tonight first published by Penguin Books India 1990

Three poems from the section 'In Other Voices' in *All You Who Sleep Tonight* were directly inspired by passages from the following books: *Ghalib: Life and Letters* by Ralph Russell and Khurshidul Islam (Harvard University Press); *Commandant of Auschwitz* by Rudolf Hoess (Weidenfeld); *Hiroshima Diary* by Michihiko Hachiya (The University of North Carolina Press). The author has been unable to trace the source of the poem 'Lithuania: Question and Answer'.

Three Chinese Poets first published in Great Britain by Faber and Faber Limited 1992
This translation copyright © Vikram Seth 1992

Beastly Tales from Here and There first published by Penguin Books India 1992

Arion and the Dolphin first published in Great Britain by Orion in 1994

Arion and the Dolphin was commissioned by the Baylis Programme of English National Opera with funds provided by the Arts Council of Great Britain. The composer was Alec Roth.

The Rivered Earth first published in Penguin Books 2011
Published by Weidenfeld & Nicolson 2015
Pipal leaf motif by kind permission of buddhapath.com

Summer Requiem first published in Great Britain by Weidenfeld & Nicolson 2015

A CIP catalogue record for this book is available from the British Library.

978 0 297 60878 3 (cased)

Typeset in Dante MT 12/14.75pt by Input Data Services Ltd, Bridgwater, Somerset

Printed and bound in Great Britain by Clays Ltd, St Ives plc

The Orion Publishing Group's policy is to use papers that are natural, renewable and recyclable products and made from wood grown in sustainable forests. The logging and manufacturing processes are expected to conform to the environmental regulations of the country of origin.

www.orionbooks.co.uk

to my parents
too often too far away

Despite the Distance
for Mama on her 61st birthday (1991)

I do not feel at all like writing wittily.
The house is empty and my mood is bleak.
To be with you today I flew from Italy
Though I'd have gladly stayed another week.
I know, of course, I should upbraid you bitterly
And growl as usual, and give way to pique;
  But still, I'm very glad to greet you here,
  In, if not on, your 62nd year.

Three stanzas, one for each of us, should show you
The measure of our feeling and our thought.
We can't begin to give you what we owe you,
Although we sometimes try – as children ought –
Nor do we love you less when we outgrow you
And seek to live our lives through what you've taught:
  Affection, independence, work and wit –
  Though we can't match your sacrifice and grit.

I hope, despite the distance to the hills,
The winding roads, the wild and windy weather,
Despite the drama of conflicting wills,
The claims of books and Buddhas, law and leather,
Magnetic Moons and diplomatic drills,
The family will spend some time together –
  And that, when we're apart, our love is what'll
  Act as your permanent hot-water bottle.

Small Things
for Papa on his 90th birthday (2013)

The start of all things, small or great
– My bronze Ganesh, embodied Om,
Tiny, but heavier than his weight –
I pack him first when leaving home.
But three things else, your gifts to me
Over the years – for use, not prayer –
Imbue me with your company,
However I may be, or where.

Your cufflinks, given in the hope
Your scruffy son might mend his ways –
Which (while he hasn't) help him cope
With airports, nervousness, and days
When the whole world seems crazy and
Two lesser globes give him at length
The sense that you are close at hand
To keep him sane and lend him strength.

The shaving brush I use each day
With fist and wrist to foam my face
In the old pre-millennial way
At my own pre-millennial pace:
I ask the eyes that stare at me,
What have I done or left undone?
What word today or deed would be
Worthy of you or of your son?

~

And your old watch, for nine pounds bought
In Norway fifty years ago –
Its mottled face so cleanly wrought,
Its hands with their nocturnal glow:
Nightly I wind it, and observe
Its fine red needle swivel fast,
Too fast, along creation's curve
From Om to Omega at last.

I hope you die before I do –
Not soon, but when you wish to go.
Both now and then, they'll speak of you:
The link, the touch, the tick, the glow.
More than the grace of trunk and tusk,
Your minor trinity will prove
– By lonely dawn or doubtful dusk –
The gift of courage and of love.

Contents

THE HUMBLE ADMINISTRATOR'S GARDEN (1985) 83

Note:

THE GOLDEN GATE: A NOVEL IN VERSE (1986)

This poem – or novel – of some 300 pages has not been included in the present volume. It is published by Faber & Faber.

Mappings

———◆———

1981

For Tim Steele & Donald Davie

Introduction to the 1994 Edition

I wrote the poems that appear in this book in my twenties, when I was a student in England and, later, California. Since I was studying Economics, not English, I stood outside the orbit of the latest critical theories, and did not realize that writing in rhyme and metre would make me a sort of literary untouchable. In due course, I sent my manuscript to almost every publisher I had heard of. After innumerable, increasingly painful rejections, I decided to typeset and publish it myself. I dedicated it to the two English teachers at Stanford who had gone out of their way to encourage, inspire, and (not least of all) criticize my efforts.

When the slim, stapled, paperbound volume of *Mappings* with its black and white cover came off the press in 1980, I proudly peddled it around various bookstores in the San Francisco Bay area. Not many, however, were willing to stock, let alone buy, the first fruits of my self-determined genius. I then forced copies on my friends and family, telling them to sell them if they could, and to give them away if they couldn't. Meanwhile, I went off to China for two years of travel and economic research. Although I had printed an address in the book for the benefit of enthusiastic readers who wished to re-order copies, I don't believe that anyone used it.

After a year in China, I returned home to Delhi for a visit. On a short trip to Calcutta I met Professor P. Lal, and he published *Mappings* in 1981 in an elegant orange sari-clad version under the imprint of the Writers Workshop. He was thus my

5

first publisher – and I, like many other Indian writers in English, owe him a debt of esteem and gratitude.

Ten years passed, and other matters took over my time and mind. Occasionally someone would tell me that they had read a copy of *Mappings* in a library or at the home of a friend. The book had gone out of print, and I had no thought of resuscitating it. Then I discovered that a second edition had been brought out by Writers Workshop in 1991, this time, unfortunately, peppered with misprints.

When my present publishers asked me for permission to republish *Mappings*, I hesitated. On the one hand, I was keen that the work should appear in an accurate version if it had to appear at all. On the other, I wondered about the poems themselves, some of which now struck me as embarrassingly callow. I did not wish to make my readers cringe by offering them a second helping of my juvenilia. But a friend (whose opinions are always forthright if sometimes eccentric) told me that she much preferred my voice in *Mappings* to that of my later books of poems. Whether I agreed with that slightly alarming judgement or not, I felt that I ought not to withdraw a book that had elicited it.

In the present edition, I have made a few amendments: I have excised two footnotes; removed the originals (more picturesque than helpful) of the four translated poems; and in two poems changed a word or phrase. In 'Guest', 'entirely' has been replaced by 'utterly'. In 'Moonless Night', the phrase 'the reciprocal certainty' has been altered, and as a result the meaning of the line is now very different from what it was before. I am not sure that all this is justifiable. Readers get attached to particular incarnations of a work, and I myself have become quite indignant when I have read an updated, 'authoritative' version of a well-loved poem. Perhaps the authority of authors should lapse with their first editions, and they should be forbidden from tampering with their own published work in the name of improvement. My excuse (for what it is worth) is that in both cases I have in fact restored the wording of an earlier draft which I had revised in what now seems to me a mistaken attempt at polish.

Delhi   *Vikram Seth*
February 1994

Panipat

My aunts sit in the courtyard,
Gossiping, shelling peas,
While around them parrots
Cackle in the neem trees.

I sit with my flute near the place
Where the well was covered up
To make a septic tank.
I glide from stop to stop

Following the scale of Lalit
Though it is afternoon;
Its mournful meditative
Mood moves into a tune

Leading me God knows where –
Into a universe
Beyond – beyond Panipat!
Well, I could have done worse

Than break my studies and come
Back home from Inglistan.   ⚹*

*   a stanza break at the end of a page is marked by ~
     no stanza break at the end of a page is marked by ⚹

Punjab, pandits, panir,
Panipat and paan,

Family, music, faces,
Food, land, everything
Drew me back, yet now
To hear the koyal sing

Bring notes of other birds,
The nightingale, the wren,
The blackbird; and my heart's
Barometer turns down.

I think of beeches, elms,
And stare at the neem tree.
My cousin slices a mango
And offers it to me.

I choose the slice with the seed
And learn from the sweet taste,
Well-known and alien,
I must be home at last.

Sea and Desert

How do I merit such happiness? To have
The moon, the Pacific, and you beside me, waking
At three to sudden cold – dew, the stiff breeze
Along the headland; I have been watching you,
Your face lit in the full moon, restless, still,
As out beyond the strip of foam near the crags
Below, the moon lights up a calm yet shifting
Track on the ocean. Your face with its
Clean lines and tousled hair is beautiful
And it is hard to believe that even in
This stark and lovely place it is the cause
Of so much of my peace. You sleep again,
And I know this unusual beauty, that you've
Neither aimed for nor deserved, will recur
Again and again for me with sea and moon,
An image changing with these changing things,
Distracting me from neither, enhancing both,
A gift you could not help but give, something
I too have neither aimed for nor deserve.

A Winter Word

Cold cold friend, Frost –
Night comes, and I
Am dispossessed.
Most cold, cold
Is this night;
And my youth old,
My spirit lost.
I cannot rest.
I walk alone.
Frost, burn upon
My every bone.

Departure Lounge

Among the lobsters and pushcarts
At Boston Airport we
Walk up and down, father and son
Knowing that we will be
Apart for years now, talking and regretting
The shortness of this meeting.

Four days of a New England Spring;
I recall one Monsoon
– Calcutta – when one night I gave
A 50-paise coin
To a girl in rags. You had forbidden it
And I cannot forget

The nature of your punishment.
It was not words or blows.
I had had beatings; as for words,
There were not many of those,
Sharp, or warm, between us. What you said
Was that you'd cut me dead.

I had ignored your stated will
And would be ignored
From that day on: the status quo
No doubt; but when I heard

You say the express words, it was to me
Unneeded cruelty.

I had few memories of your love
Or kindness, even speech.
'The chapatis are well-cooked'; 'Stop that
At once.' How could you reach
To me through those? How could I understand
What lay behind your hand?

My act to you had one intent,
To thwart you. I recall
The fear, hate, the contempt I felt
At that. It would appal
That sixteen-year-old to observe in me
The opposite of all three.

But what has changed, Papa? Those years
I'd have wished different
Are lost. Is it that fatherhood,
Perhaps now imminent,
Reframes my views of what a father means?
Or that those clear-edged scenes

Of boyhood are less focused now;
Since I no longer hate
'The self they made me' I can free
The myths that bore the freight
Of self-dislike, self-pity and despair?
Or is it that we are

In noncontiguous domains
And can afford our smiles,
Non-grating greetings and exchange
Over the frictionless miles?
All? None of the above? Whatever's true
I know that I love you

Far less for these than that I see
What I could not then know
– You doubtless thought it manifest –
Your love for us. Although
You gave us food and comforts, were obsessed
With 'Nothing but the best

Will do for *my* kids,' it was time,
The costless priceless salt
We lacked, that you spared only to
Dislodge some leechlike fault.
I never grew inured to the blurred fear
I sensed when you were near.

You screened your griefs; you sheltered us.
For one who in his youth
Is both a part of and apart
From those he loves, the truth
Of what he feels, if difficult to bear
Is harder yet to share.

Orphaned at two, you ran away
From Baoji at fifteen.
The tin shack, the Mussourie store,
Hunger, the freezing rain,

Nothing could split the shell of hurt and pride.
You would have rather died

Than faced that uneasy ease again.
Unsure of tenderness
Where you most craved it, did it grow
Too anguished to express?
You screened your love; though Mama says you cried
The day Baoji died.

Well, I was blind; but it was dark
And both of us have moved
Into a clearer sunlight. I, now
Certain that I was loved,
See you, too, mellowed. Age? Doubtless. But more;
The carapace you wore

Could have withstood that. Something's given
In your philosophy.
'Relaxing' then was one more stern
Programmed activity.
Yet today to walk a Boston square
Savouring what we share –

Threads of light rain, the reflected church,
Talk of the family;
Your work and mine; your paradigm
For paradise – greenery
And a small river; Delhi politics;
Aradhana's latest tricks –

Brings you a peace that draws me inwards;
And the unrigid heart
With which you view my views, my loves,
However far apart
From yours, seasons the warmth I newly sense
With a vivid tolerance

Of living day to day. You could,
I know, live mile to mile.
Long distance runners learn to bear
Segmented pain. But while
The college marathon and the torturous
Disease you've borne taught this,

They did not teach its partner-art,
To live with happiness
In what is an unfinished state
Till we die. You possess
What was not there then when I was a boy,
This uninvasive joy.

Yet somewhat late for me, I think.
I have moved on, my life
Twelve thousand miles from yours, my ways
Safe from paternal strife,
Paternal judgement and – how can I tell –
Paternal love as well?

Your arm around my shoulder, we
Stroll through the lounge. The hand
Arcs round the clock; flight 43
Is called; I understand

The weight of fatherhood can survive the day
That a child moves away.

We meet on neutral ground: next time
May be at home. I should
Tell you as you walk through the door
I'll miss you. If I could
Have had a better father years ago
I could not now, I know.

Quaking Bridge

So here I am again by Quaking Bridge,
Standing a moment by the water's edge,
Hearing the water's roar as it churns past
The ancient brewery; and I am cast
Back to December when by Quaking Bridge
I stood a moment by the water's edge
And heard the water's turbulence, and knew
That since no more remained that I could do
And since to think of pain itself is pain,
I should forget and not walk here again
And hear the water under Quaking Bridge
And stand in thought beside the water's edge,
And I am here again; but why delay?
Think, and walk on, and think: but walk away.

Switching Off

There are no fears of undiscovered countries
Or bournes from which no traveller returns
To one who knows this life is all there is;
So when he feels it has become oppressive,
The effort of drawing breath exhausts and strains him
And dispriz'd love, and whips and scorns etcetera
Have mangled him, why does he not switch off?

Perhaps the thought that, having once been happy
(And stirred by the analogy of life
Being a wheel) he will again be so;
Or some imagined, as yet unseen sight,
Like Halley's Comet lighting up the sky
For which he'd have to wait till '86;
Or else objective curiosity:
Who will be President in ten years' time?
Who'll win the hockey in the Olympic Games?
And then his family: although he knows
When dead there's no remorse, he cannot bear
That they, remaining, feel he did not love them –
It is such things that hold him to the earth
And not the dread of something after death.

Sonnet

O my generous and exuberant love
As the slow moon coldly slopes down the sky
The pines hum to themselves and you to yourself
And you pass your hands across my face.
My hands stray – stray? – to your breasts,
Small, such as angels probably are permitted.
You are forgiven, solely because of them
For beating me at Scrabble.

Dear friend you cannot know
How much you fill my days – and the long nights,
When outside the whole world is threatening silence,
The pine is swaying in a senseless dream,
Your hand within my hand, your warm warm body
Close by me, and in the dark your unseen smile.

Grand Canyon

Swift dawn across the falling wall below;
The billion-year-old schist – and the powdered snow
Of yesterday caught in the juniper limb
Leaning wind-warped over the sheer South Rim.

To a Fellow-Traveller

Dear Madeleine, I dip my Pepperidge Farm
Cookie into my tea and think of you
And how you laughed and held me by the arm

On Shattuck when I left. Though I'm one who
Believes that between strangers there should be
A proper distance kept – between us two

Who have not sipped each other's company
For even a day, I'd happily dispense
With distance, logic or consistency.

I love you! Let us meet again. I sense
This may be read and smiled at and rejected
As overripe Parnassian pretence;

The honesty of prose is less suspected –
This is not Florence in 1293
When rhyme was reasonable, but I've elected

To do it this way both because for me
It's fun, and – yes – to re-elicit that smile
It set my spirit yodelling to see.   ~

At Newark Airport, brooding all the while
On DC10s and engine failure
I thought I saw a sign above the aisle,

'All hope abandon, ye who enter here.
The pilot is obtuse, the plane is late,
The flight attendants flighty, and the sheer

Monotony of a sedentary state
Maintained for seven hours will likely drive
You into lunacy, or at any rate

To morbid introspection. You'll arrive
At Oakland, high-strung and (in spirits) low,
Lost in your past, scared by the future.' I've

Known many flights like this. How could I know
That what I would recall about this flight
Would not be doom and polythene, but the snow-

Fluffed cloud-terrain heavy with evening light,
Your laughter, Dante, and the darkening flare
Of the chased sunset merging with the night?

I'd always hoped somehow, sometime, somewhere
I'd meet someone like you. I also deemed
Such visions built on vodka and on air.

And so this was, and yet to me it seemed
Even when we stood on sober earth again
That neither of us wished it had been dreamed.   ~

So what do you say? I don't care where or when.
I have your number but am somewhat chary
Of using it. Will you call me? And then

The two of us could meet. You know I'm wary
Of ruffling the calm waters of your mind,
But mine are ruffled. I sip a Bloody Mary

Or dunk a pseudo-madeleine and find
Your face before me – as when two hours ago
I browsed through 'Heaven'; and when such things remind

Me of your voice, the short shard of rainbow
Above the clouds, the layered sky above –
'Chartreuse, turquoise, red sherbet, indigo . . .'

(Remember?) – I remember you with love
Richer than I believed seven swift hours
Could ever wake; perhaps some semblance of

The love that moves the sun and the other stars.

Rakhi

for Aradhana

I had forgotten the time
Of year. Your rakhi came,
Showing how things have changed
And are the same.

It was a contract of trust
With more than you. I know
I left home too many
Years ago.

I place the golden thread
Across my wrist; that done,
Struggle with my left hand
To tie it on.

You should have done that; I
Too have lost half the rite.
I promise you your gift
In '78.

Those future numerals
Look curious; and your brother
Too will be strange when next
We meet each other.

~

How we must both have changed;
Only the custom stays,
Educing from the past
The undying days.

Tomatoes

The slugs have got to the tomatoes.
The corn is dead. The wooden poles no longer
Hold up the chicken wire. Gophers'
Burrows cover the spot where I stood
And watched the sun sink below the tendrils
Still articulate with spray. Mint
And the nameless blueflowered weed
Have covered it all – quiet and quick;
One plot of a hundred similar ones,
Odd child of lazy parents.

Not now too lovesome a thing, God wot.
Nothing to mark the labour of hoeing the ground –
Bread and cheese and beer in the thorn-tree's shade, the sweat
And laughter. Marvelling at the
Bloated zucchini of the neighbouring plot;
A swim in the lake afterwards. The land
Is patient but not infinitely so.
After you went it became an effort to water,
Weed, mulch, replant, even harvest the rich
Recurring crop. I went to the Co-op instead.
Oh well,
Those tomatoes were far too expensive anyway:
My bike was punctured twice by nearby thorns.

Home Thoughts from the Bay

Down Highway 101 the van
Hurtles with all the speed it can
And all the passengers but one
Have jolted off to sleep. The sun
Strikes long apocalyptic lines
Of corrugated sheds, the tines
Of Sutro Tower, billboards, wires,
The airport, scrap, discarded tyres;
And I who must commute each day
Along the grimy-margined Bay
Dizzied by each high-octane breath
And tired of work and bored to death
And sick for home decide I ought
To check that surrogate for thought,
The Highway I-Ching – which today
States 'Yield.' 'Keep Right.' 'Go Back. Wrong Way.'
Should I fly home? Why am I here?
And yield to what? To whim? Fate? Fear?
Keep Right . . . My eyes obey and there
Pursue a jumbo-jet to where
This afternoon high in the sky
A half moon loiters absently by,
Incognizant of why or what
Or where it ought to be or not.

Rain

The rain drips quietly down
    The windowpane
Through nightfall, midnight, on
    To sublit dawn.

The sleeping bag is warm,
    The little room
Suffices for a time
    For world, for home.

May too much light not fall
    Across the sill
Onto the rug, the wall.
    For this slow while

May the cool pattering souse
    The unquenched trees
And these assuaging greys
    Rest on my eyes.

From the Memoirs of Babur, First Moghul Emperor of Hindustan

The snows near Chiraghdan
Covered the roads. Our guide,
Like us, was lost. We sent
Out men to find the road.
And still it snowed and snowed.

Four days passed: they returned.
They had not found a soul.
No sign of settlement,
No wandering tribesmen; hill
On hill, and that was all.

We knew we must advance
Into the breast-deep snow.
As the first man lost strength
He was replaced. I, too,
Helped press it down. This way

In a week we pushed ourselves
Three miles, or perhaps less.
Regardless of their rank,
Though I left them the choice,
Few men remained on horse.

We halted by a cave.
That evening the wind blew

So sharply through the fierce
And fearsome drifts of snow
We all expected to die.

I dug a prayer-mat's space
Close to the mouth with a hoe
And knelt. The cave seemed small.
Though some desired that I
Go in, I did not go.

When almost at midnight
A survey party discovered
The cave could hold us all
I shook the snow from my head
And entered. Such as had food

– Preserved flesh or stewed meat –
Produced it. Thus we moved
From the inhuman cold
Into the warmth of the cave
Where all at length were safe.

To Manijeh

O Scorpio-cat
When you have gone
My eyes will turn
To lumps of stone.

I'll look at ice
And think of how
You called it 'bairf'.
I'll eat pilao

And taste your touch
Where it won't be.
How will I bear
To read Rumi?

Raga Darbari,
The taste of dill
And all clean mirrors
Will make me ill.

Windex will lie
Where it was laid,
The record player
Sit unplayed,   ~

And dill may grow
Ten feet in height
But will no longer
Yield delight.

At reference to
Shirazi Turks
My stricken heart
Will beat in jerks –

But worst, some random
Woman's clear laugh
Will neatly cut
My liver in half.

The Walkers

They walked towards a trigonometrical point
along a ridge; as they approached, a brace
of startled ravens suddenly rose in joint
defensive chorus for their living-space.

The walkers laughed companionably; then one
who filled the other's heart with clear delight
said, pointing up at Snowdon, 'Look, the sun
has not yet thawed the snow; no, there, that white—'

The other looked; the abrasive poignancy
of the ravens' cries, their dark extended wings
spoke of no parting, and he did not see
the decay inherent in contingent things.

Time-Zones

I willed my love to dream of me last night
    That we might lie
At peace, if not beneath a single sheet,
    Under one sky.

I dreamed of her but she could not alas
    Humour my will;
It struck me suddenly that where she was
    Was daylight still.

After Three Years

Charred grass (the drought); the birch stump (last year's
    gales);
Discoloured rose-leaves. Yet at the lawn's cropped edge
Orange azaleas flame; beyond the hedge
The sunset reddens steeply towards North Wales.

Blight; change, recurrence – I am at it again.
Your illness; meaning; the old neurotic search.
Instead of the woodpecker on the birch
A crazy jackdaw hammers the window-pane.

From Mount Tamalpais

The brown-winged hawks
Hover and glide
Below the rock
While from its shade

I watch them crest
Over ridge and hill;
They seem at rest,
Not flight, for all

Their effort lies
In sensed surrender
To the heat's rise
From the earth under

In which suspense
Their cruise would appear
Less hunt than dance
With shadow and air.

Thoughts While Travelling at Night
translated from the Chinese of Du Fu

Light breeze on the fine grass.
I stand alone at the mast.

Stars lean on the vast wild plain.
Moon bobs in the Great River's spate.

Letters have brought no fame.
Office? Too old to obtain.

Drifting, what am I like?
A gull between earth and sky.

Aubade

Wake up! The smudge of dawn
Low on the hills has shot
The bay with light. Don't miss
These minutes. This is not

Pure altruism, though.
I grant I want to see
Your face against the dawn.
Wake up, therefore, for me.

The Yellow Cricket

The cricket, vivid
Wings closed fast
In caution, sits
Unnoticed. Trust

Or extreme fear
Sets him to flight,
Charging the grey
Splinter with bright

Gold flame, unthought of,
Now revealed –
Like love that has
Lain long concealed.

You will one day
Find charged in me
What wariness
Disguises. See

How he now squats,
As drab as dust.
Love, let it not
Be fear but trust.

The Sultan's Turret

Dawnlight; I wake; and wait for you, uneasy
With early dreams: r.e.m., twist and mutter –
Here, let me touch your shoulder. Hmm. Real.
Rub eyes. The room asserts itself, a clutter
Of books – my jeans, your jeans (← fertile; sleazy →)
An upset yoghurt dripping through my socks.
Dawnlight: striations on the ceiling now.
Aurora – and her sister Mocha too?
But I'm content, wombed in the quilt with you,
To let the car-hums, chirrups, ticks and tocks
And your soft breathing hold me till I feel
Far sleepier – and awaker too, somehow,
Than I . . . the light sheathes your reluctant head,
You blink, I smile. We kiss. 'Your turn.' I nod.
(Duty, Stern Daughter of the Voice of God!)
The errant Coffeeman gets out of bed.

At Evening

Let me not sleep, let me not think, let me
Not ache with inconsistent tenderness.
It was untenable delight; we're free –
Separate, equal – and if loverless,
Love consumes time which is more dear than love,
More unreplicable. With everything
Thus posited, the choice was clear enough
And daylight ratified our reckoning.

Now only movement marks the birds from the pines;
Now it is dark; the blinded stars appear;
I am alone; you cannot read these lines
Who are with me when no one else is here,
Who are with me and cannot hear my voice
And take my hand and abrogate the choice.

Moonless Night

Moonless night; no phosphorescence;
                 no line of land or sea.
Fractured noise, randomly rising
                 and falling endlessly.
Dark erratic recollection:
            the driftwood, pearls and slime;
Love; love's passing; dissipated
                 ability and time.
Patternless delight and wreckage
             without restraint or norm.
Strange, though; even here perhaps one
             discerns ingenerate form:
Certainty; pause; the return to uncertainty
           as the breakers assaulting the sand
Gather slowly, loose their power,
                then ebb away from land.

Guest

I woke. He mumbled things in the next bed.
I lay there for an hour or so. At four
The alarm rang. He got out of bed. He wore
Nothing. I felt his sleepy classic head
And long-limbed body stir my quiescent heart.
I'd thought that I was free. Wrong from the start.
I found I loved him utterly instead.

There was no real hope. 'Guy loving guy?
Man – that's a weird trip – and not for me.'
I accepted that. But next day, warily,
We coiled to snap or spring. Rash truth. To lie
Still could have spared the trust; the warmth as well.
I left his room that day. I try to tell
Myself this sorrow like this ink will dry.

The Balcony

If I have bent so far and not snapped, it
cannot destroy me now. This thing will pass
as it has passed before. Elation is
no birthright. This room is the same. The grass

in post-drought green, the violet hills, this light
of early evening are the same. I stare
out from my balcony, like one who's lost
the threads of his obsessions, hardly aware

that from the darkening sky peace falls upon
my world, or on the car-park where, below,
two lovers ferry groceries from their car
and kiss. My eyes jaywalk the road and go

to where you live, jog, laugh, toke, talk – and I
am suddenly glad that I've survived this love
and that it too survives. Now there's no hope
it's strange that this should seem almost enough.

Even Such

I saw him turn
With worried haste
And the world's fear
From me. I shall

Through month and year
Stitch up the rags
And will unlearn
The evident way.

The pain-dense tracks
Dark in the mist
Will see snow fall.
I will retaste

The tang of day,
The ceased belief
That paths exist
Outside this grief.

Close of Play

We are the last generations. Surdas, Bach,
Rembrandt, Du Fu, all life, love, work and worth
Will end in the particular rain. Computers
And chisels will rust, unpeopled city by city,
Beijing and Boston, Rome, Madras, grow still.
The kolkhoz milkmaid, the Basque goatherd, the peasant
Eking his sustenance from the Nile's silt; old
And young; black, brown; the Rio millionaire
And those who starve in the favela; without
Discrimination, justice or injustice,
Antagonist and indifferent alike
Will house the charge of death, and as the dust
Dissolves in the sea, the dolphins too, the complex
Whales. Seaweed may still survive; life's sap
May permeate a crippled grass; but we,
'The roof and crown of things', if such we are,
Will be defunct.

A mote held up against bright clouds of stars
The earth will move through universal time
And humankind will not be missed. If some
Distant intelligence scans the earth some day,
Mozart will be vibrations to them. Our relics,
Our alien skeletons, and the history
That led us to the radiance we attained
Will make them merely curious; but to assign

Human feelings to beings with their own
Is fanciful; who knows what they will sense
When data of this planet and the signs
Of an extinct consciousness reach them, its marks
Of art, its dwellings, its Great Wall, its highways,
Its books in which decipherable lie
Passion and knowledge?

The six-year-old's giant snowball slips
Down to the valley. He runs after it
To the far slope, then falls, and it rolls back
Its accreted mass to crush him. Too late we perceive
Our playthings, grown autonomous, knowledge and use,
This practical, that ideal Good at last
Rear doomtoys that will undo nine-tenths of us
Leaving the breathing dead we call survivors
On a radiant waste. Viruses perhaps
May breed despite a thousand shocks. We will not
Once so mutated see a new live child.

The custom of frenzy, pride and fear will ebb
Only with us; soon fifty nations will cluck
Over their extirpative eggs: and governments
Will get their sages, journeymen and maniacs
As randomly as in past centuries.
The toxic madmen who come to sting mankind
Every so often will not forbear to appear
In deference to changed circumstance; and Hitler
Will not grow sweetly scrupulous when next
He froths in his bunker. Someone, sooner or later,
Will view this world through the eyes of capable hate
And 'earth of the slumbering and liquid trees',

The apple-blossomed earth will nurse its dead
Or tortured and denatured crust, and our strain,
For all its promise, power and prayer, will die.

It is a pity. Life is, or can be, good.
To sing, eat, swim, work, sleep, make love – to be
Breathing and out of pain, to have the arm
Of one's friend around one, or one's ears surrounded
By the deep quilt of music, to see the stars,
To understand their fire – but here it grows
More hazardous – for what was it but that
That will now bring us death, this will to know –
And ultimate knowledge is not ultimate power
But ultimate and seeable helplessness;
And though it is for our few generations
To value living these particular days
Until the earth rejoins its fellow-planets
In common lifelessness, circling around
Their mother-star in deepening entropy,
Rejoin it will, and soon. It is a pity
But nothing new to an old universe.

Last Night

translated from the Urdu of Faiz Ahmed Faiz

Last night your faded memory came to me
As in the wilderness spring comes quietly,
As, slowly, in the desert, moves the breeze,
As, to a sick man, without cause, comes peace.

Party for the Retirement of the Oldest-Serving British Museum Reading Room Book Attendant

Yes, yes, thank you, thank you, yes, it has been
A very pleasant forty . . . fifty years.
Quite so, sir; how time does fly. I have seen
So many changes that the world appears
Peculiar now. But this place, not much change.
Well, yes, sir, that's correct, the lighting's new.
And now we're particular about checking; strange,
Recently, though, we have lost quite a few.
Marx? . . . Marx? . . . well, there *was* someone of that name;
Old gentleman he was. Sat at 10A,
Writing, writing, writing, always the same,
And foreign languages too, day after day,
Year after year. One day he left, and since then
No one has ever heard of him again.

Dubious

Some men like Jack
and some like Jill;
I'm glad I like
them both; but still

I wonder if
this freewheeling
really is an
enlightened thing –

or is its greater
scope a sign
of deviance from
some party line?

In the strict ranks
of Gay and Straight
what is my status?
Stray? or Great?

Bagatelles

1. On the Ninth Cacophony of a Modern Composer

First there's a fusillade of farts and thunder.
Then there is silence for an entire minute.
The instruments are finally torn asunder.
The audience cheers. There must be something in it.

2. Rake's Progress

'Cars, women, beer – there's nothing else in life.
This is the tripod of my youth,' said Swill.
Ten years – and now the tripod is the wife,
The television and the sleeping pill.

3. In Praise of Urban Green

When every park becomes a highwayed plain
Cemeteries and golf courses will remain;
For every thinking man who is not red
Reveres the rich; and, next to them, the dead.

4. Overheard at a Cocktail Party

But empathy with the Id is the quintessential
Je-ne-sais-quoi – as it were – of the Existential . . .   ~

5. Mere Invocation

O luminous, dark and serpent-haunted sea,
O ever-hooded, tragic-gestured sea,
O dolphin-torn, O gong-tormented sea,
And thou, thou unplumbed, salt, estranging sea,
O snotgreen sea, O scrotumtightening sea,
Incarnadined and multitudinous sea,
O finny-tribèd, much-describèd sea,
How weary of description must thou be.

The Tale of Melon City
after Idries Shah

In the city of which I sing
There was a just and placid King.

The King proclaimed an arch should be
Constructed, that triumphally

Would span the major thoroughfare
To edify spectators there.

The workmen went and built the thing.
They did so since he was the King.

The King rode down the thoroughfare
To edify spectators there.

Under the arch he lost his crown.
The arch was built too low. A frown

Appeared upon his placid face.
The King said, 'This is a disgrace.

The chief of builders will be hanged.'
The rope and gallows were arranged.

The chief of builders was led out.
He passed the King. He gave a shout,

'O King, it was the workmen's fault.'
'Oh!' said the King, and called a halt

To the proceedings. Being just
(And placider now) he said, 'I must

Have all the workmen hanged instead.'
The workmen looked surprised, and said,

'O King, you do not realize
The bricks were made of the wrong size.'

'Summon the masons!' said the King.
The masons stood there quivering.

'It was the architect . . .', they said,
The architect was summonèd.

'Well, architect,' said His Majesty.
'I do ordain that you shall be

Hanged.' Said the architect, 'O King,
You have forgotten one small thing.

You made certain amendments to
The plans when I showed them to *you*.'

The King heard this. The King saw red.
In fact he nearly lost his head;

But being a just and placid King
He said, 'This is a tricky thing.   ~

I need some counsel. Bring to me
The wisest man in this country.'

The wisest man was found and brought,
Nay, carried, to the Royal Court.

He could not walk and could not see,
So old (and therefore wise) was he –

But in a quavering voice he said,
'The culprit must be punishèd.

Truly, the arch it was that banged
The crown off, and it must be hanged.'

To the scaffold the arch was led
When suddenly a Councillor said –

'How can we hang so shamefully
What touched your head, Your Majesty?'

'True,' mused the King. By now the crowd,
Restless, was muttering aloud.

The King perceived their mood and trembled
And said to all who were assembled –

'Let us postpone consideration
Of finer points like guilt. The nation

Wants a hanging. Hanged must be
Someone, and that immediately.'   ~

The noose was set up somewhat high.
Each man was measured by and by.

But only one man was so tall
He fitted. One man. That was all.

He was the King. His Majesty
Was therefore hanged by Royal Decree.

'Thank Goodness we found someone,' said
The Ministers, 'for if instead

We had not, the unruly town
Might well have turned against the Crown.'

'Long live the King!' the Ministers said.
'Long live the King! The King is dead.'

They pondered the dilemma; then,
Being practical-minded men,

Sent out the heralds to proclaim
(In his [former] Majesty's name):

'The next to pass the City Gate
Will choose the ruler of our state,

As is our custom. This will be
Enforced with due ceremony.'

A man passed by the City Gate.
An idiot. The guards cried, 'Wait!   ~

Who is to be the King? Decide!'
'A melon,' the idiot replied.

This was his standard answer to
All questions. (He liked melons.) 'You

Are now our King,' the Ministers said,
Crowning a melon. Then they led

(Carried) the Melon to the throne
And reverently set it down.

★

This happened years and years ago.
When now you ask the people, 'So –

Your King appears to be a melon.
How did this happen?', they say, 'Well, on

Account of customary choice.
If His Majesty rejoice

In being a melon, that's OK
With us, for who are we to say

What he should be as long as he
Leaves us in Peace and Liberty?'

The principles of laissez-faire
Seem to be well-established there.

Six Octets

1

You have the slimmest body. The light fur
That covers it is lovely. Lovelier
Still is that gold-shot hair; that mouth, those eyes,
Smiling, unmetaphysical and wise.
Enough said. But beneath this you possess
That blend of gentle whim and forcefulness
That only a bartender of high class
Could have poured out. May I request a glass?

2

Hands held in friendship, hands caressed in love,
I watch you break a croissant, while above
The patio redwinged blackbirds swirl in flight.
O morning after! 'Triste' can't be right
– 'post coitum omne animal' – it's suspicious,
Even this instant coffee tastes delicious.
It's drunk with pleasure and I'm drunk with bliss;
Sleep; Doonesbury; and sitting here like this.   ~

3

You don't love me at all? O God. O shit.
You still 'respect me'. Thanks. I value it
About as much as one who's asked to use
A second hat when he's in need of shoes.
Since, I discover, my own self-respect
Is quite enough to keep my spine erect
Why is it true my ample self-affection
Will not suffice to buoy me in rejection?

4

So now, instead of Zen gardens, of why
Small Markets work, of loquats, of the sky,
Of kinship ties, of that house-shadowing tree
Propped up by iron poles, we talk only
Of us, only of us, and what went wrong.
Curious, I suppose, to note how our rich strong
Companionship has thinned to this lament.
Analysis is free when the rest is spent.

5

I've spoiled your mood. I'm sorry. Yes, I will
Keep clear of you. It will require more skill
To keep you clear of me, you who infuse
My music now, my sunsets. I could use
More fortitude and say the afterglow,
The coda too holds beauty, but I know
Too well that these diminishing chords of light
Will be resolved to soundlessness and night.   ~

6

Here are the plums. Take all you can, my friend.
We will not meet alone again. The end,
Without, alas, a happily-ever-after,
Is here, but undisgraced by covering laughter.
If bitterness there is, still there was love.
What you and I have shared reminds me of
These plums that we will separately eat.
For all their sourness, they are wild and sweet.

Distressful Homonyms

Since for me now you have no warmth to spare
I sense I must adopt a sane and spare

Philosophy to ease a restless state
Fuelled by this uncaring. It will state

A very meagre truth: love, like the rest
Of our emotions, sometimes needs a rest.

Happiness, too, no doubt; and so, why even
Hope that 'the course of true love' could run even?

Progress Report

My need has frayed with time; you said it would.
It has; I can walk again across the flood
Of gold silk popples on the straw-gold hills
Under a deep Californian sky that expels
All truant clouds; watch squads of cattle graze
By the radio-telescope; blue-battered jays
Flash raucous squawking by my swivelling head
While squirrels sine-wave past over the dead
Oak-leaves, and not miss you – although I may
Admit that near the telescope yesterday
By a small bushcovered gully I blundered on
Five golden fox-cubs playing in the sun
And wished you had been there to see them play;
But that I only mention by the way.

Point Reyes

Diagonal rain. Waves scud towards the sand,
Crestfroth blown backwards. Through the clouds a strand
Of light rifts down to a silvered zone of sea.
The buffeted gulls circle it uncertainly.

Sleep and Death

translated from the German of Heinrich Heine

How similar they are, these two
Beautiful young figures, though one is far
Paler, sterner than the other; one might
Almost say, far more distinguished than him
Who held me in his arms – how gentle was
His smile, how blessed his gaze. It might have been
The poppies wreathing his brow touched my brow too
And strangely fragrant drove all pain from my soul.
But such reprieve is brief. I will be cured
Only when he, the other brother, so
Serious and pale, lowers his torch. Sleep
Is good, Death better; of course the best would be
Never to have been born.

Mappings

Now that the windsurfers have gone, equipped
With wine, some loquats and my manuscript
I breathe the chilled gold of late afternoon
Along the lake-pier. The breeze ebbs. A tern
Pauses and plummets. Mallards manoeuvre through
The weedclogged creek. The hills slate into blue.
I stretch my towel out upon the pier
And read the bitter lines I once wrote here.

That was a younger self. I want to touch
His shoulder, make him smile, show him how each
Sorrow and failure that lacerates his heart
Can heal or numb itself: the limb-trapped hurt
Of love; the search for what remains when we
No longer animate the geography
Of cell and sense; the unassuageable urge
For ecstasy and knowledge; parting; age.

A mockingbird begins a sunset song
Patched from the passions of five birds. I'm wrong;
That was no younger counterpart but one
Of a live clutch of egos. As I scan
My mappings of these selves – despondent, witty,
Calm and uncalm, lost in self-doubt or pity . . .
The courtier, soldier, scholar – I check the pieces;
All are still here, the old familiar faces

~

In one-to-one correspondence: words and moods.
The light has lapsed. I strip and swim towards
A wooden raft. The cool enveloping lake
Merges with all I was and am. My wake,
The wine, my breathing, the recovering stars,
Venus, bright as a plane, Jupiter, Mars,
My pulse, my vagrant selves, my poetry,
Seem here to inhere in a seamless me.

Moths

The brightness stirs;
Two moths approach
The bulb; they sense
Its braising touch

Across the space
Their spiralling path
Must cross to brush
Its globe of death.

Fuddled with glare
Their wings succumb
To the taut shine;
As they draw home

No fear occurs;
There is instead
An eagerness
As they build speed.

Divali

Three years of neurotic
Guy Fawkes Days – I recall
That lonely hankering –
But I am home after all.

Home. These walls, this sky
Splintered with wakes of light,
These mud-lamps beaded round
The eaves, this festive night,

These streets, these voices . . . yet
The old insensate dread,
Abeyant as that love,
Once more shifts in my head.

Five? six? generations ago
Somewhere in the Punjab
My father's family, farmers,
Perhaps had a small shop

And two generations later
Could send a son to school
To gain the conqueror's
Authoritarian seal:

~

English! Six-armed god,
Key to a job, to power,
Snobbery, the good life,
This separateness, this fear.

English: beloved language
Of Jonson, Wordsworth's tongue –
These my 'meridian names'
Whose grooves I crawl along.

The Moghuls fought and ruled
And settled. Even while
They hungered for musk-melon,
Rose, peach, nightingale,

The land assumed their love.
At sixty they could not
Retire westwards. The British
Made us the Orient.

How could an Englishman say
About the divan-e-khas,
'If there is heaven on earth
It is this; it is this; it is this.'

Macaulay the prophet of learning
Chewed at his pen: one taste
Of Western wisdom 'surpasses
All the books of the East',

And Kalidas, Shankaracharya,
Panini, Bhaskar, Kabir,

Surdas sank, and we welcomed
The reign of Shakespeare,

The undigested Hobbes,
The Mill who later ground
(Through talk of liberty)
The Raj out of the land . . .

O happy breed of Babus,
I march on with your purpose;
We will have railways, common law
And a good postal service –

And as I twist along
Those grooves from image to image,
Violet, elm-tree, swan,
Pork-pie, gable, scrimmage

And as we title our memoirs
'Roses in December'
Though we well know that here
Roses *grow* in December

And as we import songs
Composed in the US
For Vietnam (not even
Our local horrors grip us)

And as, over gin at the Club,
I note that egregious member
Strut just perceptibly more
When with a foreigner,

~

I know that the whole world
Means exile for our breed
Who are not home at home
And are abroad abroad,

Huddled in towns, while around:
'He died last week. My boys
Are starving. Daily we dig
The ground for sweet potatoes.'

'The landlord's hirelings broke
My husband's ribs – and I
Grow blind in the smoke of the hearth.'
'Who will take care of me

When I am old? No one
Is left.' So it goes on,
The cyclic shadow-play
Under the sinister sun;

That sun that, were there water,
Could bless the dispirited land,
Coaxing three crops a year
From this same yieldless ground.

Yet would these parched wraiths still
Starve in their ruins, while
'Silkworms around them grow
Into fat cocoons'? Sad soil,

This may as well be my home.
Because no other nation

Moves me thus? What of that?
Cause for congratulation?

This may as well be my home;
I am too used to the flavour
Of tenuous fixity;
I have been brought to savour

Its phases: the winter wheat –
The flowers of Har-ki-Doon –
The sal forests – the hills
Inflamed with rhododendron –

The first smell of the Rains
On the baked earth – the peaks
Snow-drowned in permanence –
The single mountain lakes.

What if my tongue is warped?
I need no words to gaze
At Ajanta, those flaked caves,
Or at the tomb of Mumtaz;

And when an alap of Marwa
Swims on slow flute-notes over
The neighbours' roofs at sunset,
Wordlessly like a lover

It holds me – till the strain
Of exile, here, or there,
Subverts the trance, the fear
Of fear found everywhere.

~

'But freedom?' the notes would sing . . .
Parole is enough. Tonight
Below the fire-crossed sky
Of the Festival of Light

Give your soul leave to feel
What distilled peace it can;
In lieu of joy, at least
This lapsing anodyne.

'The world is a bridge. Pass over it,
Building no house upon it.'
Acceptance may come with time;
Rest, then, disquieted heart.

A Morning Walk

A web hung from the avocado tree;
The spider rested in the dew and sun
And looked about the grove contentedly
Awaiting visitors; and I was one:
Neither a Californian nor a fly,
And humming to myself in Bhairavi.

Foreigner, hence! he may have thought, but chose
Instead to squat immobile as I came
Further into his district. Did I pose
An unpredictability? The same
Was true of him – bloated, yellow, with some
Sepia blotches not like those at home.

Our spiders are much blacker and much thinner,
Patrol their webs with greater frequency
And seem perpetually anxious about dinner;
Thin . . . spindly . . . starved – Nirala suddenly
Came to me – Shyambazaar, Chowringhee, Strand –
His 'Bhikshuk' poem – all blurred in this new land.

My very turn of phrase – Foreigner, hence! –
Betrayed the web of jocularity
I had spun round me here; nor could I sense
The pain I felt at home where I could see

The hunger, half resigned, half desperate
Of those like me but for a freak of fate.

To wander through the streets of Calcutta is
To force the whole world's misery on the heart –
Children on broken stumps, staring with eyes
White and opaque, begging with hardened art.
Far from those eyes, blind in my stead, I wander
Among these affluent trees, and stop and ponder

How fine it is to share the world and not
Its need when there are those who weep for food.
Their children's limbs will atrophy, brains rot
Swollen for lack of it, while 'all things good',
Food, shelter, health, are mine; interests; loves;
The time to walk through avocado groves.

Living abroad, I have lost sight of home.
Locked in my web I have grown happily blind
And blindly happy, and few images come
To jar the fine strands of my peace of mind.
A clod is washed away; the world is less;
But why disturb my quest for happiness?

For me there is this bitter questioning.
For others life is bitter through and through.
It may be short but it is everything.
No Compassionate Being leans down to view
And balance things; there is no justice after
For those deprived this life of food or laughter.

~

I draw my easy non-consumptive breath,
Think life sweet, spin rhymes, eat my daily fly
And neither shrink before nor welcome death
But others, even those who fear to die,
Suffer with quietude, with spent relief
The final amnesty from want and grief.

Stump

translated from the Hindi of Suryakant Tripathi 'Nirala'

It is a stump now,
Its art gone,
Its ornaments all gone.

It does not stir with Spring
Nor bend like a bow when green
Nor from its flowers fly Kamadeva's arrows
Nor in its shade are sighs of travellers heard
Or tears of lovers seen.

Only one old bird
Sits remembering something.

The Humble Administrator's Garden

———◆———

1985

To my family, pictured within

Wutong

A Little Night Music

White walls. Moonlight. I wander through
The alleys skein-drawn by the sound
Of someone playing the erhu.
A courtyard; two chairs on the ground.

As if he knew I'd come tonight
He gestures, only half-surprised.
The old hands poise. The bow takes flight
And unwished tears come to my eyes.

He pauses, tunes, and plays again
An hour beneath the wutong trees
For self and stranger, as if all men
Were brothers within the enclosing seas.

Suzhou, 1981

The Master-of-Nets Garden

Magnolia petals fall, pale, fragrant, brown,
Resting on moss within a square of white;
Courtyard of quietness, of intimate stone
And latticed shadow. Outside, low at night,
Three moons – of water, mirror, sky – define
Pine and old cypress struggling against the stars,
And jasmine and gardenia combine
Their scent with that of closed magnolias.

The Humble Administrator's Garden

A plump gold carp nudges a lily pad
And shakes the raindrops off like mercury,
And Mr Wang walks round. 'Not bad, not bad.'
He eyes the Fragrant Chamber dreamily.
He eyes the Rainbow Bridge. He may have got
The means by somewhat dubious means, but now
This is the loveliest of all gardens. What
Do scruples know of beauty anyhow?
The Humble Administrator admires a bee
Poised on a lotus, walks through the bamboo wood,
Strips half a dozen loquats off a tree
And looks about and sees that it is good.
    He leans against a willow with a dish
    And throws a dumpling to a passing fish.

The North Temple Tower

On the North Temple Tower, from the fifth floor
I pull fierce faces at two boys below.
One gasps, and tells the other what he saw:
A waibin in the throes of vertigo.
They look again. I spread my arms and grunt.
Sudden delight: they point upwards and scowl.
One imitates a baby elephant.
The other glares and totters like an owl.
The camera clicks. They do not seem to mind
Involuntary immortality.
I change a reel, and spiral down to find
Them stomping through the flower-beds with glee.
      They say 'Ni hao', remembering their manners,
      Then leap away through hollyhocks and cannas.

The Gentle Waves Pavilion

A pool as green as pea-soup. Four sleek fish,
Red as pimentos, push through bubbly scum.
A vagrant sparrow from a rocky niche
Looks critically on. Two lovers come
To gaze at fish and foreigner in the park
And talk and cuddle by the moss-trunked tree
And with a pen-knife hack their names through bark
For (if the tree survives) posterity.

The Tarrying Garden

Here are no vistas. Piece by piece unfolds.
Stand by the rock. The lotus and the fish,
In still pale yellows, greens and fluid golds
Startle the rainy sky. Or if you wish
Stare at a single slab of cursive script
Sealed in the whitewash, passionate, bone-strong,
Crafted, uncrafted, singular, and stripped
Of all superfluous charm. Or walk along
The covered walks, the courtyards and the pools,
The zigzags of embodied hesitation,
A strict game where, within the given rules,
You may throw dice or follow inclination.
    The Tarrying Garden, piecemeal or entire:
    Meander, tarry, amble, pause, admire.

The Great Confucian Temple, Suzhou

Two geese strut through the balustrade, where rust
And stacks of timber marked 'Department of
Culture: for Restoration' gather dust.
The ginkgo lodges a complaining dove.
A centipede squirms over 'Hong Wu' hewn
In seal-script on the white fragmented stone
Where reign-names of the Ming and Qing lie strewn
In mint and dog-turd, creeper, tile and bone.
Before the frayed vermilion walls and eaves
The plaster statue of a man in red
With pudgy vehemence and rolled-up sleeves
Proclaims the oppressive heritage is dead.
    Inside the hall six workmen renovate
    The verveless splendour of a corpse of state.

Nanjing Night

Full moon, the Nanjing walls, bicycle bells.
Two children huddle in the 10 o'clock movie crowd
Against the plunging cold. The air foretells
Snow, moonlit snow. Low-voiced, dog-eared, heads bowed,
Students seep out from libraries into the cold.
It is the last month – the yellow plum is in bloom.
Exams, the Spring Festival; each one is to be told
His lifework by the Party. In the room
Someone grinds his teeth in his sleep and moans.
The moonlight finds two pink hot-water flasks,
Pull-up bars, a leafless ginkgo, four stones –
Either the Gang of Four or the Four Great Tasks.
    I dream of the twelve full moons of the coming year:
    Tilts of curved roof; branches; a stonewhite sphere.

Evening Wheat

Evening is the best time for wheat.
Toads croak.
Children ride buffaloes home for supper.
The last loads are shoulder-borne.
Squares light up
And the wheat sags with a late gold.
There on the other side of the raised path
Is the untransplanted emerald rice.
But it is the wheat I watch, the still dark gold
With maybe a pig that has strayed from the brigade
Enjoying a few soft ears.

The Accountant's House

We go in the evening to the accountant's house.
It is dark and the road is slush.
The fireflies fleck silver.
The ash flicked off by my companion, the barefoot doctor, is
    gold.

I want to clear up some questions on the income and
    expenditure account.
His wife and two daughters smile as I come in.
They pour tea. Their son died last Spring Festival.
We smile and discuss electricity fees.

This is my last day here. The Ministry of Education
Has decreed a two-and-a-half-week limit.
I will turn into a pumpkin soon enough
But today there is work, are pleasantries.

The green seedlings outside have been transplanted.
The accountant looks sad and my heart goes out.
No one knows how he died. He came home from play
And his head was hot, his nose bled, and he died.

Yet they laugh, yet they laugh, these lovely people,
And he clicks his abacus and she gives me a towel and the two
    girls
Smile shyly, boldly at the stranger and the father
Discussing matters of much importance together.

Research in Jiangsu Province

From off this plastic strip the noise
Of buzzing stops. A human voice
Asks its set questions, pauses, then
Waits for responses to begin.

The questions bore in. How much is
The cost and area of this house?
I see you have two sons. Would you
Prefer to have had a daughter too?

And do your private plots provide
Substantial income on the side?
Do you rear silkworms? goslings? pigs?
How much per year is spent on eggs?

How much on oil and soya sauce
And salt and vinegar? asks the voice.
The answering phantom states a figure,
Then reconsiders, makes it bigger.

Children and contraceptives, soap
And schooling rise like dreams of hope   ⨎*

---

*   a stanza break at the end of a page is marked by ~
    no stanza break at the end of a page is marked by ⨎

To whirl with radios and bikes
Round pensions, tea and alarm clocks.

'Forty square metres. Sixteen cents.
To save us from the elements.
Miscarriage. Pickle with rice-gruel
Three times a week. Rice-straw for fuel.

Chickens and fruit-trees.' In Jiangning
Green spurts the psychedelic Spring
And blossoming plum confounds the smell
Of pig-shit plastered on the soil.

Life and production, drought and flood
Merge with the fertile river mud
And maids come forth sprig-muslin drest
And mandarin ducks return to nest.

The Yangtze flows on like brown tape.
The research forms take final shape,
Each figure like a laden boat
With white or madder sails afloat.

Float on, float on, O facts and facts,
Distilled compendia of past acts,
Reveal the Grand Design to me,
Flotilla of my PhD.

On the obnoxious dreary pillage
Of privacy, imperfect knowledge
Will sprout like lodged rice, rank with grain,
In whose submerging ears obtain

~

Statistics where none grew before
And housing estimates galore,
Diet and wealth and income data,
Age structures and a price inflator,

Birth and fertility projections,
Plans based on need and predilections.
O needful numbers, and half true,
Without you what would nations do?

I switch the tape off. This to me
Encapsulates reality,
Although the beckoning plum-trees splayed
Against the sky, the fragrant shade,

Have something tellable, it seems,
Of evanescence, light and dreams,
And the cloud-busy, far-blue air
Forms a continuous questionnaire

And Mrs Gao herself whose voice
Is captive on my tape may choose
Some time when tapes and forms are far
To talk about the Japanese War,

May mention how her family fled,
And starved, and bartered her for bread,
And stroke her grandson's head and say
Such things could not occur today.

From a Traveller

The willows cut across the commune fields.
Smoke pours from stacks across persimmon trees.
The afternoon light and the jolt of the rails
Provoke the familiar nostalgia of travellers
As I read your letter (thank you for writing) once and again,
And sip warm water from my cup and think of what to say.

Thank you for writing (again) and for the poem.
It came a week ago and has been with me since.
It made me happy. It is very fine—
Latinate and resonant, the words precisely hefted.
As for craft, rhyme and metre are well
But this has more, a balanced power.
I want to know if the proximity
Of 'obvious', 'obtuse' and 'obscure' was meant or not
To be an obtrusive touch of humour or skill,
Though of course my professional opinion is not what you
    require
So much as an explication of my status
As amateur.

Returning from a journey of some length
From the Southern to the Northern capital, my mind turns
To Nanjing in its Fall loveliness
With the Ming tomb before the wooded knoll,
The acorns, chestnuts and small sprouts of oak

On the unneedled ground beneath the pines
And a few pine-rats (squirrels) scampering around
As if to reconfirm that there are few places here
To be solitary, and I realize that I
Go around the world gathering as much
Nostalgia as knowledge, for I can see that no sooner
Will I have moved to an Eccentric State
Than the whole weight of the Central Kingdom
Will ravage my memory – the rasp and swash
Of the catalpa trees, the oversize magpies, my friends,
The pleasure of walking the lanes of a poor country
Where there is no or little destitution,
This afternoon sun and these persimmon orchards
And the clank of rails, and so I often fear
That those few days we spent in each other's company
In San Francisco in the imperial months
And those nights were just another part
Of a tenuous tissue, real enough at the time
Yet changeable as the sieved light that falls
Upon this page from beyond the embanked trees
And so though I was happy it revived my disquiet
To know you thought as much about those days
As I.

When you go to The Latest Scoop next time
Buy chocolate-chocolate-chip in honour of me.
I imagine you there as often as in
Bed or the studio or your roach-frequented kitchen
(I remember you in tastes – ice-cream, garlic soup,
Cinnamon rolls, pâté) and at alternate chips
Mumble 'obtuse' and 'not obtuse' and tell me the result
(And if the latter overtip the friendly giant)

For the obtuseness you diagnosed with such acuity
Had in it an element of intention.
Apart from the aspect of physical difference,
As exciting to me as that of similarity,
And beauty that I always am a sucker for,
I loved in you that cavalier, ungiving
Self-inwardness I usually link with men,
And I suppose it worried me, this affinity and ours –
To what end should any inklings be confirmed
To be uprooted in a predictable week?
What if within this year, what if, what if
You or I were to find the all-gold baby,
Compleat and mechanical, with whom we wished
To play at birds and orchids all our life,
How would we face each other when I returned
Or revive those Vivaldian Beach-Boyish days,
Endless Summer – the most nostalgic of the seasons
For sunspoilt denizens of the Old Gold Mountain
As is Spring in the City of Dreaming Spires,
Winter in Delhi, or here by the Great River
The long slow-cooling cycles of a temperate Fall.
The fact that those days were is perhaps enough.
Time tempers natures, true; but they have existed.
Though all of it, Han, Tang, Song, Ming, Qing,
Their turbulence and life have left few marks
Upon the physical city of Nanjing
And even its tragic century is unreflected
Except for younger brick where the Qing mined in
To crush the Heavenly Kingdom of Great Peace
Or there the mausoleum of Sun Zhong Shan –
And the Guomindang killings and the Japanese horror
Are of less permanence than the coeval plane-trees

That string the streets, still it has been. I feel
Acknowledgement could not add weight to it,
Still less to the levity and gravity of our bond.
Why tax our urban idyll with admission when we,
Both of us, wish, more than we need commit
To meet and spend more than those countable days
In the repeatable magic of San Francisco?
I am honing my charm. For the interim
Though with you I basked perhaps too unfeelingly in
The luxury of not needing to compromise,
And most of what I say is still inchoate
Or irrelevant or evasive, take at least
The 'I like you' you once skilfully prised from me
As indefensible and true.

A Little Distance

A little distance from the waterfall
By a small pool the yellow beachtowel lies
On a long warm rock, and near it azaleas grow
And the shadows of thin fish fall
Across the speckled stones, and a light breeze blows
Rippling the skin of the pool, first this way, then that.
A blue-tailed lizard suns itself
And we ourselves as the sun burns through a cloud
Into the secluded valley, onto the pool,
Onto the rocks, into our cold bones.

Tired, tired, my mind melts in the sun.
An ant crawls over my ankle. I sit up: there
You lie, beautiful, half-nude on the white pebbles,
Cream-coloured breasts open to the breeze and the sky
And a few lines of silver hair in the brown
To announce the burden of your twenty-eight years.
To be chaste, how frustrating for minutes,
How uncomplicated for days – to order fish, chives,
To discuss the rats in our room when the morning gongs
Sound out the monastery routine. To be
Just friends, reverting in a richer vein
To what we were, the way that we once were,
The way I hope, for a while, we may remain.   ~

After six days, with nothing voiced, we are
Unexpectant, companionable,
Perhaps like an ageing couple. We do not
Even kiss goodnight yet wake to friendliness.
It is perhaps the tiredness in my mind
Or the fear of a structure set. Unsettledness
Is what I have come to fear. We sit away
From the noise of the waterfall, by a clear pool,
Less conscious of the risk that is not worthwhile
Than of the warm grey boulders and the slopes
That circumscribe our peace, and the warmth of the sun
Melting us into the stones, and the azaleas
Mauve against a sea of pine.

A Hangzhou Garden

Wistaria twigs, wistaria leaves, mauve petals
Drift past a goldfish ripple. As it settles
Another flower drops. Below, redly,
The fish meander through the wistaria tree.

From an 'East Is Red' Steamer

The old man in grey reproves the women's tears
And shouts from dock to deck. The sailor hears,
Smiles, flings a cigarette to a shorebound mate.
The Wuhan steamer hoots – two minutes late –
Plays martial music, exhorts us to do more
For the Four Modernisations, moves from shore,
While I the tourist view the mother and daughter
Waving across the broadening rift of water,
The grey and sunflecked water and the seagulls flying
Between the son and father, who now himself is crying.

Neem

Profiting

Uncomprehending day,
I tie my loss to leaves
And watch them drift away.

The regions are as far,
But the whole quadrant sees
The single generous star.

Yet under star or sun,
For forest tree or leaf
The year has wandered on.

And for the single cells
Held in their sentient skins
An image shapes and tells:

In wreathes of ache and strain
The bent rheumatic potter
Constructs his forms from pain.

The They

They have left me the quiet gift of fearing.
I am consumed by fear, chilling and searing.

I shiver at night. I cannot sleep. I burn
By night, by day. I tremble. They return.

They bear an abstract laser to destroy
Love-love and Live-live, little girl and boy.

Thus my heart jolts in fear. For they are known
To liquidate the squealers, sparing none.

Needless to say, the death is always long.
I weep to think of it; I am not strong.

Who are the They? Why do they act this way?
Some of us know, but no one dares to say.

The Comfortable Classes at Work and Play

A squirrel crawls on top of Ganesh.
Oscar turns over on his stomach and rolls about.
Seven satbhai-champas chatter and burble below the bignonia
    trellis.
The raat-ki-rani and malati and harsingar mingle their scent.
Above, two crows on the eaves upset Divali diyas on the
    ground,
And in the evening a hoopoe pecks at the lawn
While mynahs frolic at the edge of the mango's shade
And parrots flash across the sky.

Early in the morning the mew-like wail
Of peacocks from the grounds of Nehru's old house,
Now the Teen Murti Library, comes down the lanes,
And down the lanes and across the garden hedges
The peacocks themselves, turquoise-necked,
    turquoise-breasted
(With tail-feathers all robbed to make peacock fans)
Walk primly to our neighbours' houses and ours
Conducting a progress through the vegetable garden.

Sona the gardener does not chase them out
From by the banana tree and the gourd-vines.
He prunes the roses, the hedge, the champa, the two
Lantana elephants that welcome walkers in
To walk, after drinking ginger tea against the chill,   ✗

In chappals on the dew-soft dew-greyed lawn
Or to sit on the large white swing
And swing and stare or read.

The eldest son brings down his surpeti
And mumbles a snatch of Lalit, then hums and lapses.
Oscar bores out of the hedge from the neighbour's garden
And hurls himself barking at the singer's feet.
The eldest son says, 'No, Oscar, no!'
But is persuaded by a sequence of short nips
To run Oscar down the red path
As far as the whitewashed gate.

The second son brings down *The Women's Room*,
Of Woman Born, *My Mother/My Self* and *Sexual Politics*.
His girlfriend is feminist, and he is feminist.
When his girlfriend was anarchist, he was anarchist.
He has begun of late to talk in psychobabble
And his elder brother does not improve energy interflows
By cynical imitation of his style of speech
Or cynical puncturing of his current ism.

The daughter of the house sits in her room
Immersed in sociology and social visits
Paid her at any hour by many friends,
And talks about their coming field-trip south
Where they, like earlier cohorts from their college
('A shock of sociologists'), will examine
The much-examined customs of the Todas
(Who have learned now to exploit their data-pickers).   ~

In the long sunlit closed verandah
The mother takes a volume in half-calf
From off the wall, and wrestles with a judgement
Of Justice Krishna Iyer of the Supreme Court.
He must mean something, but what does he mean?
'The endless pathology of factious scrimmage' – and now
'Crypto-coercion'. She knits her forehead
And asks for another cup of ginger tea.

The father sits in bed reading the *Indian Express*,
Inveighing against politicians and corruption.
'India could do so much . . .' he says.
'Even in the time of the British . . .' he says.
'Can you believe it – on every bag of cement –
And still he continues to be a minister!
The rot has gone too deep. Let's go for a walk.'
He and the elder son drive to Lodi Gardens.

There against the exquisite morning sky
The Arab domes of the tombs sit formed and fine
And neem and semal, ashok and amaltas
And casuarina lend the air freshness, the heart peace.
On the enamel-striped domes the vultures nest.
Along the casual paths three joggers thump.
A group of eight old citizens wearing safas
Gossip in the growing sun and laugh with abandon.

At home the grandmother has sat down to breakfast
And complains that she is ignored, unloved.
Her blood pressure is high, her spirits low.
She is not allowed to eat gulabjamuns.
The doctor has compiled an Index of Foods

And today, to compound things, is a non-grain fast.
Her dentures hurt. She looks at a stuffed tomato
And considers how to darn her grandson's sweater.

The Gift

Awake, he recalls
The district of his sleep.
It was desert land,
The dunes gold, steep,
Warm to the bare foot, walls
Of pliant sand.

Someone, was he a friend?,
Placed a stone of jade
In his hand
And, laughing, said
'When this comes to an end
You will not understand.'

He is awake, yet through
The ache of light
He longs to dream again.
He longs for night,
The contour of the sand, the rendezvous,
The gift of jade, of sight.

Homeless

I envy those
Who have a house of their own,
Who can say their feet
Rest on what is theirs alone,
Who do not live on sufferance
In strangers' shells,
As my family has all our life,
And as I probably will.

A place on the earth, untenured,
Soil, grass, brick, air;
To know I will never have to move;
To review the seasons from one lair.
When night comes, to lie down in peace;
To know that I may die as I have slept;
That things will not revert to a stranger's hand;
That those I love may keep what I have kept.

From the Babur-Nama: Memoirs of Babur, First Moghul Emperor of India

1.

A lad called Baburi lived in the camp-bazaar.
Odd how our names matched. I became fond of him –
'Nay, to speak truth, distracted after him.'
I had never before this been in love
Or witnessed words expressive of passion, but now
I wrote some Persian verses: 'Never was lover
So wretched, so enamoured, so dishonoured
As I'; and others of this type. Sometimes
Baburi came to see me, and I, Babur,
Could scarcely look him in the face, much less
Talk to him, amuse him, or disclose the matter
Weighing on me. So joyful was I I could not
Thank him for visiting; how then could I
Reproach him for departing? I lacked even
The self-command to be polite to him.
Passing one day through a narrow lane with only
A few companions, suddenly, face to face,
I met him, and I almost fell to pieces.
I could not meet his eyes or say a word.
Shame overcame me. I passed on, and left him,
And Muhammed Salih's verses came to my mind –
'I am abashed whenever I see my love.
My friends look at me; I look another way.'
This passion in my effervescent youth

Drove me through lane and street, bare-foot, bare-headed,
Through orchard, vineyard, neglecting the respect
And attention due both to myself and to others:
'During my passion I was deranged, nor knew that
Such is the state of one who is in love.'
Sometimes, afflicted, I would roam alone
Over the mountains and deserts, sometimes I wandered
From street to street, in suburbs and in gardens.
'To such a state did you reduce me, O heart—'
I could not stand or walk; remain or go.

2.

At dawn we left the stream and resumed our march.
I ate a maajun. Under its effect
I visited some gardens, dense with yellow
And purple flowers; some beds yellow, some purple,
And some so intermingled – sprung up together
As if they had been flung and scattered abroad.
I sat down on a hillock. On every side
The gardens lay before me, shaped into beds,
Yellow on one side, purple on another,
Laid out in hexagons, exquisitely.

On Saturday we had a drinking party.
The following day, when we had nearly arrived
At Khwajeh Sehyaran, a serpent was killed,
As thick as an arm, as long as two outstretched.
Out of this large one crept a thinner one,
Yet all its parts were sound and quite uninjured;
Out of this thinner serpent came a mouse,

Perfectly sound again, with no limb injured.
(When we arrived, we had a drinking party.)

Hindustan is a land of meagre pleasures.
The people are not handsome, nor have they
The least conception of the charms of friendship.
They have no spirit, no comprehension, kindness
Or fellow-feeling – no inventiveness
In handicraft or skill in design – no method,
Order, principle, rule in work or thought;
No good flesh or bread in their bazaars,
No ice, cold water, musk-melons, grapes; no horses;
No aqueducts or canals in palace or garden,
Not a single bath or college in the whole land,
No candles, no torches; not even a candlestick.

A splendid bird, more known for colour and beauty
Than bulk, is the peacock. Its size is that of the crane.
The head of the male has an iridescent lustre;
His neck is a fine blue, his back is rich
With yellows, violets, greens and blues, and stars
Extend to the very extremity of his tail.
The bird flies badly, worse indeed than the pheasant:
Where peacocks choose to live, jackals abound.
The doctrines of Hanifeh state that the bird
Is lawful food, its flesh quite pleasant, quail-like;
But eaten somewhat with loathing – like that of the camel.

The frogs of Hindustan are worthy of notice.
Although their species is the same as ours,
They will run seven yards on the face of the water.   ~

3.

Noblemen and soldiers – every man
Who comes into this world is subject to
Dissolution. When we pass away
God alone survives, unchangeable.
Whoever tastes the feast of life must drink
The cup of death. The traveller at the inn
Of mortality sooner or later leaves
That house of sorrow, the world. Is it not better
To die with honour than live with infamy?
'With fame, even to die makes me content.
Let me have fame, since Death has my body.'
The Most High God has been propitious to us
For we are placed in such a crisis that
Should we now die we die the death of martyrs
And should we live we will have served his cause.
Let us all swear then not to turn from battle
Nor desert the slaughter ensuing until we die.

4.

To Humayun, whom I long to see; much health.
On Saturday your letters came from the Northwest.
Praise be to God, who has given you a child;
To you a child, to me an object of love
And comfort. You name him Al Amaan. Consider,
'The protected' – Al Amaan – is pronounced by some
Alaaman, which means 'plunderer' in our tongue!
Well, may God prosper his name and constitution;
May he be happy, and we made happy by
The fame and fortune of Al Amaan. Indeed

God from his grace and bounty has accomplished
Most unprecedentedly all our desires.

On the eleventh I heard the men of Balkh
Had opened the city. I sent word to your brother
And to the Begs to join you against Merv,
Hissar or Samarkand as you deem fittest,
That through God's mercy you might be enabled
To scatter the enemy, seize their lands, and make
Your friends rejoice in their discomfiture.
This is the time to expose yourself to danger.
Exert yourself, and meet things as they come,
For indolence suits ill with royalty.
If through God's favour Balkh and Hissar are ours,
You rule Hissar; let Kamran be in Balkh.
If Samarkand should fall, it falls to you.
Six parts are always yours, and five Kamran's;
Remember this; the great are generous.

I have a quarrel with you. Your letters are
Illegible. They take hours to decode –
The writing crabbed, the style, too, somewhat strange.
(A riddle is not normally written in prose.)
The spelling is not bad (though *iltafaat*
Is spelt with *te* not *toeh*); yet even when read
The far-fetched diction you delight in veils
Your meaning. This is affectation. Write
From now on, clearly, using words that cost
Less torment both to your reader and to you.

In several of your letters you are saddened
By separation from your friends. Consider –   ⚡

'If you are independent, follow your will.
If circumstances fetter you, submit.'
There is no bondage greater than a king's.
Of this, my son, do not therefore complain.

This letter goes to you with Bian Sheikh
Who will tell you much else by word of mouth.
Maintain the army's discipline and force.
Farewell. The thirteenth day of the first Rabi.

5.

Humayun left Badakhshan after a year,
Journeying via Kabul to Agra to see me.
He sent no word. His mother and I were talking
Of him when he appeared. His presence made
Our hearts blossom like rosebuds, and our eyes shine
Like torches. It had been my daily custom
To hold an open table, yet when he arrived
I threw a feast in his honour and treated him
In both a distinguished and most intimate manner.
The truth is that his conversation held
An inexpressible charm, and he realized
For me the very type of the perfect man.

When the time came Humayun took his leave
To go to Sambhal, his appointed seat,
Where he remained six months. He became ill.
The climate did not suit him. Fever attacked him
And worsened daily. I ordered that he be brought
To Agra, so the best doctors might prescribe
Some treatment. He travelled by water several days.

Despite the remedies he got no better.
His life was despaired of. I was in despair
Till Abdul Kasim said, 'In such a case
A sacrifice of great value may incline God
To restore the patient's health.' Nothing was dearer
Than his life save my own. I offered it.
My friends protested, saying the great diamond
That came to me with Agra would suffice.
I entered the chamber where my son was lying
And circled his bed three times, saying each time,
'I take upon myself all that you suffer.'
I forthwith felt myself depressed and heavy
And in much pain. He rose in perfect health.
I called my noblemen. Placing their hands
In Humayun's as a mark of investiture,
I proclaimed him heir and placed him on the throne.
Those there concurred, and bound themselves to serve him.

Live-Oak

Curious Mishaps

As I was clipping my nails out in the yard
A squirrel came to take a look at me.
He twitched his rat-like face, stared at me hard,
Raised his right paw with smart solemnity

And placed it on his chest, as if on oath.
From a live-oak against the twilight sky
An owl swooped downwards to survey us both,
Judged distances, and with a hybrid cry –

Half dog, half pigeon – fell upon his prey.
The squirrel had no chance, being far from cover.
Incurious, he would have got away.
One hoot: one squeak; and things were quickly over.

The owl curved off. I stood, too stunned to move
Indoors, or to continue clipping nails.
A bowl of soup boiled over on my stove,
Adding to my more nugatory travails.

Song: 'Coast Starlight'

Some days I am so lonely, so content.
The dust lifts up. The trees are weatherbent.
The cypresses lean down against the sea.
The Californian poppies close early.

The poppies close at five. The Coast Starlight
Will get me to the City by tonight,
Will get me to the City and my friend,
Will get me to my month-long journey's end.

The cattle rest among the mustard flowers.
The Starlight circles past the prison towers.
The golfers pull their carts along the green.
The blackbird flies across the deep ravine.

Some days I feel a sadness not of grief.
The shadows lengthen on the earth's relief.
Salinas flows by like a silver shawl.
A girl waves from the ruined mission wall.

Now darkness falls – the moon gives little light.
O Starlight, ride into the gentle night.
O travellers, may starlight see you home.
O travellers, may you not sleep alone.

From California

Sunday night in the house.
The blinds drawn, the phone dead.
The sound of the kettle, the rain.
Supper: cheese, celery, bread.

For company, old letters
In the same disjointed script.
Old love wells up again,
All that I thought had slipped

Through the sieve of long absence
Is here with me again:
The long stone walls, the green
Hillsides renewed with rain.

The way you would lick your finger
And touch your forehead, the way
You hummed a phrase from the flute
Sonatas, or turned to say,

'Larches – the only conifers
That blend honestly with Wales.'
I walk with you again
Along those settled trails.   ~

It seems I started this poem
So many years ago
I cannot follow its ending
And must begin anew.

Blame, some bitterness,
I recall there were these.
Yet what survives is Bach
And a few blackberries.

Something of the 'falling sunlight',
In the phrase of Wang Wei,
Falls on my shadowed self.
I thank you that today

His words are open to me.
How much you have inspired
You cannot know. The end
Left much to be desired.

'There is a comfort in
The strength of love.' I quote
Another favourite
You vouchsafed me. Please note

The lack of hope or faith:
Neither is justified.
I have closed out the night.
The random rain outside

~

Rejuvenates the parched
Foothills along the Bay.
Anaesthetized by years
I think of you today

Not with impassionedness
So much as half a smile
To see the weathered past
Still worth my present while.

Song: 'Waiting'

As I stood on Dolores Street
With thoughts of sadness and defeat
A cat came from across the way
And sat beneath a Chevrolet.

The sun was hot. His grey-green eyes
Surveyed the scene with small surprise.
I plied my pencil furtively.
The cat took no account of me.

I drew the cat with stubby strokes.
I gave the cat appealing looks.
I walked to him. Without demur
He let me stroke his friendly fur.

My friend had gone to run a race.
My heart beat at an urgent pace.
In my mind's eye I saw him breast
The tape, then fall to earth and rest.

I wished that I could touch his hair
And be to him some comfort there,
But here I was, and here the cat,
And there he was, and that was that.

~

Since when my friend said we would meet
An hour has passed along the street.
The cat purrs in the noonday sun.
O cat, I know my friend has won!

Between Storms

The hills are green again, the lake
Murky. Continual storms
Over California have washed away
Houses, gouged the coastline,
Stranded bewildered seals,
Swept away walkers in aberrant waves
And left a limpness in my brain.
There is no cure –

Except that the light that comes
In the late afternoon after a storm
Enters my room and transfigures
Books, computer print-outs,
The wooden seal the fruitsellers gave me,
And my blue plastic poncho.
Beautiful beautiful light,
Heavy as honey, redolent

Of Cotswold stone
And of lemon groves on drier hills,
Drawing from the heart a music,
Departing suddenly.
Tonight another storm is forecast.
I look out at the two trees,
Uprooted, not yet cleared away,
And hear the squirrels chatter in distress.

And Some Have Madness Thrust upon Them

Salesmen have come in throughout the day
Bearing photocopying machines into my house.
They have copied graphs onto computer paper,
Bach onto tracing paper,
Academic documents onto sheets of plastic.
Prices have been quoted, reduced.
The more grief-stricken I look, the more they reduce their
　　prices,
And throw in bottles of toner.
I tell them I will think about the matter.

The Toshiba salesman says gently:
'Do yourself a favour – ask the others
If they have selenium drums.
To tell you the truth, those Sharp machines may be cheaper,
But that's because they're cheap. After a thousand copies
They look like dirt.' The Gestetner man,
Tight-jawed, grim
– His demonstration machine is being undemonstrative –
Says, 'Sure, there's an edge-void, but to be honest,
You'll find that on any machine, and as for the Minolta –
Look – these independent assessments speak for themselves.
I'll leave the machine here for you to . . . no, no, I insist.
You just think about it. It's a steal.'　　　　　　　　　～

I stare at the Gestetner 2000,
Squat, immovable on my dining table.
I set two places around it
And turn the lights low.
Outside the wind flings itself into the March trees
And I wait for my darling to appear.
I will place the wine on the lid.
It cannot be allowed to come between us.

Spring of Content

Since you have gone, it has grown fresh and still;
The blond hills have turned green, the winter rain
Has pressed the dust back to the earth again.
The ophthalmologist's almond tree is full,
No, swathed with frost-fine blossom, and the scent,
Pressing and light, converts the colourless air;
Grapes of wistaria are everywhere
Usurping walls where climbing roses aren't
Jostling each other in the breeze and sun;
Wild oats and barley intersperse with grass
And boisterous dandelions – and I lie hours
Cat-curled and narcoleptic on the lawn
And think of nothing – not even that you're away
Or that today is – is it? – Saturday.

Moonlight

Some lines from Trakl come to me: moonlight;
His sister plays the sonata once again.
It is as short of hope, as clear with pain.
I listen to the road outside. Despite
Years, despite years, tears blur my steadied sight
Like a bad joke irrelevant words arouse.
Through pylons, as before, the moon tonight
Sears with a fire new time and loves won't douse.

I see some things are much the same. If you
Knocked at my door some year I could not say,
'He lived here once, but now has moved away.'
Most things have lost their power to hurt. A few
Exceptions, moonlight, a quintet or two,
May cause these fits to re-occur, but now
I know there is not much that I can do.
I know that they will pass, somehow, somehow.

At any rate I've come to recognize
It's I who built this bleached cairn, stone by stone –
The first time that you spoke to me by phone,
Walks, Wordsworth, woodpeckers, Colombian highs,
The last time that I looked into your eyes:
A derelict memorial on a plain,
Its architect must in time realize
His plan to see beyond his work again.   ~

And as for you, my love of many years,
Who are so fine, quiet and unobsessed,
I wish you what you have already, rest
Of spirit. To you memory appears
Too little worth analysis or tears.
In my heart too I will it not to last,
Nor do I wish that when the moonlight sears
It should inveigle you into the past.

Abalone Soup

Grateful for the resin-scented night
And for the great full moon above the sea
With few remarks we drive to where the light
Brightens the crests of waves tentatively,
Dreaming, while dawn's left hand is in the sky
Of seabed shelves where abalone lie.

Smell of a skunk, coyote on the road,
The redwoods of the coast, a seagull's mew,
Twist to the cove where we now halt to unload
Weights, ab-knives made from leaf-springs, one or two
Yellow string bags to trail the catch to land.
I touch the water and pull back my hand.

They tug their wetsuits on. Jim strips a plant:
'It smells like liquorice.' The oval moon,
Squeezed by a fog-bank, loses shape. I can't
– No wetsuit – go with them. 'We'll be back soon.'
Custodian of their spectacles and keys,
I sit upon the least moist rock and freeze,

Watching them bob and strain to the far rock,
Four buoyant blots against a lightening blue.
Eight thirty. Where are they? At nine o'clock
I'll call up next of kin. 'How do you do –

Mrs Gebhart? Your son was lost at sea,
A martyr to cuisine.' Ah, abalone,

The gourmet's edelweiss, of the four A's
Of California – asparagus,
Ab, avocado, artichoke – you raise
Our palates to the most vertiginous
Conception of sublimity . . . . But here
Four heads, four snorkels, once again appear.

Beyond the narrow rocks, a stronger swell
Delays the last foray towards the shore,
And now, each twisting in its open shell,
Lie sixteen abalone; no, one more.
He is replaced – four abs each is the quota –
Upon a nearby reef below the water.

We climb the hillside on a path between
Wild sweetpea and convolvulus to the car.
One man with cramp (tight beavertail) is keen
On breakfast and on bed. Domestic war
Sputters around a mask and an ab-knife
Lost to the surge. Ah, well, no loss of life –

Or, rather, only sixteen. Beer and Brie
Resuscitate us as we view the catch,
Anticipating oral ecstasy.
Facing the slow Pacific swell we watch
Seven pelicans flap laxly across the sky,
Unperturbed by the traffic blustering by.   ~

Having three times had abalone steak,
Each time with (and by courtesy of) Jim,
Back at his house my pampered tastebuds ache
With lust for ab and gratitude to him.
Once having tasted abalone soup
Little is left to do in life but hope

That Mrs Chen – Jim's Chinese neighbour who,
Though reticent, one evening chanced to see
Him pounding abs in the yard and as he threw
The scraps away, exclaimed, 'Give those to me!',
One night appearing with two tureens at the door –
May grant her avid addicts an encore.

Love and Work

The fact is, this work is as dreary as shit.
I do not like it a bit.
While at it I wander off into a dream.
When I return, I scream.

If I had a lover
I'd bear it all, because when day is over
I could go home and find peace in bed.
Instead

The boredom pulps my brain
And there is nothing at day's end to help assuage the pain.
I am alone, as I have usually been.
The lawn is green.

The robin hops into the sprinkler's spray.
Day after day
I fill the feeder with bird-seed,
My one good deed.

Night after night
I turn off the porch light, the kitchen light.
The weight lodged in my spirit will not go
For years, I know.

~

There is so much to do
There isn't any time for feeling blue.
There isn't any point in feeling sad.
Things could be worse. Right now they're only bad.

Ceasing upon the Midnight

He stacks the dishes on the table.
He wants to die, but is unable
    To decide when and how.
    Why not, he wonders, now?

A piece of gristle catches his eye.
The phone rings; he turns to reply.
    A smell of burning comes
    From somewhere. Something hums.

The fridge. He looks at it. This room
Would make an unpacific tomb.
    He walks outside. The breeze
    Blows warmly, and he sees

A sky brushed clean of dust and haze.
He wanders in a lucid daze
    Beneath the live-oak tree
    Whose creaks accompany

The drifting hub of yellow light
Low on the hillcrest. Ah, tonight,
    How rich it seems to be
    Alive unhappily.   ~

'O sähst du, voller Mondenschein,
Zum letztenmal auf meine Pein,'
        He murmurs to convince
        Himself its force will rinse

The pus of memory from his mind,
Dispel the dust he's swept behind
        The furniture of days,
        And with beneficent rays

Kindle the taut and tearless eyes
With the quick current of surprise,
        Joy, frenzy, anything
        But this meandering

Down a dead river on a plain,
Null, unhorizoned, whose terrain,
        Devoid of entity,
        Leads to no open sea.

The moon, himself, his shadow, wine
And Li Bai's poem may define
        A breath, an appetite,
        His link to earth tonight.

He gets a bottle, pours a glass,
A few red droplets on the grass,
        Libation to the god
        Of oak-trees and of mud,   ~

Holds up its colour to the moon,
Drinks slowly, listens to the tune
    The branches improvise,
    Drinks, pours, drinks, pours, and lies

Face down on the moist grass and drinks
The dewdrops off its leaves. He thinks
    Of other moons he's seen
    And creatures he has been.

The breeze comforts him where he sprawls.
Raccoons' eyes shine. A grey owl calls.
    He imitates its cries,
    Chants shreds, invents replies.

The alcohol, his molecules,
The clear and intimate air, the rules
    Of metre, shield him from
    Himself. To cease upon

The midnight under the live-oak
Seems too derisory a joke.
    The bottle lies on the ground.
    He sleeps. His sleep is sound.

Unclaimed

To make love with a stranger is the best.
There is no riddle and there is no test. –

To lie and love, not aching to make sense
Of this night in the mesh of reference.

To touch, unclaimed by fear of imminent day,
And understand, as only strangers may.

To feel the beat of foreign heart to heart
Preferring neither to prolong nor part.

To rest within the unknown arms and know
That this is all there is; that this is so.

All You Who Sleep Tonight

1990

For Shantum and Aradhana

I *Romantic Residues*

Round and Round

After a long and wretched flight
That stretched from daylight into night,
Where babies wept and tempers shattered
And the plane lurched and whisky splattered
Over my plastic food, I came
To claim my bags from Baggage Claim.

Around, the carousel went around.
The anxious travellers sought and found
Their bags, intact or gently battered,
But to my foolish eyes what mattered
Was a brave suitcase, red and small,
That circled round, not mine at all.

I knew that bag. It must be hers.
We hadn't met in seven years!
And as the steel plates squealed and clattered
My happy memories chimed and chattered.
An old man pulled it off the Claim.
My bags appeared; I did the same.

Protocols

What can I say to you? How can I now retract
    All that that fool, my voice, has spoken –
Now that the facts are plain, the placid surface cracked,
    The protocols of friendship broken?

I cannot walk by day as now I walk at dawn
    Past the still house where you lie sleeping.
May the sun burn away these footprints on the lawn
    And hold you in its warmth and keeping.

A Style of Loving

Light now restricts itself
To the top half of trees;
The angled sun
Slants honey-coloured rays
That lessen to the ground
As we bike through
The corridor of Palm Drive.
We two

Have reached a safety the years
Can claim to have created:
Unconsummated, therefore
Unjaded, unsated.
Picnic, movie, ice-cream;
Talk; to clear my head
Hot buttered rum – coffee for you;
And so not to bed.

And so we have set the question
Aside, gently.
Were we to become lovers
Where would our best friends be?
You do not wish, nor I
To risk again
This savoured light for noon's
High joy or pain.

Across

Across these miles I wish you well.
May nothing haunt your heart but sleep.
May you not sense what I don't tell.
May you not dream, or doubt, or weep.

May what my pen this peaceless day
Writes on this page not reach your view
Till its deferred print lets you say
It speaks to someone else than you.

Equals

It's evening. I lack courage.
The sun has set behind the fogbound hill.
The breeze has died, even the jays are silent.
The lake is still.

I sit down. I am tired.
To speak my mind's beyond my power to do.
I have no warranty against the vision
I have of you.

You're close, and cannot help me.
The concrete slab is cold. The arcing stars
Pass too high overhead for easy grasping
Even if ours.

But frogs' songs, quiet ripples,
These we may claim, and for this while concede
We are, at least in hope, unequal equals,
If not in deed.

Mistaken

I smiled at you because I thought that you
Were someone else; you smiled back; and there grew
Between two strangers in a library
Something that seemed like love; but you loved me
(If that's the word) because you thought that I
Was other than I was. And by and by
We found we'd been mistaken all the while
From that first glance, that first mistaken smile.

Sit

Sit, drink your coffee here; your work can wait awhile.
You're twenty-six, and still have some of life ahead.
No need for wit; just talk vacuities, and I'll
Reciprocate in kind, or laugh at you instead.

The world is too opaque, distressing, and profound.
This twenty minutes' rendezvous will make my day:
To sit here in the sun, with grackles all around,
Staring with beady eyes, and you two feet away.

The Room and the Street

After a few short bars
You stop and look at me.
The last of our few hours
Is over. I am free.

Free now to leave this room,
Its broken chords, its light,
Its scent of lilac bloom,
And be elsewhere tonight.

You wrestle for reserve
And its keen dignity.
Now is the time to serve
Eviction upon me.

'I will not see you out.
I hope you understand.'
Only your mouth speaks doubt.
I take your chordless hand.   ~*

---

*   a stanza break at the end of a page is marked by ~
    no stanza break at the end of a page is marked by ⸜

I see my younger grief
Accusing with your eyes.
I cannot give relief
Nor can you give me lies.

But do not say I've wrecked
Your peace and caused you pain.
I've done that, I suspect,
But won't do so again.

You see me to the street.
The cars slosh past. It's true
That I may have light feet.
I'm not in love with you.

And yet with half my heart
I wish I were – that we,
Knowing that we must part,
Could share this equally.

Great city, harsh and tall,
In the cold throes of spring –
Numb and distract us all
That love may lose its sting.

A cab. You take my hand,
Then stand and frown awhile.
At my express demand
You undertake to smile.

Walk

I walked last night with my old friend
Past the old house where we first met,
Past each known bush and each known bend.
The moon shone, and the path was wet.

No one passed by us as we strolled
At our sad ease. Though hand in hand
We did not speak. Our hands grew cold,
Yet we walked on as we had planned.

We did not deal in words or tears.
At the dead light we did not rage.
What change had crept through our forked years
We did not have the will to gauge.

The lights went out. Who lived here now,
Paid rent, and saw spring come and go
Lived past the range of why and how
For those who had no wish to know.

II *In Other Voices*

To Wei Ba, Who Has Lived Away from the Court

translated from the Chinese of Du Fu

Like stars that rise when the other has set,
For years we two friends have not met.
How rare it is then that tonight
We once more share the same lamplight.
Our youth has quickly slipped away
And both of us are turning grey.
Old friends have died, and with a start
We hear the sad news, sick at heart.
How could I, twenty years before,
Know that I'd be here at your door?
When last I left, so long ago,
You were unmarried. In a row
Suddenly now your children stand,
Welcome their father's friend, demand
To know his home, his town, his kin –
Till they're chased out to fetch wine in.
Spring chives are cut in the night rain
And steamed rice mixed with yellow grain.
To mark the occasion, we should drink
Ten cups of wine straight off, you think –
But even ten can't make me high,
So moved by your old love am I.
The mountains will divide our lives,
Each to his world, when day arrives.

Lithuania: Question and Answer

To Ephraim Oshry, rabbi, this is the case:
A woman of a good family in Kovno
Came to me weeping, comfortless. The Germans
Had raped her and had tattooed on her arm
The legend, 'Whore for Hitler's troops.' She found
Her husband recently, and they intended
To build again a proper Jewish home.
(Their children had been killed.) But when he saw
The words he was appalled, and felt constrained
To ask, 'Is she permitted me or not?
Was there consent in this?' She came to me,
Eyes asking mercy. Tell me what to do.

★

This took place in the city, not the field.
Nor did she cry out, therefore we may assume
That she consented. But Maimonides
Has said a sword above the head spells force.
Would it avail her to cry out? A sword
Was over all our heads. She could not wish
To lie with the abominable wolves.

This leads to the conclusion in this case
That she was forced. For in addition to

What we have used above, some others say
Even in the city with no witnesses
Such words are to be trusted.

                         Far be it
From anyone to cast aspersion on
These honourable women. He who hears
The pleadings of the poor will heal their sorrow.
I know that some men have divorced such wives.
Alas for us this happens in our times.

Preserve those words. They bear no tint of shame.
They will remind you that we yet shall see
The fall of the transgressors from whose face
Is blotted any human semblance – wolves,
Beasts of the forest and voracious wolves
Who hasten to spill innocent blood and kill
The pious and the upright. Read those words
But think of Moses' words, the man of God:
'Sing aloud, O you nations, of His people;
For he avenges the blood of his servants, and
Renders revenge upon His adversaries.'

Work and Freedom

Even small events that others might not notice,
I found hard to forget. In Auschwitz truly
I had no reason to complain of boredom.
If an incident affected me too deeply
I could not go straight home to my wife and children.
I would ride my horse till the terrible picture faded.
Often at night I would wander through the stables
And seek relief among my beloved horses.
At home my thoughts, often and with no warning,
Turned to such things. When I saw my children playing
Or observed my wife's delight over our youngest
I would walk out and stand beside the transports,
The fire-pits, crematoriums, or gas-chambers.
My wife ascribed my gloom to some annoyance
Connected with my work but I was thinking,
'How long will our happiness last?' I was not happy
Once the mass exterminations had started.

My work, such unease aside, was never-ending,
My colleagues untrustworthy, those above me
Reluctant to understand or even to listen –
Yet everyone thought the commandant's life was heaven.
My wife and children, true, were well looked after.
Her garden was a paradise of flowers.
The prisoners, trying no doubt to attract attention,
Never once failed in little acts of kindness.

Not one of them, in our house, was badly treated:
My wife would have loved to give the prisoners presents –
And as for the children, they begged for cigarettes for them,
Especially for those who worked in the garden and brought
    them
Tortoises, martens, lizards, cats. Each Sunday
We'd walk to the stables, never omitting the kennels
Where the dogs were kept. My children loved all creatures
But most of all our foal and our two horses.
In summer they splashed in the wading pool, but their
    greatest
Joy was to bathe together with Daddy – who had
Limited hours, alas, for these childish pleasures.
My wife said, 'Think of us, not only the service.'
How could she know what lay so heavily on me?
(It made life hard, this excessive sense of duty.)

When Auschwitz was divided, Pohl in a kindly
And quite exceptional gesture gave me the option
– Perhaps as recompense for the last assignment –
To head DK or to run Sachsenhausen.
I had one day to decide. At first the thought of
Uprooting myself from Auschwitz made me unhappy,
So involved had I grown in its tasks and troubles.
But in the end I was glad to gain my freedom.

Ghalib, Two Years After the Mutiny

Dear Yusuf Mirza, none but God can know my plight.
Men have gone mad from cares far less than those I fight.
But grief and cares for what? you ask – what do I claim? –
For death, for parting, for my livelihood, my name.

Whose deaths? I leave aside the stricken Mughal court;
In Delhi proper – not the Inauspicious Fort –
Your uncle; Ashur Beg; and Mir Nāsir-ud-din;
My sister's grandson too, a mere child of nineteen;

Mustafa Khan; his sons; the blood flows from my pen.
The names go on; O God! What can replace such men?
Those of my friends who live, like Miran and Majruh,
Condemned to roam the world, may God preserve them too.

My brother died insane; his children and his wife,
Stranded in Jaipur, eke their pittance of a life.
The children of high lords go begging in the street.
My household, God knows how, finds just enough to eat.

Nor is my time my own. I have grown old. How can
I bear this load? I am no giant but a man.
I leave my sickbed, try to sit an hour or two
To write, to plan, to think – but there's too much to do.   ~

As for sustaining wine, my cash won't spill that far –
Still less to buy a gift if called to the durbar.
They used to call me once. Will they do so again? –
I who have neither helped nor harmed the Englishmen.

I'm sending you an ode about my life, which night
And day for two long months I've sweated blood to write.
Say if you think my skill has cheated fortune's knife
Even if my heart lacks fire – why fire? even life.

In my old eulogy, for Amjad Ali's name
I've slotted 'Wājid' in; but God has done the same.
Such verse in praise of kings, just notch it down a peg:
I wrote it not to show my prowess but to beg.

More news. That gentle boy, Shivji Ram's son and pride,
Fell ill, lay two days thus, and on the third day died.
His father is distraught with grief, and for my part
I have lost two more friends, one dead, one sick at heart.

Another twenty months, and I too will be dust:
My body to Rampur, my soul to light, I trust.
What grief, joy, praise or shame afflict me in this spell
I will find strength to face. Goodbye. May all be well.

A Doctor's Journal Entry for August 6, 1945

The morning stretched calm, beautiful, and warm.
Sprawling half-clad, I gazed out at the form
Of shimmering leaves and shadows. Suddenly
A strong flash, then another, startled me.
I saw the old stone lantern brightly lit.
Magnesium flares? While I debated it,
The roof, the walls and, as it seemed, the world
Collapsed in timber and debris, dust swirled
Around me – in the garden now – and, weird,
My drawers and undershirt had disappeared.
A splinter jutted from my mangled thigh.
My right side bled, my cheek was torn, and I
Dislodged, detachedly, a piece of glass,
All the time wondering what had come to pass.
Where was my wife? Alarmed, I gave a shout,
'Where are you, Yecko-san?' My blood gushed out.
The artery in my neck? Scared for my life,
I called out, panic-stricken, to my wife.
Pale, bloodstained, frightened, Yecko-san emerged,
Holding her elbow. 'We'll be fine,' I urged –
'Let's get out quickly.' Stumbling to the street
We fell, tripped up by something at our feet.
I gasped out, when I saw it was a head:
'Excuse me, please excuse me—' He was dead:
A gate had crushed him. There we stood, afraid.
A house standing before us tilted, swayed,

Toppled, and crashed. Fire sprang up in the dust,
Spread by the wind. It dawned on us we must
Get to the hospital: we needed aid –
And I should help my staff too. (Though this made
Sense to me then, I wonder how I could
Have hoped, hurt as I was, to do much good.)
My legs gave way. I sat down on the ground.
Thirst seized me, but no water could be found.
My breath was short, but bit by bit my strength
Seemed to revive, and I got up at length.
I was still naked, but I felt no shame,
This thought disturbed me somewhat, till I came
Upon a soldier, standing silently,
Who gave the towel round his neck to me.
My legs, stiff with dried blood, rebelled. I said
To Yecko-san she must go on ahead.
She did not wish to, but in our distress
What choice had we? A dreadful loneliness
Came over me when she had gone. My mind
Ran at high speed, my body crept behind.
I saw the shadowy forms of people, some
Were ghosts, some scarecrows, all were wordless, dumb –
Arms stretched straight out, shoulder to dangling hand;
It took some time for me to understand
The friction on their burns caused so much pain
They feared to chafe flesh against flesh again.
Those who could, shuffled in a blank parade
Towards the hospital. I saw, dismayed,
A woman with a child stand in my path –
Both naked. Had they come back from the bath?
I turned my gaze, but I was at a loss
That she should stand thus, till I came across

A naked man – and now the thought arose
That some strange thing had stripped us of our clothes.
The face of an old woman on the ground
Was marred with suffering, but she made no sound.
Silence was common to us all. I heard
No cries of anguish, or a single word.

Soon

I shall die soon, I know.
This thing is in my blood.
It will not let me go.
It saps my cells for food.

It soaks my nights in sweat
And breaks my days in pain.
No hand or drug can treat
These limbs for love or gain.

Love was the strange first cause
That bred grief in its seed,
And gain knew its own laws –
To fix its place and breed.

He whom I love, thank God,
Won't speak of hope or cure.
It would not do me good.
He sees that I am sure.

He knows what I have read
And will not bring me lies.
He sees that I am dead.
I read it in his eyes.   ~

How am I to go on –
How will I bear this taste,
My throat cased in white spawn –
These hands that shake and waste?

Stay by my steel ward bed
And hold me where I lie.
Love me when I am dead
And do not let me die.

III *In Other Places*

Hill Dawn

Sudden and swift I hear
A distant avalanche.
The last stars disappear.
The blue snows flush and blanch.

As shadows, then as mass,
The mountains of Garhwal
Serrate and curve by pass
And peak towards Nepal.

The rising mist now fills
The forest rifts below:
Peninsulas of hills
And lakes of fluid snow.

Oak, rhododendron, pine
And cedar freed from night
Recede in a design
As visionless as white.

Suzhou Park

Magnolia trees float out their flowers,
Vast, soft, upon a rubbish heap.
The grandfather sits still for hours:
His lap-held grandson is asleep.
Above him plane trees fan the sky.
Nearby, a man in muted dance
Does tai-qi-quan. A butterfly
Flies whitely past his easy trance.
A magpie flaps back to its pine.
A sparrow dust-rolls, fluffs, and cheeps.
The humans rest in a design:
One writes, one thinks, one moves, one sleeps.
    The leaves trace out the stencilled stone,
    And each is in his dream alone.

Night in Jiangning

A glass of tea; the moon;
The frogs croak in the weeds.
A bat wriggles down across
Gold disc to silver reeds.
The distant light of lamps.
The whirr of winnowing grain.
The peace of loneliness.
The scent of imminent rain.

Lion Grove, Suzhou

Like life, there is a plan but little sense.
Each step, each cryptic path, each stone and plane,
Each thwarting twist implies intelligence
Far more than playful and far less than sane.
Yet children love it, gulp with shocking glee
When parents, desperate that they may have drowned,
Hunt through the pool-pierced maze of masonry
And are too pleased for anger when they're found.

Tourists

She looked at him, he at the guide.
The facts rolled on; they walked outside
To where confinement seemed less dense,
Breath quieter, rinsed of the pretence
Of the group-jollity that swore
And clucked and posed and clicked before
The turtle stele. The last light
Eased them as travellers into night.

They did not speak the language though
They'd lived here forty years ago
In hopeless times and cleaner air
And had been happy. A despair
Of change had led them back again,
Though group-contained, to an old scene.
Yet now the unaltered steps had made
Him breathless, her therefore, afraid.

There on the Drum Tower, sipping tea,
They watched the sun set lingeringly
Across the black bricks, leaves and dust
That were the city. They discussed
Their next day's pre-planned enterprise
And turned their unexpectant eyes
To where, smoke-red and unentire,
There glowed out an uncertain fire.

Qingdao: December

Here by the sea this quiet night
I see the moon through misted light.
The water laps the rocks below.
I hear it lap and swash and go.
The pine-trees, dense and earthward-bent,
Suffuse the air with resin-scent.
A landward breeze combs through my hair
And cools the earth with salted air.

Here all attempt in life appears
Irrelevant. The erosive years
That built the moon and rock and tree
Speak of a sweet futility
And say that we who are from birth
Caressed by unimpulsive earth
Should yield our fever to the trees,
The seaward light and resined breeze.

Here by the sea this quiet night
Where my still spirit could take flight
And nullify the heart's distress
Into the peace of wordlessness,
I see the light, I breathe the scent,
I touch the insight, but a bent
Of heart exacts its old designs
And draws my hands to write these lines.

The Monk at Han Shan Temple

He fingers his dark rosary
And sounds the gong, again, again,
Blinks at the flash photography
Of the grave Japanese businessmen.
They leave. He turns and, with a smile,
Asks me, *Are Indian people poor?*
Are they all Buddhist? In a while
He talks about the Gang of Four.
Ten Years – we were sent down – He stares
In contemplation at a face,
Gold, calm, unsorrowing, that bears
Pain, age, death, vandals, and disgrace –
Then sees my puzzled eyes, and brings
Himself to earth, and milder things.

On the Fiftieth Anniversary of the Golden Gate Bridge

The grey Pacific, curved and old,
    Indented, bare,
Flings out, day after day, its cold
    Breakers to where

Marin and San Francisco shore
    The rapid strait
Christened a century before,
    The Golden Gate.

Both counties know this still might be
    A wistful view
If Strauss had not resolved to see
    The matter through.

Though courts twice threatened it, though storms
    Once washed away
The trestles of his bridge, two forms
    Inched day by day

Closer so that the ocean's rift
    Might disappear.
Two stubborn decades were his gift;
    He died next year.

~

How fortunate such greatness stirred
 In his small frame
That even obstacles deferred
 To set his fame.

How sad that he should be so small
 In his great mind
To disacknowledge after all
 Him who designed

This shape of use and loveliness
 And to subject
Ellis, his partner in success,
 To long neglect.

Two towers hold the cable; ton
 On ton of it
Hangs chainlike from their peaks, yet one
 Alone is lit.

But let us leave blurred facts behind
 In the plain hope
That each will be at last assigned
 His equal scope

– A claim that justice can in no
 Clear light refuse –
And glimpse the fifty years that flow
 Down from those views.

         ~

How much of life has passed above,
　　Below, upon.
How much of hatred and of love
　　Has come and gone!

What portion of the soldiers who
　　Sailed out to war
Sailed back beneath the bridge they knew
　　Four years before?

How many lovers who have found
　　A world of mist
To cloak them from the world around
　　Have stood and kissed

Where others, who have walked alone
　　On a bright day,
In unsupported grief have thrown
　　Their lives away.

How many more have been impelled
　　From death they craved,
By force or by persuasion held,
　　And somehow saved.

'I would have been happy and dead,
　　I'm sure, by now,
If it weren't for those heroes,' said
　　One saved somehow.

And surely, if one had to die,
    What happier place
To quit that over-salted pie,
    The human race?

Indeed this morning's pilgrimage
    Just after light
Saw us frail lemmings on the bridge
    Jammed in so tight,

Breathing against a neighbour's face,
    Gasping for air,
We almost quit the human race
    Right then and there.

But panic could not scuttle love,
    A love half-blind,
An amiable affection of
    A civic kind

For what we've known for years, for all
    Who feel the same,
As when in darkness we recall
    A common name.

It is as if the bridge's core,
    Its grace, its strength
Could not have not been on this shore,
    And that at length   ~

The green and empty hills agreed
        That humankind
Might be allowed this binding deed –
        Which brings to mind

The engineering dean's reply
        To her who said,
'If such a manmade thing should lie,
        Metalled and dead

Across God's natural world, why should
        We think it best?' –
'That's a fine pendant on your God-
        created breast.'

Cool repartee; but would it still
        Suffice to douse
The later, enigmatic will
        Of Mrs Strauss?

The plaque upon his tomb displays
        The bridge; on hers
The bridgeless strait, as if she says
        That she demurs.

The Scent of Sage and Bay

The yellow lupins bloom, and far below I see
    The distant cars in soundless motion.
Below the strip of road the cliffs drop brokenly
    Down to a placid blur of ocean.

High on the hill I sit and watch an errant jay
    Set a low twig of redwood swinging.
Wild columbines are here, the scent of sage and bay,
    The slanting light, a cricket singing.

IV *Quatrains*

Telephone

I see you smile across the phone
And feel the moisture of your hair
And smell the musk of your cologne . . .
Hello? Is anybody there?

God's Love

God loves us all, I'm pleased to say –
Or those who love him anyway –
Or those who love him and are good.
Or so they say. Or so he should.

Dark Road

The road is dark, and home is far.
Sleep now, in the poor state you are.
Tonight be dreamless, and tomorrow
Wake free from fear, half-free of sorrow.

Pigeons

The pigeons swing across the square,
Suddenly voiceless in mid-air,
Flaunting, against their civic coats,
The glossy oils that scarf their throats.

Pomegranate

The most impassioned of all trees,
The home of three intensities:
Gnarled trunk, dark concentrated leaf,
And flowers that burn in love and grief.

Southward Bound

From the grey willows of the North
Bright sprays of green now fountain forth,
For each train-hour towards Nanjing
Is two days' journey into Spring.

Pendulum

The nervous mother shouting ceaselessly
At her roped children swinging from the tree
Remembers with a start she once was young
And terrified her mother as she swung.

Advice to Orators

In speech it's best – though not the only way –
Indeed the best, it's true, can be the worst –
Though often I . . . as I had meant to say:
Qualify later; state the premise first.

Cant

In Cant's resilient, venerable lies
There's something for the artist to take heart.
They tell the truth that fiction never dies,
And that tradition is the soul of art.

Malefic Things

Imagining the flowerpot attacked it,
The kitten flung the violets near and far.
And yet, who knows? This morning, as I backed it,
My car was set upon by a parked car.

Door

He dreams beyond exhaustion of a door
At which he knocked and entered years before,
But now no street or city comes to mind
Nor why he knocked, nor what he came to find.

Night Watch

Awake for hours and staring at the ceiling
Through the unsettled stillness of the night
He grows possessed of the obsessive feeling
That dawn has come and gone and brought no light.

Condition

I have to speak – I must – I should – I ought . . .
I'd tell you how I love you if I thought
The world would end tomorrow afternoon.
But short of that . . . well, it might be too soon.

Half Out of Sleep

Half out of sleep I watch your sleeping face.
Behind your eyelids' restlessness I see
A dream that waking may not quite displace:
If there were equity you'd dream of me.

Prandial Plaint

My love, I love your breasts. I love your nose.
I love your accent and I love your toes.
I am your slave. One word, and I obey.
But please don't slurp your coffee in that way.

Interpretation

Somewhere within your loving look I sense,
Without the least intention to deceive,
Without suspicion, without evidence,
Somewhere within your heart the heart to leave.

The End

A towel, fig-bars, and a bottle of mead.
The End. I cannot grasp it, and I plead.
You cannot 'keep me hanging', as you say.
Well, cut me down tomorrow, not today.

Promise

I will be easy company; the blur
Of what I longed for once will fade to space.
No thought that could discomfort you will stir.
My eyes will painlessly survey your face.

Reunion

If you had known . . . if I had known . . . ah well,
We played our cards so suavely, who could tell?
Ten years ago, so suavely, with such pain . . .
And, being wise, will do so once again.

Passage

Your eyes, my understanding, all will rot;
The trees we see, the books we read, will go;
The way that we use words, as like as not;
And we are fortunate that this is so.

V Meditations of the Heart

The Stray Cat

The grey cat stirs upon the ledge
Outside the glass doors just at dawn.
I open it; he tries to wedge
His nose indoors. It is withdrawn.
He sits back to assess my mood.
He sees me frown; he thinks of food.

I am familiar with his stunts.
His Grace, unfed, will not expire.
He may be hungry, but he hunts
When need compels him, or desire.
Just yesterday he caught a mouse
And yoyo'd it outside the house.

But now he turns his topaz eyes
Upon my eyes, which must reveal
The private pressures of these days,
The numb anxieties I feel.
But no, his greyness settles back
And yawns, and lets his limbs go slack.

He ventures forth an easy paw
As if in bargain. Thus addressed,
I fetch a bowl, and watch him gnaw
The star-shaped nuggets he likes best.
He is permitted food, and I
The furred indulgence of a sigh.

Poet

for Irina Ratushinskaya

She lived for six years in a cage. When I
Am inclined to regret the way things are, I think
Of her who through long cold and pain did not
Betray the ones she loved or plead for mercy.
They censored the few letters they allowed.
Cabbage and bread, rotten and stale, were food.
While outside governments and springs went round
And summits, thaws, and great events occurred,
Here inside was no hope. Years of her youth
Were sickened for no crime. She did not even
Know if her lover knew she was alive.
The paper she'd written poems on was removed.
What could she find? – the swirls in the cold blue light
Through bars so thick her hands could not pass through
     them –
Those swirls of blue light and the heels of bread
She shared with some companionable mouse.
Her poems she memorised line by line and destroyed.
The Contents were what was difficult to remember.

Adagio

Fate is against me (though only in Vienna)
                    – Wolfgang Amadeus Mozart, Letters

No need for *dolce*; once more, unemphasised,
The theme's slow clarity curves above the strings.
He does not awe us yet for while we listen
There is no more than this plain tapestry.
He never, like the great Beethoven thunders,
'My stomach's aching and my heart is breaking
And you will hear me,' yet to hear him is
To suffer all heartbreak, to assume all sorrow
And to survive. Where does his music cry,
'I could not sleep all night for pain. Dear Friend,
Picture my situation – ill and full
Of grief and care. I am in want – could you
Assist me with a trifle? O God, here I am
With fresh entreaties instead of with thanks.' . . . 'Death
When we think of it is the true goal of our life.'
'I could not write for very grief; black thoughts
(Which I must forcibly banish) . . .'

                                        We listen to
The adagio of the Clarinet Quintet; if
We see the abyss, as who can not, who can
Resist the enveloping tranquillity
Drawn from the heart of 1789
In the clear supple lilt of one who like
The nightingale, his breast against the thorn,   ⚡

Sang jubilantly in sorrow, who defied
The immobility of childhood fame
To work this web of tenderness between
The freedom of a child and a man's power
Two years before an endless requiem.

Mist

The wires sink into the mist.
The red madrone trunks blur to grey.
The roadway shortens at each twist.
The headlights contradict the day.

In the bright valley that we left,
Each needle, leaf and cone distinct,
In clarity's excessive heft
Like baffled owls we winced and blinked.

Did we expect this height might give
Far air to shape what lay below?
Or did we wish for mist to sieve
Even the nearness we should know?

Here on a lesser planet's crust
How may we hope that we exist
To mark a vision in our trust
Too bright for us and dim for mist? –

To see clear through this muffled light
That grants no needle, leaf or cone,
Or hold unchanged in changing sight
The redness of the grey madrone.

How Rarely These Few Years

How rarely these few years, as work keeps us aloof,
    Or fares, or one thing or another,
Have we had days to spend under our parents' roof:
    Myself, my sister, and my brother.

All five of us will die; to reckon from the past
    This flesh and blood is unforgiving.
What's hard is that just one of us will be the last
    To bear it all and go on living.

Things

Put back the letter, half conceived
From error, half to see you grieved.
Some things are seen and disbelieved.

Some talk of failings, some of love –
That terms are reckoned from above –
What could she have been thinking of?

As if aloneness were a sign
Of greater wisdom in design
To bear the torque of me and mine.

As if the years were lists of goods,
A helve of dares, a head of shoulds
To hack a route through rotten woods.

As if creation wrapped the heart
Impenetrably in its art,
As if the land upon the chart

Were prior to the acred land
And that a mark could countermand
The houses and the trees that stand.   ~

Though she would fell them if she could,
They will stand, and they will have stood
For all the will of dare and should.

Put it away. You cannot find
In a far reading of this kind
One character for heart or mind.

Read into things; they will remain.
Things fall apart and feel no pain.
And things, if not the world, are sane.

Voices

Voices in my head,
Chanting, 'Kisses. Bread.
Prove yourself. Fight. Shove.
Learn. Earn. Look for love,'

Drown a lesser voice.
Silent now of choice:
'Breathe in peace, and be
Still, for once, like me.'

Heart

I wake at three, in some slight pain.
I hear no sound of clock or rain,
No chorus of the stars, no gong,
Mosquito, siren, horn or plane.

Only my heart beats slow and strong.
I listen to its certain song.
It does not sympathise but strives
To beat all night and all day long.

Whether my spirit soars or dives,
My blood, at its compulsion, drives
Through its elastic chambers, through
My arteries, my veins, my lives.

Above all, to my heart I'm true.
It does not tell me what to do.
It beats, I live, it beats again.
For what? I wish I knew it knew.

The Wind

The bay is thick with flecks of white.
The freezing air is honed and thinned.
The gulls sleep on the stones tonight,
Wings locked against the prising wind.
With no companion to my mood,
Against the wind, as it should be,
I walk, but in my solitude
Bow to the wind that buffets me.

All You Who Sleep Tonight

All you who sleep tonight
Far from the ones you love,
No hand to left or right,
And emptiness above –

Know that you aren't alone.
The whole world shares your tears,
Some for two nights or one,
And some for all their years.

Three
Chinese Poets

1992

Translations of poems by
Wang Wei, Li Bai and Du Fu

To Yin Chuang

Professor Chuang, whose stern pen drew
Red rings around my puerile scrawling,
I hope this book appears to you,
If not appealing, not appalling.

Enthusiastic and sardonic,
Exacting, warm and too soon past,
Your classes, once my daily tonic,
Have borne eccentric fruit at last.

Acknowledgements

I have consulted a number of books for explanations and original text. I am particularly indebted to *A Little Primer of Tu Fu* by David Hawkes (Oxford University Press); *The Poetry of Wang Wei* by Pauline Yu (Indiana University Press); and *Li Tai Bai Quan Ji* (Collected Poems of Li Bai, 2 vols; Xianggang Guangzhi Shuju, i.e., Kwong Chi Book Company, Hong Kong).

I would like to thank my friend Andrew Andreasen, who looked over these translations and made many valuable suggestions; and David Hawkes, who helped me greatly with two of Wang Wei's poems – 'Autumn Nightfall at My Place in the Hills' and 'Ballad of the Peach Tree Spring'.

V.S.

Note on Pronunciation

I have used Pinyin, the standard transliteration of Mandarin Chinese used in mainland China, throughout this book except for well-known names like the Yangtze. In certain older transliterations Li Bai and Du Fu are written as Li Po and Tu Fu.

Most Pinyin consonants sound roughly the same in Chinese as in English. The notable exceptions are: c pronounced as 'ts'; q as 'chh'; x as 'sh'; z as 'dz'; zh as 'j'.

Most Pinyin vowels sound roughly the same in Chinese as in English, except for i in the following syllables: chi pronounced as 'chhrr'; ci as 'tss'; ri as 'rr'; shi as 'shrr'; si as 'ss'; zhi as 'jrr'; zi as 'dzz'.

Introduction

Works in translation from languages I do not understand have had as deep an influence on my own writing as works I can read in the original. In some cases the translations have so moved me that I have tried to learn the original language of the work. In others, the form or the spirit of the writing has served as a template for my own inspiration. Life is short, and I doubt I will ever have the delight of reading Pushkin in Russian, Molière in French, or Homer in Greek. But to have at hand Charles Johnston's *Eugene Onegin*, Richard Wilbur's *Tartuffe* or Robert Fitzgerald's *Iliad* has allowed me at least some ingress into worlds that would otherwise be unreachable and most likely unimaginable.

This book is presented as a dual offering – as thanks to those three translators of one generation who have meant so much to me, and as thanks to the three Chinese poets of another generation whose original poems have meant even more. If you, who are reading this, get some pleasure from their poems, it will be in spite of the unremovable barriers of language, which are passable only in part. Much – possibly most – of what they say will be lost, but I hope that even such limited access to the works of Wang Wei, Li Bai and Du Fu as these translations provide will be worthwhile.

The Chinese is one of the richest and certainly the oldest continuous tradition of poetry, stretching back to the *Book of Songs*, which was recorded 2,500 years ago. The three Tang dynasty poets translated in the present volume fall about midway along the line of time stretching from then until now. They lived in the eighth century AD, in an age of great cultural glory interrupted by a disastrous civil war.

The Tang dynasty was founded in 618 by a young man who, after crushing his military rivals and filially installing his father on the throne for eight years, took over as emperor himself under the name of Tai Zong. He recruited talent, honed the administration, expanded China's frontiers and founded an academy at the capital Changan, which became the foremost seat of learning in the world. After his death and that of his somewhat incompetent son and successor, one of Tai Zong's erstwhile concubines installed herself on the throne of China as the Empress Wu. She ruled through intrigue and force for fifteen years until 705, and is one of the most controversial figures in Chinese history. One of her innovations was the inclusion of poetry composition as a compulsory subject in the imperial civil service examinations, which until then had dealt mainly with Confucian texts. This measure was to have a profound influence in contributing to the remarkable reflowering of poetry in the next generation.

Wang Wei, Li Bai and Du Fu grew up under the Emperor Ming Huang, whose long reign began in 713 and lasted for most of their lives. The first decades of his reign were seen both at the time and ever afterwards as a golden age, marked by unprecedented efficiency in government, peace at home and on the borders, economic prosperity and brilliance in the arts. Then, after a long decline, disaster struck.

The emperor, increasingly under the influence of his favourite concubine Yang Guifei, lost all taste for his duties. He became obsessed with extravagant expenditure at court and on military expansion, which he financed by increases in taxation levied on the common people. Honest officials were dismissed, and Yang Guifei's rapacious relatives and favourites were installed in high office. One such favourite was the fat, sinister and capable barbarian general An Lushan, who at first was ingratiatingly jolly and gratefully absorbed the gifts, resources and positions lavished on him. In 755, however, he declared rebellion on the throne, and marched on Changan. The imperial family and court fled in panic, and An Lushan's forces took control of the capital. It took years to crush the rebellion and the subsidiary rebellions it spawned, and the cost was terrible. Over ten million lives were lost, the economy was devastated, and the country divided into what were virtually military fiefdoms with only nominal imperial sway. The Tang empire staggered on for another century and a half, but its days of grandeur and strength were over.

Tang dynasty China, a huge and diverse country in an age of slow communications, was ruled from the capital by imperial fiat transmitted through and tempered by an elite civil service spread throughout the country. This highly literate elite, recruited largely through rigorous competitive examinations, was both the creator of and the major audience for poetry. The ability to compose poetry was considered to be one of the accomplishments of a scholar-gentleman even before it was made a compulsory subject in the examinations; afterwards it became a necessity. It was moreover accepted as a profound medium not only of self-expression but also of the indirect expression of moral or political philosophy.

The world into which the three almost exactly contemporary poets – Wang Wei, Li Bai and Du Fu – were born can be sensed in many specific aspects of their poetry; for example, their stance with respect to the court and affairs of state, and the value they placed on friendship in a world of slow transport and great distances, where parting from a friend held the real possibility of never seeing him again. There is a large common zone of sentiment among the three – their appreciation of music, their acute perception of nature, their bent towards nostalgia.

But despite this and despite the fact that many of the poems of these three poets are in identical forms, their personalities and the spirit of their writing could not have been more different. The standard trichotomy of Wang Wei as Buddhist recluse, Li Bai as Taoist immortal and Du Fu as Confucian sage has been rejected by some critics as unsubtle and artificial, but it can act as a clarifying approximation for those approaching Chinese poetry of this period for the first time. The centre of gravity of their work, the characteristic emphasis of their most characteristic poems, is distinct and individual.

Wang Wei's typical mood is that of aloneness, quiet, a retreat into nature and Buddhism. What one associates with him are running water, evening and dawn, bamboo, the absence of men's voices. The word 'empty' is almost his signature. Li Bai's poetry sparkles with zest, impulsiveness, exuberance, even at the risk of bombast and imbalance. Sword, horse, wine, gold, the moon, the Milky Way and impossibly large numbers are recurring features of his work. He attempts alchemically to transmute life through the intoxication of poetry or music or wine into delight and forgetfulness. Du Fu's poetry is informed by deeply suggestive and often sad reflections on society, history, the state and his own disturbed times, all central concerns of Confucianism. But what especially endears him to the Chinese is his wry self-deprecation combined with an intense compassion for oppressed or dispossessed people of every kind in a time of poverty, famine and war.

Wang Wei, the first of the three poets translated here, was born into a distinguished literary family on his mother's side;

his father was a local official. He was a prodigy – an accomplished musician, artist, calligrapher and poet who wrote the classic 'Ballad of the Peach Tree Spring' at seventeen. When he and his younger brother Wang Jin went up to the capital they were readily absorbed into aristocratic society. Wang Wei passed the imperial examinations at twenty-three. He was appointed to the post of Assistant Secretary for Music, but soon afterwards, probably for some small dereliction of duty, was transferred to a minor provincial post, where he served for several years before resigning and returning to the capital. He bought an estate in the hills on the Wang River about thirty miles away from Changan. Here he lived whenever he was on holiday or out of office, and its landscape was the source of much of his painting and poetry. Not long afterwards, Wang Wei's wife died. He was under thirty, and childless, but he never married again.

He filled a series of posts, none of which seem to have involved him as much as the calm pleasures of his country estate: nature, friends and Buddhist philosophy were his preoccupations. He survived the recurrent court intrigues unscathed; this was probably because he was not much interested in what went on at court even though he wrote the occasional court poem upon request.

When rebellion struck and An Lushan established his bloody rule in Changan, Wang Wei, after some resistance, accepted office under him. His dear friend and fellow poet Pei Di, fifteen years his junior, managed to visit him during the occupation, and Wang Wei recited to him a poem touching upon his sorrow and dismay at the recent events. When the rebellion was crushed and imperial control re-established in Changan, it was very likely this poem together with the intercession of his brother Wang Jin – who had followed the emperor into exile and established impeccable loyalist credentials – that saved him from execution.

Wang Wei died four years later at the age of sixty-one. After his death Wang Jin, then prime minister, ordered that his scattered poems be collected, but many – possibly most – of his poems (like those of Li Bai and Du Fu) have been lost. As for his paintings – and Wang Wei was at least as famous in his lifetime for his painting as for his poetry – nothing remains except much later copies (several times removed) of his work. It was said of him by a later poet, Su Dongpo, that 'there was poetry in his painting and painting in his poetry'. His landscapes, like his poetry, are said to have embodied a sense of distance, space and the pervading presence of 'emptiness'.

Li Bai was born in Chinese Turkestan in 701 and moved to Sichuan around the age of five. He travelled a great deal throughout China, never sat the imperial examinations or held a post for long, and rarely mentioned specific contemporary events in his poetry. As a result not a great deal is known about his life or his exact movements.

He is known to have been married several times, to have had children, and to have made a great impression on his contemporaries as a paradigm of the intoxicated and impulsive poet with his flashing eyes and great iconoclastic energy. He was interested in alchemy and in Taoism.

In his early forties he was presented to the emperor in Changan and given a position in the Imperial Academy, but this did not last long; he was unseated in a court intrigue. When the An Lushan rebellion broke out he was in his mid-fifties. He left for the south and entered the service of Prince Yong, but the prince was himself later killed by the emperor who feared that he might usurp his throne. Li Bai too was implicated in the plot and exiled to the south-west. Before he got there, however, he was pardoned, and so continued his wanderings. He died in 762 while visiting a relative, a famous calligrapher.

The vigour and flamboyance of much of Li Bai's poetry hides a deep core of loneliness. He achieved great fame in his lifetime, and seems only on occasion to have known want; for the most part those who met him felt honoured to provide him with generous hospitality. But he saw himself as a man in heroic and romantic opposition to the universe and was torn by nostalgia. He never settled down, and the restless energy of his life found its counterpart both in the speed with which he set down his compositions and in their propulsive sweep. His longer poems in irregular metres are particularly heady and daring, and provide a sense of escape into a height beyond the dross and boredom of daily life. Some of his nature poetry – for example, 'The Road to Shu' – is tumultuous, almost at times bizarre, in its dramatic detail.

Though Li Bai was born in the same year as Wang Wei and died just a year before him, it is not clear whether they ever met. They did however have a common friend in the poet Meng Haoran, twelve years their senior, and each wrote poems addressed to him or to his memory. Meng Haoran could be said to have combined in his work two threads of Chinese nature poetry – the quietistic stream which was to find its most intense expression in the poetry of Wang Wei, and the sense of natural grandeur that found expression in some of the poetry of Li Bai.

Du Fu's attitude to nature is somewhat different from that of either Wang Wei or Li Bai. He sees nature not as retreat or drama but as an emotional or moral entity set in juxtaposition to human life and human events, whether in sympathy or antipathy. The noble cypress that is not uprooted by violent storms, the flowers that insist on returning in spring to a devastated war-stricken country – these appear to him to be intimately tied through either consciousness or heedlessness to human vicissitudes and griefs.

Du Fu experienced a great deal of both during his life. He was born in 712 into a distinguished but not wealthy family; his grandfather was a famous poet. Although – like both Wang Wei and Li Bai, his seniors by a decade – he displayed great literary promise in his teens, he failed the imperial examinations in his early twenties, and was to fail them again in his mid-thirties. In the meantime he travelled widely in south-central China, visiting historical sites and meeting (among other poets) Li Bai, one of his great heroes, who was to become a lifelong friend. In 752 Du Fu took a special examination in the capital, and failed yet again.

For Du Fu, repeated lack of success in the examinations was a triple failure. He needed the salary of an official: unlike some other poets he had not been able to obtain economic support through a personal patron, and had to live apart from his wife and children, whom he could not afford to keep in the capital. Secondly, his natural ambition for office was continually thwarted. Thirdly, his wish to be of use to his country was frustrated. For a man bred in Confucian traditions, unselfish service to the emperor, to the state and to the people was what gave life meaning. Li Bai and Wang Wei, each in his own way, felt that the essential purposes of life lay elsewhere; this was not possible for Du Fu.

In 755, Du Fu was awarded a minor office low in the official hierarchy. But soon thereafter the An Lushan rebellion broke out, and in 756 the capital fell to the rebels. Du Fu was not in Changan at the time but arrived there later; it is said that he was captured by the rebels and brought to Changan, but the facts are unclear. Many of his greatest poems date from this period; these include 'Grieving for the Young Prince' and 'Spring Scene in Time of War'. He was again separated from his family. One of his children had already died of starvation, and once more his family was faced with penury.

Du Fu managed to leave Changan and join the court in exile. In 757 he was appointed to a higher rank as a reward for his loyalty. This he lost shortly afterwards; his defence of a general who had lost a battle caused him to fall out of imperial favour, and he was exiled to Shaanxi. A couple of years later he left for Sichuan, where in semi-retirement, in the last decade of his life, he wrote over half of the 1,450 poems of his that survive. In 765 he undertook a journey down the Yangtze. He fell ill on the way and was forced to remain at Kuizhou for two years. In 768 he continued towards Henan, where he had been born; but in 770, while still travelling, he died.

Neither Du Fu's personality nor his poetry made a great impression on most of his contemporaries. Unlike Li Bai and Wang Wei, he was not included in major poetry anthologies for several generations after his death. But from before the turn of the millennium and continuously since then he has been considered to be one of China's greatest poets. His feeling for the things of consequence of his times, his realism and honesty, the richness of his technique and language, the moral force of his writing, his affection and concern for those around him and his sense of fun have ensured immortality for the poet who received meagre literary acclaim in his lifetime. Even his unsuccess in office, his long periods of unemployment, can with time be seen in a different light. As with that other diligent bureaucrat Chaucer, we would not have as much of his work as we do if he had escaped what must have seemed to him fallow and frustrating times.

***

Partly as a matter of interest, and partly in order to illustrate those effects attained by Chinese poetry that are lost in these translations, it may be worthwhile briefly to analyse one of the original poems included in this book. A quick look at the longer poems of Du Fu or Li Bai shows that several forms using irregular line-lengths were popular during this period. However, the most commonly used of all forms for several centuries – more standard even than the sonnet in Europe – was an eight-line regular form with the same number of syllables in each line throughout the poem, either five or seven. The second, fourth, sixth and eighth lines of the octet rhymed with one another, thus reinforcing the basic division of four couplets within the octet. (Sometimes the first line rhymed with them as well.)

In the strict or 'regulated' form of the octet that increased in popularity during the Tang there were two additional features. One was a prescribed sequence of so-called 'tones' for successive syllables of the poem once a certain pattern had been chosen. In classical Chinese, syllables – each exactly one written character long – were classified into tones depending on the direction of pitch of the sound. (The meaning of the syllable depended then, as now, upon this pitch-direction.) The pattern of tones in the regulated octet set up expectations and provided musical satisfactions that are impossible to provide in a non-tonal language like English. This is part of what is necessarily lost in translation.

The other feature was exact grammatical parallelism and contrast of meaning between lines three and four, and again between lines five and six. This parallelism within each of the second and third couplets is a particular pleasure of the Chinese regulated octet, but in my translations I have often let natural English syntax override strict parallelism in order to avoid what might otherwise emerge as a choppy or a rigid rendering. In the example of the poem by Wang Wei given below (see p. 244) it should be borne in mind that Chinese parts of speech are not the same as English ones, and that the requirement of grammatical parallelism has in fact been strictly adhered to in the middle couplets. (As it happens, in this particular poem parallelism holds within each of the four couplets, but that is not a requirement of the form.)

Much of the pleasure of rhymed and metred poetry depends, obviously enough, on rhyme and metre; and these are intrinsic to the enjoyment of classical Chinese verse. This is true even though over the centuries most characters have changed in pronunciation, not always consistently with each other, and as a result what were once exact rhymes are now sometimes half-rhymes or less. I felt in my translations that wherever I could I should maintain rhyme, and also wherever possible retain a sense of the regularity or irregularity of the metrical movement. The joy of poetry for me lies not so much in transcending or escaping from the so-called bonds of artifice or constraint as in using them to enhance the power of what is being said.

With so much by way of general explication, I would invite the reader to look at 'Living in the Hills: Impromptu Verses' by Wang Wei – reproduced on page 244 with its eight-by-five grid of characters, their pronunciation in modern Mandarin Chinese, their meaning, and a line-by-line prose translation.

This is an immensely simple poem, yet one which, once read, I have never been able to forget. To compare the incomparable, if the difficulty of translating Wang Wei is akin to the difficulty of playing Mozart, the difficulty of translating Du Fu with his rich counterpoint of historical allusion can be compared to that of playing Bach. As for translating the wild and romantic Li Bai – it is rather like playing Beethoven, often

1. 寂　寞　掩　柴　扉　[Rhyme]
   JÍ　MÒ　YǍN　CHÁI　FĒI
   lonely　　　close　brushwood　door
   Lonely, I close my brushwood door.

2. 蒼　茫　對　落　暉　[Rhyme]
   CĀNG　MÁNG　DÙI　LÙO　HŪI
   vast/misty　　face　falling　light/brilliance
   I face the vast expanse as the sunset falls.

3. 鶴　巢　松　樹　徧
   HÉ　CHÁO　SŌNG　SHÙ　BIÀN
   cranes　nest　pine　tree　everywhere
   Cranes nest everywhere in the pine trees.

4. 人　訪　蓽　門　稀　[Rhyme]
   RÉN　FÁNG　BÌ　MÉN　XĪ
   men　visit　wicker　gate　few
   I have few visitors at my wicker gate.

5. 嫩　竹　含　新　粉
   NÈN　ZHÚ　HÁN　XĪN　FĚN
   tender　bamboo　holds　new　powder
   The tender bamboo holds new powder.

6. 紅　蓮　落　故　衣　[Rhyme]
   HÓNG　LIÁN　LÙO　GǓ　YÌ
   red　lotus　sheds　old　clothes
   Red lotuses shed their old clothes.

7. 渡　頭　燈　火　起
   DÙ　TÓU　DĒNG　HǓO　QǏ
   at the ford　　lantern fires　rise
   Lantern fires are lit at the ford.

8. 處　處　採　菱　歸　[Rhyme]
   CHÙ　CHÙ　CǍI　LÍNG　GŪI
   everywhere　water-chestnut pickers　return home
   Everywhere water-chestnut pickers go home.

Grammatically parallel pair of lines (lines 3–4)

Grammatically parallel pair of lines (lines 5–6)

full of sound and fury, signifying (usually) a great deal. But in each poem, as important as the texture or tone of the work is the exact content of what is being said – and the translator's task is not to improvise cadenzas in the spirit of the piece but to stick, as tellingly as he can, to the score.

There is a school of translation that believes that one can safely ignore many of the actual words of a poem once one has drunk deeply of its spirit. An approximate rendering invigorated by a sense of poetic inspiration becomes the aim. The idea is that if the final product reads well as a poem, all is well: a good poem exists where none existed before. I should mention that the poems in this book are not intended as transcreations or free translations in this sense, attempts to use the originals as trampolines from which to bounce off on to poems of my own. The famous translations of Ezra Pound, compounded as they are of ignorance of Chinese and valiant self-indulgence have remained before me as a warning of what to shun. I have preferred mentors who, like the three translators I mentioned before, admit the primacy of the original and attempt fidelity to it. Like them, I have tried not to compromise the meaning of the actual words of the poems, though I have often failed. Even in prose the associations of a word or an image in one language do not slip readily into another. The loss is still greater in poetry, where each word or image carries a heavier charge of association, and where the exigencies of form leave less scope for choice and manoeuvre. But if it is felt that the limited access to the worlds of these poems that translation can reasonably hope to provide has been given, I will be more than happy.

王　維　　　　　　　　　　　　　　　Wang Wei

Deer Park

Empty hills, no man in sight –
Just echoes of the voice of men.
In the deep wood reflected light
Shines on the blue-green moss again.

Birdsong Brook

Idly I watch cassia flowers fall.
Still is the night, empty the hill in Spring.
Up comes the moon, startling the mountain birds.
Once in a while in the Spring brook they sing.

Lady Xi

No present royal favour could efface
The memory of the love that once she knew.
Seeing a flower filled her eyes with tears.
She did not speak a word to the King of Chu.

Grieving for Meng Haoran

I will not ever see my friend again.
Day after day Han waters eastward flow.
Even if I asked of the old man, the hills
And rivers would seem empty in Caizhou.

Remembering My Brothers in Shandong on the Double-Ninth Festival

Alone, a stranger in a distant province –
At festivals I'm homesick through and through.
In my mind's eye, my brothers climb the mountain,
Each carrying dogwood – but there's one too few.

The Pleasures of the Country

Peach blossom's red; again it holds night rain.
Willows are green, clad once more in spring mist.
The houseboy's not yet swept the fallen flowers.
The orioles chirp, but don't wake my hill guest.

Autumn Nightfall at My Place in the Hills

In the empty mountains, after recent rain,
A sense of Fall comes with the evening air.
The moon is bright and shines between the pines.
Over the stones the spring-fed stream runs clear.
Bamboos rustle: washerwomen go home.
Lotuses stir: fishing boats make their way.
At its own will, the scent of Spring has gone.
But you, 'O prince of friends', of course may stay.

Zhongnan Retreat

In middle age I'm quite drawn to the Way.
Here by the hills I've built a home. I go
– Whenever the spirit seizes me – alone
To see the spots that other folk don't know.
I walk to the head of the stream, sit down, and watch
For when the clouds rise. On the forest track
By chance I meet an old man, and we talk
And laugh, and I don't think of going back.

In Answer to Vice-Magistrate Zhang

Late in my life I only care for quiet.
A million pressing tasks, I let them go.
I look at myself; I have no long-range plans.
To go back to the forest is all I know.
Pine breeze: I ease my belt. Hill moon: I strum
My lute. You ask – but I can say no more
About success or failure than the song
The fisherman sings, which comes to the deep shore.

Living in the Hills: Impromptu Verses

I close my brushwood door in solitude
And face the vast sky as late sunlight falls.
The pine trees: cranes are nesting all around.
My wicker gate: a visitor seldom calls.
The tender bamboo's dusted with fresh powder.
Red lotuses strip off their former bloom.
Lamps shine out at the ford, and everywhere
The water-chestnut pickers wander home.

Lament for Yin Yao

How long can one man's lifetime last?
In the end we return to formlessness.
I think of you, waiting to die.
A thousand things cause me distress –

Your kind old mother's still alive.
Your only daughter's only ten.
In the vast chilly wilderness
I hear the sounds of weeping men.

Clouds float into a great expanse.
Birds fly but do not sing in flight.
How lonely are the travellers.
Even the sun shines cold and white.

Alas, when you still lived, and asked
To study non-rebirth with me,
My exhortations were delayed –
And so the end came, fruitlessly.

All your old friends have brought you gifts
But for your life these too are late.
I've failed you in more ways than one.
Weeping, I walk back to my gate.

Ballad of the Peach Tree Spring

A fisherman sailed up-river; he loved the hills in Spring.
On either bank of the old ford stood peach trees blossoming.
He stared at the red trees. The miles passed; unaware,
He reached the green creek's end but saw no human
  anywhere.
A gap – a hidden path twisted and turned about –
Then suddenly among the hills a vast plain opened out.
From far, a host of clouds and trees – but as he neared
Among bamboos and scattered flowers a thousand homes
  appeared.
Woodcutters with Han names and surnames passed them on.
The villagers still wore the clothes of Qin times, long since
  gone.
Together all of them now lived at Wuling Spring,
Tilling their gardens and their fields away from everything.
Moon bright below the pines – their houses all lay quiet.
When the sun rose among the clouds, roosters and dogs ran
  riot.
A visitor from the world! They gathered round and vied
To ask him home and question him on how things were
  outside.
From village lanes at dawn they swept the flowers away.   ⤴*

---

*   a stanza break at the end of a page is marked by ~
    no stanza break at the end of a page is marked by ⤴

Woodsmen and fishermen rowed home towards the close of
    day.
At first they'd come to flee the world and, some maintain,
Had then become immortals and decided to remain.
From these ravines who'd guess human affairs exist? –
And from the world you'd only see blank mountains cloaked
    in mist.
He did not think such realms were hard to hear or see;
His heart, still dusty with the world, longed for his own
    country.
He went out through the cave, not heeding stream or hill,
To take his leave from home and then return here at his will.
Certain he could not lose what he had just passed through,
How could he know when he returned the landscape would
    look new?
He'd gone into deep hills – but nothing else was clear.
How often into cloudy woods do green creeks disappear?
All over every stream in Spring peach blossom lies.
Who can discern where he should seek the spring of paradise?

李 白 Li Bai

In the Quiet Night

The floor before my bed is bright:
Moonlight – like hoarfrost – in my room.
I lift my head and watch the moon.
I drop my head and think of home.

A Song of Qiu-pu

The Qiu-pu shore teems with white gibbons.
They leap and bounce like flying snow.
They tug their young down from the branches
To drink and play with the moonglow.

The Waterfall at Lu Shan

In sunshine, Censer Peak breathes purple mist.
A jutting stream, the cataract hangs in spray
Far off, then plunges down three thousand feet –
As if the sky had dropped the Milky Way.

Question and Answer in the Mountains

They ask me why I live in the green mountains.
I smile and don't reply; my heart's at ease.
Peach blossoms flow downstream, leaving no trace –
And there are other earths and skies than these.

Seeing Meng Haoran Off to Yangzhou

Yellow Crane Terrace: my old friend bids me goodbye.
To Yangzhou in the mists and flowers of Spring he goes.
His single sail's far shadow melts in the blue void.
All I see is the sky to which the Yangtze flows.

Parting at a Wineshop in Nanjing

Breeze bearing willow-cotton fills the shop with scent.
A Wu girl, pouring wine, exhorts us to drink up.
We Nanjing friends are here to see each other off.
Those who must go, and those who don't, each drains his
    cup.
Go ask the Yangtze, which of these two sooner ends:
Its waters flowing east – the love of parting friends.

Listening to a Monk from Shu Playing the Lute

The monk from Shu with his green lute-case walked
Westward down Emei Shan, and at the sound
Of the first notes he strummed for me I heard
A thousand valleys' rustling pines resound.
My heart was cleansed, as if in flowing water.
In bells of frost I heard the resonance die.
Dusk came unnoticed over the emerald hills
And autumn clouds layered the darkening sky.

The Mighty Eunuchs' Carriages

The mighty eunuchs' carriages
Raise a great swirl of dust that shrouds
The fields in darkness though it's noon.
What wealth! Their mansions touch the clouds.

They bump into a cockfight now.
Bright canopies! Superb headgear!
A double rainbow tints their breath.
Folk by the roadside quake with fear.

Since Xu You washed his ears in shame
When offered a place at court, who can
Distinguish between Yao and Zhi –
The brigand and the virtuous man?

Drinking Alone with the Moon

A pot of wine among the flowers.
I drink alone, no friend with me.
I raise my cup to invite the moon.
He and my shadow and I make three.

The moon does not know how to drink;
My shadow mimes my capering;
But I'll make merry with them both –
And soon enough it will be Spring.

I sing – the moon moves to and fro.
I dance – my shadow leaps and sways.
Still sober, we exchange our joys.
Drunk – and we'll go our separate ways.

Let's pledge – beyond human ties – to be friends,
And meet where the Silver River ends.

Bring in the Wine

The waters of the Yellow River come down from the sky,
Never once returning as towards the sea they flow.
The mirrors of high palaces are sad with once-bright hair:
Though silken-black at morning it has changed by night to
    snow.
Fulfil your wishes in this life, exhaust your every whim
And never raise an empty golden goblet to the moon.
Fate's loaded me with talent and it must be put to use!
Scatter a thousand coins – they'll all come winging homeward
    soon.
Cook a sheep, slaughter an ox – and for our further pleasure
Let's drink three hundred cups of wine down in a single
    measure.
        So here's to you, Dan Qiu –
        And Master Cen, drink up.
        Bring in, bring in the wine –
        Pour on, cup after cup.
        I'll sing a song for you –
        So lend your ears and hear me through.
Bells and drums and feasts and jade are all esteemed in vain:
Just let me be forever drunk and never be sober again.
The sages and the virtuous men are all forgotten now.
It is the drinkers of the world whose names alone remain.
Chen Wang, the prince and poet, once at a great banquet
    paid

Ten thousand for a cask of wine with laughter wild and free.
How can you say, my host, that you have fallen short of cash?
You've got to buy more wine and drink it face to face with me.
    My furs so rare –
    My dappled mare –
Summon the boy to go and get the choicest wine for these
And we'll dissolve the sorrows of a hundred centuries.

The Road to Shu Is Hard

Ah! it's fearsome – oh! it's high!
The road to Shu is hard, harder than climbing to the sky.
    The kings Can Cong and Yu Fu
    Founded long ago the land of Shu.
    Then for forty-eight thousand years
    Nothing linked it to the Qin frontiers.
    White Star Peak blocked the western way.
A bird-track tried to cut across to Mount Emei –
And only when the earth shook, hills collapsed, and brave men
    died
Did cliff-roads and sky-ladders join it to the world outside.
Above – high peaks turn back the dragon-chariot of the sun.
Below – great whirlpools turn around the waves that rush and
    stun.
    Not even yellow cranes can fly across –
    Even the clambering apes are at a loss.
    At Green Mud Ridge the path coils to and fro:
Nine twists for every hundred steps – up a sheer cliff we go.
The traveller, touching the stars, looks upwards, scared out of
    his wits.
He clutches his heart with a deep sigh – down on the ground
    he sits!

Sir, from this journey to the West, will you return some day?
How can you hope to climb the crags along this fearful way?
Mournful birds in ancient trees – you'll hear no other sound

Of life: the male bird follows his mate as they fly round and
  round.
    You'll hear the cuckoo call in the moonlight,
      Sad that the mountain's bare at night.

The road to Shu is hard, harder than climbing to the sky.
Just speak these words to someone's face – you'll see its colour
  fly.
A hand's breadth from the sky peaks join to crown a precipice
Where withered pines, bent upside down, lean over the abyss.
Swift rapids, wrestling cataracts descend in roaring spasms,
Pound cliffs, boil over rocks, and thunder through ten thousand
  chasms.
    To face such danger and such fear,
Alas, from such a distance, Sir, what could have brought you
  here?
    Dagger Peak is high and steep –
    Even a single man can keep
    The pass from thousands – though he may
Become a wolf or jackal – and betray.
By day we dread the savage tiger's claws,
    By night the serpent's jaws,
    Its sharp, blood-sucking fangs bared when
It mows down like hemp stalks the lives of men.
    Though Chengdu is a pleasure dome,
    Better to quickly turn back home.
The road to Shu is hard, harder than climbing to the sky.
Leaning, I stare into the west and utter a long sigh.

杜　甫　　　　　　　　　　　　　　　　　　　　*Du Fu*

Thoughts While Travelling at Night

Light breeze on the fine grass.
I stand alone at the mast.

Stars lean on the vast wild plain.
Moon bobs in the Great River's spate.

Letters have brought no fame.
Office? Too old to obtain.

Drifting, what am I like?
A gull between earth and sky.

Spring Scene in Time of War

The state lies ruined; hills and streams survive.
Spring in the city; grass and leaves now thrive.
Moved by the times the flowers shed their dew.
The birds seem startled; they hate parting too.
The steady beacon fires are three months old.
A word from home is worth a ton of gold.
I scratch my white hair, which has grown so thin
It soon won't let me stick my hatpin in.

Moonlit Night

In Fuzhou, far away, my wife is watching
The moon alone tonight, and my thoughts fill
With sadness for my children, who can't think
Of me here in Changan; they're too young still.
Her cloud-soft hair is moist with fragrant mist.
In the clear light her white arms sense the chill.
When will we feel the moonlight dry our tears,
Leaning together on our window-sill?

The Visitor

South and north of my house lies springtime water,
And only flocks of gulls come every day.
The flower path's unswept: no guests. The gate
Is open: you're the first to come this way.
The market's far: my food is nothing special.
The wine, because we're poor, is an old brew –
But if you wish I'll call my ancient neighbour
Across the fence to drink it with us two.

Thoughts on an Ancient Site: The Temple of Zhu-ge Liang

The name of Zhu-ge Liang resounds through time.
The statesman's likeness awes: revered, sublime.
The empire, split in three, curbed his great aim
But not the soaring feather of his fame.
He equalled Yi and Lü; if he'd gained power
Great names like Cao and Xiao would have ranked lower –
But time would not restore the Han again.
He died, devoid of hope, his plans all vain.

The Chancellor of Shu

The Chancellor of Shu, where may his shrine be seen?
Among dense cypress trees beyond the city walls.
Unviewed against the steps the grass greets spring in green.
Sweet-voiced, leaf-screened, unheard, a yellow oriole calls.
Begged thrice to plan the world, he finally complied.
He founded or maintained two reigns with faithfulness.
Before his armies proved victorious he died.
Heroic men shed tears to think of his distress.

An Autumn Meditation

I've heard it said Changan is like a chessboard, where
Failure and grief is all these hundred years have brought.
Mansions of princes and high nobles have new lords.
New officers are capped and robed for camp and court.

North on the passes gold drums thunder. To the west
Horses and chariots rush dispatches and reports.
Dragon and fish are still, the autumn river's cold.
My ancient land and times of peace come to my thoughts.

Dreaming of Li Bai

The pain of death's farewells grows dim.
The pain of life's farewells stays new.
Since you were exiled to Jiangnan
– Plague land – I've had no news of you.

Proving how much you're in my thoughts,
Old friend, you've come into my dreams.
I thought you still were in the law's
Tight net – but you've grown wings, it seems.

I fear yours is no living soul.
How could it make this distant flight?
You came: the maple woods were green.
You left: the pass was black with night.

The sinking moonlight floods my room.
Still hoping for your face, I stare.
The water's deep, the waves are wide.
Watch out for water-dragons there.

To Wei Ba, Who Has Lived Away from the Court

Like stars that rise when the other has set,
For years we two friends have not met.
How rare it is then that tonight
We once more share the same lamplight.
Our youth has quickly slipped away
And both of us are turning grey.
Old friends have died, and with a start
We hear the sad news, sick at heart.
How could I, twenty years before,
Know that I'd be here at your door?
When last I left, so long ago,
You were unmarried. In a row
Suddenly now your children stand,
Welcome their father's friend, demand
To know his home, his town, his kin –
Till they're chased out to fetch wine in.
Spring chives are cut in the night rain
And steamed rice mixed with yellow grain.
To mark the occasion, we should drink
Ten cups of wine straight off, you think –
But even ten can't make me high,
So moved by your old love am I.
The mountains will divide our lives,
Each to his world, when day arrives.

The Old Cypress Tree at the Temple of Zhu-ge Liang

Before the temple stands an ancient cypress tree.
Its boughs are bronze, its roots like heavy boulders lie.
Its massive frosty girth of bark is washed by rain.
Its jet-black head rears up a mile to greet the sky.

Princes and ministers have paid their debt to time.
The people love the tree as they did long ago.
The clouds' breath joins it to the long mists of Wu Gorge.
It shares the moon's chill with the high white peaks of snow.

Last year the road wound east, past my old home, near where
Both Zhu-ge Liang and his First Ruler shared one shrine.
There too great cypresses stretched over the ancient plain,
And through wrecked doors I glimpsed dim paintwork and
   design.

But this lone tree, spread wide, root-coiled to earth, has held
Its sky-high place round which fierce blasts of wind are hurled.
Nothing but Providence could keep it here so long.
Its straightness marks the work of what once made the world.

If a great hall collapsed, the oxen sent to drag
Rafters from this vast tree would turn round in dismay.
It needs no craftsman's skills, this wonder of the world.
Even if felled, who could haul such a load away?   ~

Although its bitter heart is marred by swarms of ants,
Among its scented leaves bright phoenixes collect.
Men of high aims, who live obscure, do not despair.
The great are always paid in disuse and neglect.

A Fine Lady

There is a lady, matchless in her beauty.
An empty valley's where she dwells, obscure.
Her family, she says, was once a good one.
She lives with grass and trees now, spent and poor.

When lately there was chaos in the heartlands
And at the rebels' hands her brothers died,
Their high rank failed them, as did her entreaties:
Their flesh and bones remained unsanctified.

The busy world, as fickle as a lamp-flame,
Hates what has had its day or is decayed.
The faithless man to whom she once was married
Keeps a new woman, beautiful as jade.

Those trees whose leaves curl up at night sense evening.
Without its mate a mandarin duck can't sleep.
He only sees the smile of his new woman.
How can he then hear his old woman weep?

Among the mountains, spring-fed streams run clearly.
Leaving the mountains, they are soiled with dross.
Her maid has sold her pearls and is returning.
To mend the thatch they drag the vines across.   ~

Her hands are often full of bitter cypress.
The flowers she picks don't go to grace her hair.
She rests against tall bamboo trees at nightfall.
The weather's cold and her blue sleeves threadbare.

Grieving for the Young Prince

From Changan walls white-headed crows took flight
And cawed upon the Western Gate at night –
Then on officials' roofs they pecked and cawed
To warn them to escape the barbarian horde.
The gold whips broke, so hard were they applied.
The exhausted horses galloped till they died.
The court fled, panicked – those they could not find
Of the imperial line were left behind.

Below his waist, blue coral, glints of jade –
I see a young prince, weeping and afraid
By the cross-roads. Although he won't confess
His name to me he begs in his distress
To be my slave. Thorn scrub he's hidden in
For months has left no untorn shred of skin –
But the imperial nose betrays his birth:
The Dragon's seed is not the seed of earth.

Wolves, jackals roam the city. In the wild
The Dragon and his court remain exiled.
Take care, dear Prince. I daren't speak long with you,
But for your sake will pause a breath or two.

Last night the east wind's blood-stench stained the air
And camels filled the former capital's square.

The Shuofang veterans, bright in their array,
How bold they seemed once, how inane today.
I hear the Son of Heaven has abdicated,
And in the North the Khan, it is related,
And each of his brave warriors slashed his face
 – So moved were they by the imperial grace –
And swore to wipe this great dishonour out.
But we must mind our words, with spies about.
Alas, poor Prince, be careful. May the power
Of the Five Tombs protect you hour by hour.

Ballad of the Army Carts

Carts rattle and squeak,
Horses snort and neigh –
Bows and arrows at their waists, the conscripts march away.
Fathers, mothers, children, wives run to say goodbye.
The Xianyang Bridge in clouds of dust is hidden from the eye.
They tug at them and stamp their feet, weep, and obstruct
their way.
The weeping rises to the sky.
Along the road a passer-by
Questions the conscripts. They reply:

They mobilize us constantly. Sent northwards at fifteen
To guard the River, we were forced once more to volunteer,
Though we are forty now, to man the western front this year.
The headman tied our headcloths for us when we first left
here.
We came back white-haired – to be sent again to the frontier.
Those frontier posts could fill the sea with the blood of those
who've died,
But still the Martial Emperor's aims remain unsatisfied.
In county after county to the east, Sir, don't you know,
In village after village only thorns and brambles grow.
Even if there's a sturdy wife to wield the plough and hoe,
The borders of the fields have merged, you can't tell east
from west.

It's worse still for the men from Qin, as fighters they're the
    best –
And so, like chickens or like dogs, they're driven to and fro.

> Though you are kind enough to ask,
> Dare we complain about our task?
> Take, Sir, this winter. In Guanxi
> The troops have not yet been set free.
> The district officers come to press
> The land tax from us nonetheless.
> But, Sir, how can we possibly pay?
> Having a son's a curse today.

Far better to have daughters, get them married –
A son will lie lost in the grass, unburied.

> Why, Sir, on distant Qinghai shore

The bleached ungathered bones lie year on year.
New ghosts complain, and those who died before
Weep in the wet grey sky and haunt the ear.

Notes to Poems

1 *Lady Xi (Wang Wei)*
The King of Chu in the seventh century BC defeated the ruler of Xi and took his wife. She had children by him but never spoke to him.

Fourteen centuries later Wang Wei, then twenty years old, wrote this poem in the following circumstances. One of his patrons, a prince, had acquired the wife of a cake-seller. A year later he asked her if she still loved her husband, and she gave no answer. The man was sent for, and when she saw him her eyes filled with tears.

This took place before a small but distinguished literary gathering, and the prince, moved, asked for poems on the subject. Wang Wei's poem was finished first, and when it was read out, everyone else agreed it was pointless to try to write something better.

The prince reportedly returned the cake-seller's wife to her husband.

2 *Autumn Nightfall at My Place in the Hills (Wang Wei)*
The reason for Wang Wei's unseasonable merging of the disappearance of spring with the onset of autumn is that he is referring to and contrasting his lines with an ancient poem that was well-known to Tang dynasty readers. In that poem, while attempting to draw a reclusive gentleman (the so-called 'prince') back to civilization, the anonymous poet mentions the dense spring grass as one of the features of the

mountain wilderness that the recluse has retreated to, and where he 'should not stay long'.

3 *Lament for Yin Yao (Wang Wei)*
In Buddhism, 'non-rebirth' (*wu-sheng*: literally, non-birth) denotes nirvana or liberation from the cycle of eternal rebirth.

4 *Ballad of the Peach Tree Spring (Wang Wei)*
If the character for 'woodcutter' in line 9 is a miscopying of the original character for 'fisherman' – which is possible since the two written characters are quite similar – a reading would result which accords far better with Wang Wei's original prose source for the legend. Lines 9 and 10 could then read:
　'The fisherman was the first to spread news of the Han.
　The folk here still wore clothes in vogue before that age
　　began.'

5 *In the Quiet Night (Li Bai)*
This is the well-known, well-loved and much-quoted version of the quatrain. In the version of the poem found in most anthologies of Li Bai, the moon in line 3 is specified as a hill moon or mountain moon.

6 *Listening to a Monk from Shu Playing the Lute (Li Bai)*
See note 10.

7 *Drinking Alone with the Moon (Li Bai)*
The Silver River is the Chinese name for the Milky Way.

8 *The Road to Shu Is Hard (Li Bai)*
See note 10.

9 *Thoughts While Travelling at Night (Du Fu)*
The Great River is the Yangtze.

10 *Thoughts on an Ancient Site: The Temple of Zhu-ge Liang (Du Fu)*
Shu is the name for the ancient kingdom approximating
modern-day Sichuan, and is a term still used to refer to that
province. It consists mainly of a vast, fertile, densely populated,
mountain-ringed basin in the upper reaches of the Yangtze. In
Tang times it was connected to the outside world either by
precipitous mountain paths or via the three gorges (including
the long Wu Gorge) that led to the middle and lower reaches
of the Yangtze.

The legend, ancient even in Tang times, goes that a king
of Qin promised his five daughters to a king of Shu, and five
brave men of Shu were sent to fetch them. On the way back
they tried to pull the tail of a huge serpent that had fled into
a cave. The mountains crumbled and everyone perished, but
a path of sorts was thus created between the two kingdoms.

Ancient China consisted of a large number of independent
kingdoms. A few centuries after Confucius, a ruler of Qin
conquered Shu and the other rival kingdoms and unified China
for the first time. (It is in fact from 'Qin' that the word 'China'
derives.) His brief dynasty was followed by the long Han
dynasty (206 BC to AD 220), after which the empire split again,
this time into three kingdoms – Shu, Wu and Wei – each of
which vainly attempted to swallow the other two, ostensibly
to return the country to the peace and unity it had enjoyed
under the Han. (It was only just before the Tang dynasty, almost
four centuries later, that the empire was once again unified.)

The period of the Three Kingdoms is the basis of much
chivalric legend and romance built around several striking
historical characters. These include the great general Zhu-ge

Liang, the so-called 'Chancellor of Shu', who was one of Du Fu's particular heroes. Du Fu admired him for his loyalty, strategic ability, astuteness and breadth of vision, and placed him among the greatest soldiers and statesmen in history.

Zhu-ge Liang, living in retirement, was requested three times by the adventurer Liu Bei (who considered himself the legitimate heir to the Han empire) to act as his adviser before he finally consented and helped establish Liu Bei as the First Ruler of the re-created Shu kingdom. Liu Bei on his deathbed asked Zhu-ge Liang to set his own incapable son Liu Chan aside and become emperor, but Zhu-ge Liang made Liu Chan the Second Ruler and served him as loyally as he had served his father. In AD 228 Zhu-ge Liang personally led a campaign against the kingdom of Wei, but he died before it came to a decisive outcome.

Several shrines in Shu were dedicated to Zhu-ge Liang. In 'Thoughts on an Ancient Site' the likeness referred to is his portrait in a temple in Kuizhou. In 'The Chancellor of Shu' the shrine mentioned in the poem stands outside the city walls of Chengdu, the capital of Sichuan. In 'The Old Cypress Tree' the scene is again the temple in Kuizhou, but the common shrine to Zhu-ge Liang and Liu Bei referred to in line 10 hearkens back to Chengdu once more.

Li Bai lived in Shu for much of his youth; he moved here from Chinese Turkestan when he was five. Du Fu lived in Shu in his old age and wrote much of his greatest poetry here. Even today in Chengdu, his 'thatched hut' is a much visited tourist spot.

11 *The Chancellor of Shu (Du Fu)*
See note 10.

12 *An Autumn Meditation (Du Fu)*
This is one of a group of eight meditations Du Fu wrote while recuperating in Kuizhou. The chessboard is in fact a go board; the streets of Changan were laid out in a square grid.

13 *The Old Cypress Tree at the Temple of Zhu-ge Liang (Du Fu)*
See note 10.

14 *Grieving for the Young Prince (Du Fu)*
The Dragon and the Son of Heaven are references to the Emperor.

The Shuofang veterans were the loyalist troops raised to defend the pass that was the key to the capital. They were unwisely ordered to attack the large rebel army of An Lushan rather than to hold the pass defensively. As a result they were defeated, and the capital was laid open to the cavalry and camelry of the rebels.

The Five Tombs mentioned in the last line of the poem refer to the tombs of the early Tang emperors, the prince's ancestors.

Beastly Tales from Here and There

1992

Illustrations by
Ravi Shankar

For Usha Mami and Sashi Mama

Introduction

Because it was very hot in my house one day and I could not concentrate on my work, I decided to write a summer story involving mangoes and a river. By the time I had finished writing 'The Crocodile and the Monkey' (in a cool room lent to me by a friend), another story and other animals had begun stirring in my mind. And so it went on until all ten of these beastly tales were born – or reborn.

Of the ten tales told here, the first two come from India, the next two from China, the next two from Greece, and the next two from the Ukraine. The final two came directly to me from the Land of Gup.

I hope you enjoy them all and have a beastly time.

New Delhi,   *Vikram Seth*
January 1992

The Crocodile and the Monkey

On the Ganga's greenest isle
Lived Kuroop the crocodile:
Greeny-brown with gentle grin,
Stubby legs and scaly skin,
He would view with tepid eyes
Prey below a certain size –
But when a substantial dish
– Dolphin, turtle, fatter fish –
Swam across his field of view,
He would test the water too.
Out he'd glide, a floating log,
Silent as a polliwog –
Nearer, nearer, till his prey
Swam a single length away;
Then he'd lunge with smiling head,
Grab, and snap, and rip it dead –
Then (prime pleasure of his life)
Drag the carcass to his wife,
Lay it humbly at her feet,
Eat a bit, and watch her eat.

All along the river-bank
Mango trees stood rank on rank,   ⤴*

And his monkey friend would throw
To him as he swam below
Mangoes gold and ripe and sweet
As a special summer treat.
'Crocodile, your wife, I know
Hungers after mangoes so
That she'd pine and weep and swoon,
Mango-less in burning June.'
Then Kuroop the crocodile,
Gazing upwards with a smile,
Thus addressed his monkey friend:
'Dearest monkey, in the end,
Not the fruit, but your sweet love,
Showered on us from above,
Constant through the changing years,
Slakes her griefs and dries her tears.'
(This was only partly true.
She liked love, and mangoes too.)

One day, Mrs Crocodile,
Gorged on mangoes, with a smile
– Sad, yet tender – turned and said:
'Scalykins, since we've been wed,
You've fulfilled my every wish
– Dolphins, turtles, mangoes, fish –
But I now desire to eat,
As an anniversary treat,
Something sweeter still than fruit,
Sugar-cane or sugar-root:
I must eat that monkey's heart.'
'What?' 'Well, darling, for a start,
He has been so kind to me;

Think how sweet his heart must be.
Then, the mango pulp he's eaten
Year on year must serve to sweeten
Further yet each pore and part,
Concentrating in his heart.'

'Darling, he's my friend.' 'I know;
And he trusts you. Therefore go –
Go at once and fetch him here.
Oh, my breath grows faint, I fear . . .'
'Let me fan you – it's the heat – '
'No – I long for something sweet.
Every fruit tastes bitter now.
I must eat his heart somehow.
Get him here, my love, or I,
Filled with bitterness, will die.'

When the monkey saw Kuroop
He let out a joyful whoop,
Jumped from branch to branch with pleasure,
Flinging down the golden treasure:
'Eat, my friend, and take your wife
Nectar from the tree of life –
Mangoes ripe and mangoes rare,
Mangoes, mangoes everywhere.'
Then Kuroop the crocodile
Gazed up with a gentle smile:
'Monkey, you are far too kind,
But today, if you don't mind,
Dine with both of us, and meet
Her whose life you've made so sweet.
When you meet her you will see

Why she means so much to me.
When she takes you by the paw
Something at your heart will gnaw.
When you gaze into her eyes
You will enter Paradise.
Let us show our gratitude:
Share our friendship and our food.'

'Dear Kuroop, dear crocodile,
You can swim from isle to isle.
I can leap from limb to limb,
But, my friend, I cannot swim.
And your island's far away.
If I get a boat some day . . .'
'Nonsense; jump upon my back.
You're no heavier than my sack
Filled with mangoes to the crown.'
So the monkey clambered down,
Bearing mangoes, and delighted
With such warmth to be invited.

They were just halfway across
When the crocodile said: 'Toss
All those mangoes in the water.'
'But these fruit are all I've brought her.'
'You yourself are gift enough,'
Said Kuroop in accents gruff.
'Ah, my friend, that's very gracious.'
'Well, my wife's not so voracious –
And I'm certain that today
She won't eat fruit. By the way,
Tell me what your breast contains.

Mango nectar fills your veins.
Does it also fill your heart?'
Said the monkey with a start:
'What a very curious question.'
'Well, she might get indigestion
If it's too rich, I suspect.'
'What?' 'Your heart.' 'My heart?' 'Correct.'

'Now,' Kuroop said with a frown,
'Which would you prefer – to drown
In the Ganga or to be
Gutted by my wife and me?
I will let you choose your end.
After all, you are my friend.'
Then he slowly started sinking.
'Wait—' the monkey said, 'I'm thinking.
Death by drowning, death by slaughter
 – Death by land or death by water –
I'd face either with a smile
For your sake, O crocodile!
But your wife's felicity –
That's what means the most to me.
Noble lady! How she'll freeze,
Dumb with sorrow, when she sees,
Having prised my ribs apart,
That my breast contains no heart.
If you had not rushed me so,
I'd have found the time to go
To the hollow where I keep
Heart and liver when I sleep,
Half my brain, a fingernail,
Cufflinks, chutney, and spare tail.

I had scarcely woken up
When you asked me here to sup.
Why did you not speak before?
I'd have fetched them from the shore.'

Now Kuroop the crocodile
Lost, then quickly found, his smile.
'How my sweetheart will upbraid me!
Monkey, monkey – you must aid me.'
'Well . . .' – the monkey placed his paw
Thoughtfully upon his jaw –
'Well, although the day is hot
And I'd really rather not –
We could go back, fetch my heart,
Check its sweetness, and depart.'

So the crocodile once more
Swam the monkey back to shore,
And, with tears of thankfulness
Mingled with concern and stress,
Worried what his wife would say
With regard to his delay,
Begged his friend: 'Come back at once.'
'I'm not such a double-dunce,'
Yelled the monkey from on high;
'Tell your scaly wife to try
Eating her own wicked heart
– If she has one – for a start.
Mine's been beating in my breast
Night and day without a rest.
Tell her that – and as for you,
Here's my parting gift—' He threw

Mangoes – squishy, rotten, dead –
Down upon the reptile's head,
Who, with a regretful smile,
Sat and eyed him for a while.

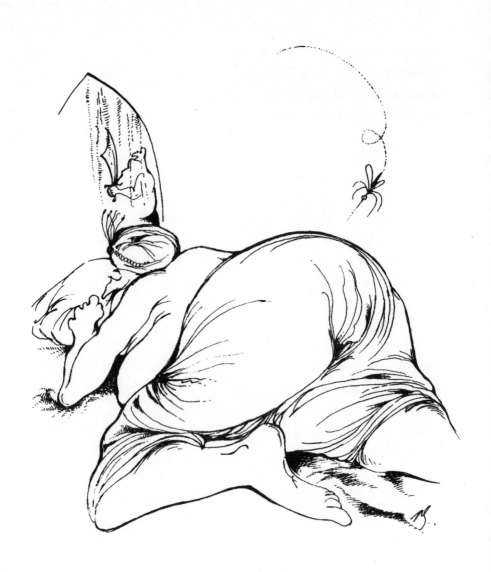

The Louse and the Mosquito

In the King's bed, Creep the louse
Lived in her ancestral house.
They had dwelt here as of right
For three decades, and each night
She and her enormous brood
Drank the King's blood for their food.
Once the signal came from Creep
That the King was fast asleep,
Quietly, discreetly, they
Nipped and sipped and drank away.
Sons and grandsons, sisters, brothers,
Great-granddaughters, great-grandmothers,
Second cousins and their wives
Thus pursued their gentle lives
– Lives of undisturbed delight –
Growing plump and smooth and white.

One day a mosquito flew
Through the window. As he drew
Closer to the velvet bed
Canopied with gold, he said:
'Lovely! Just the place for me.
Ah, what perfume – let me see –
Rose – no, jasmine. And the quilt –
Smooth as banks of Ganges silt!
Let me test the bedsprings now.'

So he jumped up – and somehow,
In a parabolic leap,
Landed not too far from Creep.

'Sir Mosquito, flap your wings.
Leave at once. This bed's the King's.'
'Who may you be, Lady Louse?'
'I'm the guardian of this house.'
'House?' 'This quilt. It's mine,' said Creep,
'There's no place for you, Sir Leap.'
'Let me sleep here for one night
And I'll catch the morning flight.'
Thus the sad mosquito pleaded,
And at last his prayers were heeded
For the tender-hearted Creep
Could not bear to watch him weep.

'Well, come in,' she said at last,
'But tonight you'll have to fast,
For on no account may you
Bite him, as we're trained to do.
We can drink and cause no pain,
Loss of royal sleep, or stain.
You, I fear, would cause all three.
I can't risk my family.'
But the glib mosquito cried:
'Now you've let me come inside,
Lady Louse, how can you be
Cold in hospitality?
Just one bite – I ask no more –
For I've learned from learned lore
That the royal blood contains

Remedies for aches and pains –
Ginger, honey, sugar, spice,
Cardamom, and all things nice.
Save me. I'm in broken health.
Let me bite him – once – by stealth.
He won't even shift or sigh.
Cross my heart and hope to die.'

Finally the louse agreed.
'Right!' she said, 'but pay close heed.
Wait till wine, fatigue, or deep
Dream-enriched, unbroken sleep
Has enveloped him. Then go:
Lightly nip his little toe.'
'Yes, yes, yes. That's all old hat,'
Said Sir Leap; 'I know all that.
Keep your stale advice.' He smiled:
'Seriously – I'm not a child.'

It was only afternoon
– Fairly early, fairly soon –
When the King came for a snooze,
Doffed his crown and shirt and shoes,
Lay down on the bed, and sighed.
The mosquito almost died
From excitement, shock, and sweat.
'No!' the louse cried: 'No! Not yet!'
But too late! The self-willed bumbler
– Oh, if only he'd been humbler –
Rushing to the rash attack,
Leapt upon the royal back,

And with fierce and fiery sting
Deeply dirked the dozing king.

'Help! a scorpion! a snake!'
Screamed the King, at once awake.
'I've been bitten! Search the bed!
Find and strike the creature dead!'
When they made a close inspection
The mosquito foiled detection,
Hidden in the canopy;
But the louse clan could not flee.
All were killed without ado.
   Meanwhile, the mosquito flew,
Looking out for further prey,
Humming mildly on his way.

The Mouse and the Snake

One fine morning two small mice,
Much against their friends' advice,
Visited a room where grain
Undisturbed for months had lain.
Other mice had entered; none
Lived to eat and tell – not one.
But the two friends, unpoliced,
Broke in and began to feast;
And their laughter fell and rose,
Till their blood with horror froze.

Gold and shiny, vicious, long,
Venom-fanged, hypnotic, strong –
Slid a snake towards the pair,
Swallowed one right then and there,
Hissed obscenely at the other:
'That's the first; and here's another!',
And, when she stood shocked and still,
Sprang at once to make his kill.

Suddenly the mouse unfroze,
Glared at him, and twitched her nose.
Every time he slid or sprang,
Dripping venom from each fang,
Out beyond his reach she leapt,
Till the snake, grown tired, crept

To his hole, slid first his head,
Then his gleaming, overfed
Trunk in, so that just his tail
Jutted out to thrash and flail.
Swift as rage the little mouse
Rushed towards the killer's house,
Bit his tail once, twice, again,
Clung to it till, wild with pain,
Hissing wrath, the snake backed out,
Swerved his body round about,
Lunged towards the mouse and tried
Swallowing her – but she leapt wide
Every time he lunged, till he,
Wriggling back exhaustedly,
Slid inside his hole once more.
Then, exactly as before,
Down she clamped with might and main
On his tail till, mad with pain,
Yet again the snake emerged.
   Thus the battle ebbed and surged
And the mouse fought on and on
Till her strength was almost gone
– When the snake, without a sound,
Spat the dead mouse on the ground,
And, with mangled slither, stole
Unopposed into his hole.

Then the mouse came up and cried
Bitter tears for her who'd died.
Squeaking sadly, and bereft,
Corpse in mouth, she sobbed and left.   ~

This was seen by Mr Yang.
    When his friend the poet Chang
Heard the mouse's story later,
Eager to commemorate her,
As he walked back to his house,
He composed 'The Faithful Mouse' –
Where in elegiac metre
He extols the Snake-Defeater
And in couplets sad and stoic
Celebrates her acts heroic –
Acts that prove that shock and pain,
Death and grief are not in vain –
Which fine lines, alive or dead,
Neither of the mice has read.

The Rat and the Ox

Once, the Chinese zodiac
Wandered slightly off its track
And a scholar-deity
Was assigned to go and see
What the gods could do about it
For they couldn't do without it.
Since the zodiac had swerved
Everything had topsy-turved:
All the years had gone awry –
Springs were cold, and monsoons dry.
Bears came out of hibernation
In midwinter with elation;
Then they saw the sky and scowled,
Shook their frozen fists, and growled.
Rabbits raged and voles grew vicious.
All these signs were inauspicious,
And the gods were much resented
By a world so discontented.

So the deity descended,
And, until his task was ended,
Workaholically obsessed,
He took neither food nor rest –
But with undiminished vigour
Questioned every fact and figure
– Size of sunspots, times of tides,

Weights of whitefish – and, besides,
Cross-examined train-commuters,
Crunched the data in computers,
Tested truths, refuted guesses,
Curved his Ts and crossed his Ss,
Asked the planets piercing questions,
Took down sensible suggestions,
Went to the original sources,
Studied all impinging forces,
Multiplied his calculations,
Grilled the sages of six nations,
And to the celestial court
Made this interim report
After three and thirty years:

'Gods and godlings, it appears
That the twelve-year zodiac
Will resume its former track
If we hasten to assign
Guards to make it toe the line—'

'Guards? What kind of guards?' 'My lords,
If I may—' 'You mean with swords?'
'Not exactly.' 'Well, what then?
Who, precisely, are these men?'
'Well, my lords, not men—' 'Then what?'
'Here's the list of guards I've got.'
When the gods looked down the list,
They hired a psychiatrist.
Only when he said he'd found
That the godling's brains were sound
Did they read the list once more:

'Rabbit, monkey, tiger, boar,
Dog, sheep, dragon, ox, cock, snake,
Horse, and rat! There's some mistake!
You have made a fool of us.
This is quite ridiculous.'
'It's an interim report,'
Came the godling's mild retort;
'If you quash my findings I
Could attempt a second try –
But it might take five and fifty—'
'No!' the gods cried, somewhat swiftly:
'No, no, no, we're sure you're right.
Sorry we were impolite.
Please, please, please don't be offended.
Do what you have recommended.
Yes, yes, yes, we do endorse it,
And, when final, we'll enforce it.'

When the godling went again
To the world of beasts and men,
He assigned, then tried to steer
Each beast to his proper year.
Several animals objected
To the years that he'd selected.
Sheep and dog, for instance, hated
To be harshly separated,
And the boar, assigned the rear,
Threatened to boycott his year.
Both the tiger and the rabbit
Felt the other should inhabit
Distant regions, and the sheep
Silently began to weep

(Why he wept was never clear
So it can't be stated here),
While the snake and dragon hissed,
'We can never coexist.
Why is he my next-door neighbour?'
But, at last, with love and labour,
Pleas and patience, they agreed
To accept the pressing need
To control the zodiac
And bring peace and order back.
Only one refused, and that
Selfish creature was the rat.

Now the rat was always reckoned
Difficult, and so the second
Year had been assigned to him –
Though in fact his claims were slim
To the quite unprecedented
Honour that this represented.
But the rat was far from grateful
And he screamed in accents hateful:
'Are you trying to ignore me?
Why's this ox been placed before me?
Equity has been denied!
Merit has been thrust aside!
Justice, faith, and truth have gone!'
On he screamed, and on and on.
Though the scholar-godling tried,
He would not be mollified.
'If the ox is great, I'm greater.
Ask a neutral mediator!
If the ox is big, I'm bigger.'

'Nonsense!' groaned the ox, 'Your figure
Is as tiny as a tit.
Ask the deity, you twit.'
But the rat screamed: 'I refuse!
For his biased, spiteful views
I don't give a flying fig!
Ask the public who is big.
Put it to a public test;
Then we'll see who comes off best.'

To defuse this first-class row
And since he was anyhow
Sure to win, the ox complied,
And the press was notified.

Then the rat feigned gloom and grief.
One night, creeping like a thief,
Snivelling to the ox he came
And he wept, 'I'll die of shame.
How can I face public scorn?
Oh, why was I ever born?
Look at my pathetic figure!
If I were a little bigger,
Just a little bigger, I
Would not wish to shrink and die.
I know you deserve first place.
Save me from my just disgrace.'

Now the ox felt rather sad.
'Cheer up, rat, don't feel so bad.
Even if your size were doubled
I would still be quite untroubled.'

'You don't mind?' 'Not in the least.
I am much the bigger beast.
Ask the godling for permission.
I will second your petition.'
'Well, I'll do as you have bid,'
Said the smirking rat, and did.

Soon he'd grown to twice his size
From his ankles to his eyes –
And, on the appointed day,
Ox and rat went on their way,
Wandering jointly through the town.
Women threw their baskets down,
Screaming: 'O my god! that rat –
Nothing quite as big as that
Have I seen – or ever will.
Just to see it makes me ill!'
Nonetheless they crowded round,
And a shocked and rattled sound
Emanated from the horde
While the ox was quite ignored.
Though they wandered side by side
Everywhere the people cried:
'What a beast! How huge! How massive!'
Then the ox, so far impassive,
Thought the people had gone blind
Or that he had lost his mind.
'Am I all that small?' he said
To the dog, who shook his head:
'No, I wouldn't say you're small –
Or the tiger – not at all –

Or the horse or sheep or pig.
But that rat – he's really big!'

That is how the ox lost face,
Sinking down to second place
In the zodiac, while the worst
Beast of all is still the first.

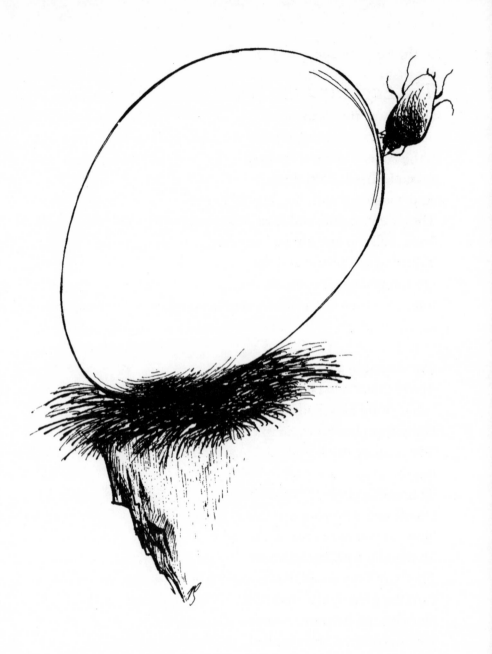

The Eagle and the Beetle

A beetle loved a certain hare
And wandered with him everywhere:
They went to fairs and feasts together,
Took walks in any kind of weather,
Talked of the future and the past
On sunny days or overcast,
But, since their friendship was so pleasant,
Lived for the most part in the present.

One day, alas, an eagle flew
Above them, and before they knew
What cloud had shadowed them, the hare
Hung from her talons in mid-air.
'Please spare my friend,' the beetle cried.
But the great eagle sneered with pride:
'You puny, servile, cloddish bug –
Go off and hide your ugly mug.
How do you dare assume the right
To meddle with my appetite?
This hare's my snack. Have you not heard
I am the great god Zeus's bird?
Nothing can harm me, least of all
A slow, pathetic, droning ball.
Here, keep your friend's head—' And she tore
The hare's head off, and swiftly bore

His bleeding torso to her nest,
Ripped off his tail, and ate the rest.

The beetle stared at her friend's head,
And wished that she herself was dead.
She mixed her tears with his dark blood
And cloaked his face with clods of mud.
She swore that till her dying breath
She would avenge his cruel death,
That she would make the eagle pay
For what she had performed today.

Next day she slowly tracked the trail
From drop of blood to tuft of tail,
Till, high up on a mountain crest,
She found the huge unguarded nest,
And at the hour that yesterday
The bird had plunged towards her prey,
The beetle with her six short legs
Rolled out the mighty eagle's eggs.
She left at once, but she could hear
The eagle's screams of pain and fear
When later she returned and found
The broken eggshells on the ground.

Next day the eagle moved her nest
Ten miles or more towards the west,
But still the beetle's scrutiny
Followed her flight from rock to tree.
When finally the eagle laid
Another clutch, the beetle made
Straight for the nest in which they lay,

And, when the bird was hunting prey,
With much fatigue but little sound
Rolled the great eggs onto the ground.

When this had gone on for a year
The eagle, crazed with rage and fear,
Would turn back, screeching, in mid-air
Whenever she would sight a hare.
The far drone of the beetle's flight
Shattered her calm by day or night.
For weeks on end she scarcely slept.
She laid her eggs in grief, and wept
When what she'd feared had come to pass –
And her smashed brood lay on the grass.

At last she cried: 'What is the use
Of bearing your protection, Zeus –
When that small, evil clot of mud
Has massacred my flesh and blood?
King of the gods, where may I rest?
Where may I safely build my nest?
Where lay my eggs without mishap?'
'Here—' said the god. 'Here, in my lap.'

And so the eggs lay, more secure
Than they had ever lain before.
What in the universe could be
More safe than Zeus's custody?
So thought the eagle, till one day
The beetle saw them where they lay –
And, aiming with precision, flung
A microscopic ball of dung

Into the lap of mighty Zeus –
Who, rising, spewed divine abuse,
And, shaking dirt from off his legs,
Unthinkingly tipped out the eggs.

Past hope, the eagle pined away
And died of grief – and to this day
They say that eagles will not nest
In months when beetles fly their best;
But others, not so superstitious,
Merely assert that Fate's capricious,
And that the strong who crush the weak
May not be shown the other cheek.

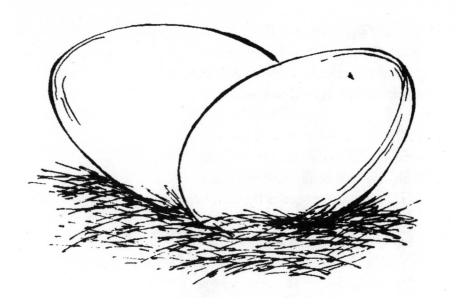

The Hare and the Tortoise

Once or twice upon a time
In the land of Runnyrhyme
Lived a hare both hot and heady
And a tortoise slow and steady.

When at noon the hare awoke
She would tell herself a joke,
Squeal with laughter, roll about,
Eat her eggs and sauerkraut,
Then pick up the phone and babble,
– 'Gibble-gabble, gibble-gabble' –
To her friends the mouse and mole
And the empty-headed vole:
'Hey, girls, did you know the rat
Was rejected by the bat?'
'Good for her! The rat's a fool!'
'Oh, I think he's kinda cool.'
'Too bad, darling, now he's dating
Lady Lemming's maid-in-waiting.'
'What – that hamster? You don't say!'
Gibble-gabble every day!
Gibble-gabble everywhere
Went the mouse and mole and hare –
Gibble-gabble, gibble-gabble.
Oh, what riffraff! Oh, what rabble!   ~

But the tortoise, when he rose,
Daily counted all his toes
Twice or three times to ensure
There were neither less nor more.
Next he'd tally the amount
In his savings bank account.
Then he'd very carefully
Count his grandsons: one, two, three –
Ed, and Ned, and Fred by name.
And his sermon was the same:
'Eddy, Neddy, Freddy – boys –
You must never break your toys.
You must often floss your gums.
You must always do your sums.
Buy your own house; don't pay rent.
Save your funds at six per cent.
Major in accountancy,
And grow up to be like me.
Listen, Eddy, Neddy, Freddy –
You be slow – but you be steady.'

One day by the Fauna Fountain
Near the noble Mammal Mountain
Where the ducks and ducklings dabble,
Hare and mouse went: 'Gibble-gabble,
Gibble-gabble – look who's coming!'
And the hare began a-humming
And the mouse began a-giggling:
'Well, it isn't Samuel Pigling
– That's for sure – or Peter Rabbit
Or Sir Fox in hunting habit.
Even Hedgehog Roly-Poly

Wouldn't ever walk so slowly.
Inch by inch by inch he's crawling.
How pathetic! how appalling!
He won't get here in an hour
If he uses turtle-power.'

'Teddy Tortoise, go and grab
Tram or train or taxi-cab!'
Squealed the hare; 'I have no doubt
You can shell the money out!'
And at this disgraceful pun
Hare and mouse both squealed with fun,
Ran around the tortoise twice,
Fell into the fountain thrice,
Swam, and sang out as they swam:
'I'm a tortoise – yes, I am!
See me swimming! Glug, glug, glug!
I'm a tortoise! No, a slug!'

Now the tortoise snapped the air,
And addressed the hare-brained hare:
'Madam, you are rash and young
And should mind your mindless tongue.
Doubtless, Madam, hares exceed
Tortoises by far in speed.
But, were we to run a race,
I, not you, would win first place.
Slowly, surely I'd defeat you.
Trust me, Madam, I would beat you.'

'Darling Tortoise,' drawled the hare,
'I would thrash you anywhere –

Marsh or mountain, hill or dale,
Field or forest, rain or hail!'
Snapped the tortoise slow and steady:
'Choose your place, and I'll be ready.
Choose your time, and make it soon.'
'Here!' the hare said: 'Sunday noon.'

So, at the appointed time
All the beasts of Runnyrhyme
– Every reptile, bird, or mammal
From the koala to the camel –
Gathered to behold the race,
Bet on first and second place,
Gobbled popcorn, guzzled beer,
And exclaimed: 'They're here! They're here!'
At the starting block the steady
Tortoise flexed his toes, quite ready;
But the flighty hare, still wearing
Her silk nightie, kept on staring
At a mirror while the press
Took her words down, more or less.
Young reporters sought her views
For the *Rhyme & Runny News.*
'What's at stake besides the honour?'
'Is the tortoise, Ma'am, a goner?'
'Why did you agree to run?'
'Is the race already won?'
Pouting out her scarlet lips,
Sweetly wiggling head and hips,
Making wolves feel weak inside,
Languidly Ms Hare replied:
'Teddy Tortoise, don't you see,

Has this awful crush on me.
Why, he thinks I'm simply stunning.
That's why, darlings, I am running.
And I've staked the cup I won
When I was Miss Honeybun . . .
Who will win? Why – can't you tell?
Read the lipstick on his shell.'
There she'd smeared a scarlet '2'
And the words: 'Mock Turtil Stew.'

Soon the starting gun was heard
And a secretary bird
Gently murmured: 'It's begun.
Ma'am, perhaps you ought to run.'
'No,' the hare laughed – 'Oh, no, no!
Teddy Tortoise is so slow.
Let him have a little start.
I don't want to break his heart.'

But the tortoise plodded on
Like a small automaton,
Muttering, as he held his pace:
'I have got to win this race.'

Two hours passed. In satin shorts
Cut for fashion more than sports,
Ms Hare once again appeared,
Yawning softly as she neared:
'Two o'clock! My beauty sleep!'
'Ma'am, the race—?' 'The race will keep.
Really, it's already won.'
And she stretched out in the sun.   ~

Two hours passed. The hare awoke
And she stretched and yawned and spoke:
'Where's the tortoise?' 'Out of sight.'
'Oh—' the hare said: 'Really? Right!
Time to go—' and off she bounded,
Leaving all her friends astounded
At her rocket-fuelled pace.
'Sure!' they said, 'She'll win this race.'
She was out of sight already
On the heels of Tortoise Teddy.

Suddenly the dizzy hare
Saw a field of mushrooms where
Champignons and chanterelles
Mixed with devils-of-the-dell.
(This last mushroom, I suspect,
Has a cerebral effect.
Every time I eat one, I
Feel I'm floating in the sky.)
'How delicious! What a treat!'
Said the hare: 'I'll stop and eat.'
So she did, and very soon
She was singing out of tune,
And she lurched towards the wood,
Shouting to the neighbourhood:
'Boring, boring, life is boring.
Birdies, help me go exploring.
Let's go off the beaten track.
In a minute I'll be back—'
Off the hare went, fancy-free.
One hour passed, then two, then three.

But the tortoise plodded on
Now the day was almost gone
And the sun was sinking low –
Very steady, very slow –
And he saw the finish line
And he thought, 'The race is mine!' –
And the gold cup was in sight
Glinting in the golden light –
When with an impassioned air
Someone screamed: 'Look! look! the hare!' –
And the punters started jumping,
And the tortoise heard a thumping
Close behind him on the track,
And he wanted to look back –
For the hare was roused at last
And was gaining on him fast –
And had almost caught him up
And retrieved her golden cup
When the tortoise, mouth agape,
Crossed the line and bit the tape.

After the announcer's gun
Had pronounced that he had won,
And the cheering of the crowd
Died at last, the tortoise bowed,
Clasped the cup with quiet pride,
And sat down, self-satisfied.
And he thought: 'That silly hare!
So much for her charm and flair.
So much for her idle boast.
In her cup I'll raise a toast
To hard work and regularity.

Silly creature! Such vulgarity!
Now she'll learn that sure and slow
Is the only way to go –
That you can't rise to the top
With a skip, a jump, a hop –
That you've got to hatch your eggs,
That you've got to count your legs,
That you've got to do your duty,
Not depend on verve and beauty.
When the press comes, I shall say
That she's been shell-shocked today!
What a well-deserved disgrace
That the fool has lost this race.'

But it was in fact the hare,
With a calm insouciant air
Like an unrepentant bounder,
Who allured the pressmen round her.
'Oh, Miss Hare, you're so appealing
When you're sweating,' said one, squealing.
'You have tendered gold and booty
To the shrine of sleep and beauty,'
Breathed another, overawed;
And Will Wolf, the great press lord
Filled a gold cup – on a whim –
With huge rubies to the brim
– Gorgeous rubies, bold and bright,
Red as cherries, rich with light –
And with an inviting grin
Murmured: 'In my eyes you win.'

~

And perhaps she had; the hare
Suddenly was everywhere.
Stories of her quotes and capers
Made front page in all the papers –
And the sleepy BBC
– Beastly Broadcast Company –
Beamed a feature with the news:
'All the World Lost for a Snooze'.
Soon she saw her name in lights,
Sold a book and movie rights,
While a travel magazine
Bought the story, sight unseen,
Of her three-hour expedition
To the wood – called 'Mushroom Mission'.
Soon the cash came pouring in,
And to save it was a sin –
So she bought a manor house
Where she lived with mole and mouse –
And her friends, when they played Scrabble
– Gibble-gabble, gibble-gabble,
Gibble-gabble all the way –
Let her spell 'Compete' with K.

Thus the hare was pampered rotten
And the tortoise was forgotten.

The Cat and the Cock

Once a certain cat and cock,
Friendship founded on a rock,
Lived together in a house
In the land of Fledermaus.
Each loved music in his way,
And the cock, at break of day
Chanted: 'Cock-a-doodle-doo!
Kiki-riki – Kuk-ru-koo!',
While his cat-friend, in the middle
Of the night, would play the fiddle.
Sometimes they would play together
– Handsome fur and fancy feather –
And the pair would dance and sing
While the house with joy would ring.

When the cat would range and roam
Far away from hearth and home
He would leave his friend the cock
To rewind the cuckoo-clock,
Read the papers or a book,
Shine the window-panes, and cook.
On departing he would say,
'Cocko, have a happy day.
But do not step out of doors:
Don't trust other carnivores.
Please avoid your usual scrapes.

You've had many close escapes.
Do things, if you would, my way.'
'Sure . . .' the cock said. 'Sure, OK.'

But one day a red-tailed fox
Who liked eating hens and cocks
– She had slaughtered twelve or more –
Drooled demurely at the door,
Whispering with a gentle knock,
'It's the postman, Mr Cock.'
'Yes, I'm sure,' the cock replied,
'But I cannot come outside.
As you know, my friend the cat
Says there's no excuse for that.
Slip the mail beneath the door
Like you've always done before.'

For a while the fox was foiled,
But, in accents smoothly oiled,
After he had counted ten
He began to speak again:
'Parcel post for you to sign
Here, sir, on the dotted line.
Really sorry, Mr Cock.
Would you please undo the lock,
Step outside, and sign, and pay?
Sir, I can't stand here all day.'
'Bother! Bother!' said the cock,
But he did undo the lock,
Step out, and bend down to sign
Neatly on the dotted line.
Quick as quoits the fox's paw

Clamped down on his inky claw,
And she seized him by the comb,
Bit his scruff, and dragged him home.

Now the cock called to the cat:
'Catto, Catto, save my fat!
Save my feathers, save your friend
From a truly wretched end –
Butchered by a vixen vicious
Who finds cocks and hens delicious.'
But the cat was far away
And when at the close of day
He returned, he gasped to find
Pen and parcel left behind,
And red fur, black ink, and blood
Mixed with feathers in the mud.

First he tried to trace their track;
Then he shivered and came back;
Then with head on paw he cried,
For the night was dark outside
And he could not guess or know
What to think or where to go:
'O, dear Cocko, will your claw
Never rest upon my paw?
Will we never dance and sing,
Share our house and everything?
Will I never see your wattle
Rise like dawn above this bottle?'
Then the Cat, who had been drinking,
Dried his tears, and started thinking –
Stared at feathers, ink, and fur,

All at once began to purr,
Grabbed his fiddle and a sack,
And set forth upon the track
Leading to the fox's house,
Silent as a yawning mouse.

Now the fox had tied her prey
So he couldn't fly away
And had gone to pay a call,
Dressed in foxgloves, hat and shawl.
She had told her eldest daughter:
'Darling, boil a pot of water.
I'll be gone an hour or two.
When I'm back I'll make some stew:
One plump cock, a pound of carrots,
Parsley, and a pair of parrots.
And, all five of you, take care
Of each other, and beware –
Never go out on your own.
Always use the telephone.
Never let a stranger in.
Heed my words through thick and thin:
These are sad and troubled times
Marred by bold and vicious crimes.
Things have changed so much—' she sighed,
'Since the year your father died.
So, my darlings, bolt the lock,
Heat the pot, and guard the cock.'

Off she went, and now the cat
– Glaring at her yellow hat
As it glimmered, gleamed and glowed,

Disappearing down the road –
Tuned his fiddle with a twang,
Coughed, and cleared his throat, and sang:

'Madame Fox's manor hall
Is so splendid, wide and tall.
Her four daughters and her son
Are a match for anyone.
Valentina and Velveeta,
Vera, Violet and Peter –
Come, all five, and hear my song –
Step outside, and sing along.
Yes, and dance, for I'm a dancer!'
But from inside came no answer.

So he changed the inclination
Of his musical temptation
And, like prince or politician,
Tried to split the opposition.
After counting three times ten,
He began to sing again –
Sing again and sing again
To a modified refrain:
'Madame Fox's manor hall
Is so splendid, wide and tall.
Her four daughters and her son
Are a match for anyone.
Valentina – heart of health –
Meet me, lovely maid, by stealth.
Just for you I'll sing a song –
Come outside, and sing along.'   ~

On and on the cat persisted
Till he couldn't be resisted,
And when finally he spied
Valentina step outside,
Lifting up his fiddle he
Plucked the open string of G,
Gave her nose a frightful whack –
And he popped her in his sack.

'That's the first, and now I've caught her,
I must catch another daughter,'
Said the cat, 'and in the end
I will surely free my friend.
I will surely save his life
From the pot and kitchen-knife.'
Twiddling on a fiddle-string
He began once more to sing:
'Madame Fox's manor hall
Is so splendid, wide and tall.
Her four daughters and her son
Are a match for anyone.
Smooth Velveeta, plump as cheese,
Meet me in the moonlight, please.
Just for you I'll sing a song –
Come outside, and sing along.'

On and on the cat persisted
Till he couldn't be resisted,
And when finally he spied
Smooth Velveeta step outside,
Lifting up his fiddle he
Plucked the open string of D,

Gave her nose a frightful whack –
And he popped her in his sack.

'That's the second; now I've caught her,
I must catch another daughter,'
Said the cat, 'and in the end
I will surely free my friend.
I will surely save his life
From the pot and kitchen-knife.'
Twiddling on a fiddle-string
He began once more to sing:
'Madame Fox's manor hall
Is so splendid, wide and tall.
Her four daughters and her son
Are a match for anyone.
Vera Vixen, fox of truth,
Let me see your grace and youth!
Just for you I'll sing a song –
Come outside, and sing along.'

On and on the cat persisted
Till he couldn't be resisted,
And when finally he spied
Vera Vixen step outside,
Lifting up his fiddle he
Plucked the A-string gallantly,
Gave her nose a frightful whack –
And he popped her in his sack.

'That's the third, and now I've caught her,
I must catch another daughter,'
Said the cat, 'and in the end

I will surely free my friend.
I will surely save his life
From the pot and kitchen-knife.'
Twiddling on a fiddle-string
He began once more to sing:
'Madame Fox's manor hall
Is so splendid, wide and tall.
Her four daughters and her son
Are a match for anyone.
Violet, so fresh and fragrant,
Leave your home and be a vagrant.
Just for you I'll sing a song –
Come outside, and sing along.'

On and on the cat persisted
Till he couldn't be resisted,
And when finally he spied
Violet emerge outside,
Lifting up his fiddle he
Plucked the open string of E,
Gave her nose a frightful whack –
And he popped her in his sack.

'That's the fourth; and now that's done
I must somehow catch the son,'
Said the cat, 'and in the end
I will surely free my friend.
I will surely save his life
From the pot and kitchen-knife.'
Twiddling on a fiddle-string
He began once more to sing:
'Madame Fox's manor hall

Is so splendid, wide and tall.
Her four daughters and her son
Are a match for anyone.
Plucky Peter, pert and proud,
Leave your house and join the crowd.
Just for you I'll sing a song –
Come outside, and sing along.'

On and on the cat persisted
Till he couldn't be resisted,
And when finally he spied
Plucky Peter step outside,
Lifting up his fiddle he
Crept towards him silently,
Gave his nose a frightful whack –
And he too went in the sack.

Then the cat skipped round and round,
Making a triumphant sound
– Half miaowing and half mewing,
Half guffawing and half cooing
(This adds up to more than one,
But it really can be done) –
And he heaved the hefty sack
Happily upon his back,
Murmuring – and now his voice
Purred like a well-oiled Rolls-Royce –
'Madame Fox's manor hall
Is so splendid, wide and tall.
Her four daughters and her son
Came outside to join the fun!
Valentina and Velveeta,

Vera, Violet and Peter –
Now I'll cook you in a pot
And I'll serve you piping hot.'

But the little foxes cried
Till the cat grew teary-eyed,
So he let the sack hang free
High upon a willow tree.
'Now get down as best you can,'
Said the cat, and off he ran
To the house to save the cock
From the execution block.

First they hugged, and then the cat
Played a prelude in E flat,
While the cock, concurrently,
Sang a serenade in D.
Then with appetite and ardour,
Commandeering fridge and larder,
Cat and cock both feasted on
Till the fox's food was gone,
Spilled the water on the boil,
Soaked her sheets in mustard oil,
Strained her toothpaste through her comb,
And before they ran back home
Bent the spoons and broke the dishes.
'Now,' the cat said, 'heed my wishes.
When we're back at home at last,
Learn a lesson from the past.
Do things, if you would, my way.'
'Sure . . .' the cock said. 'Sure, OK.'

The Goat and the Ram

An old man and his wife possessed
A zebra of enormous zest,
A white ram of enormous size,
A small black goat with yellow eyes,
Four ducks, a peacock, and a sow,
A gosling, and a purple cow.

The cow gave cream for apple tart,
The zebra drew an apple-cart,
The four fat ducks were good at laying,
The sow excelled at piano-playing,
The gosling could predict the weather,
The peacock flashed a brilliant feather,
But there was really no competing
With ram and goat for over-eating.

They ate all day, they ate all night.
They ate with beastly appetite.
They fed on grapes and grass and grain.
They ate, and paused to eat again.
They ate with pride, as if to balance
Their total lack of other talents.
They raided farmers' kitchens late
At night – and drank the milk – and ate
Both à la carte and table d'hôte.
The ram was nervous; not the goat.

She got the big fat ram to knock
The door down and to break the lock –
And told him: 'Boy, this is the life!'

One night the man said to his wife:
'My dear, that goat and ram mean trouble.
They eat their share – and more than double.
You'd hardly think a small black goat
Could force six bushels down her throat.
She and her friend have eaten all
The apples on our farm this fall.
We can't afford to house and feed
Creatures of such enormous greed.
It's reached the limit. Let's get rid
Of both of them.' And so they did.

Next day the man said: 'Goat and ram –
We've had enough of you. So scram!
Put your belongings in a sack.
And go at once. And don't come back.'
Some of the animals were glad
To see them go, but most were sad,
And the sow snivelled as she played
Dido's lament, 'When I am laid . . .'

The ram said to the goat: 'Alas –
Now that we've been put out to grass,
Now that we've lost our house and home –
What shall we do, where shall we roam?'
He sobbed and trembled till the goat,
Said rather shortly – and I quote:
'You great big booby, quit this fuss.

Who, after all, is bothering us?
Things aren't that bad. We've not been beaten.
We could have been, but were not, eaten.
Some time we'll find some home somewhere.
Let's keep on walking. What's that there?'

The ram, who was already shivering
At the word 'eaten', started quivering:
For what the goat had pointed out
Was a huge wolf's head – fangs and snout
And bloody mouth with tongue revealed –
Lying discarded in a field.
'I think—' the poor ram started bleating;
'I think we shouldn't talk of eating.
I'm feeling rather, well, upset—'
'Nonsense!' the goat said; 'Go and get
That wolf's head here.' 'Oh,' said the ram,
'I actually believe I am
Going to be sick.' 'Shut up and go!'
The goat commanded him, and so –
Despite the grey ears caked with mud,
The grizzled mane smeared thick with blood,
The yellow teeth of ghastly size,
And the dull, terrifying eyes –
The ram obeyed and, coming back,
Dropped the great wolf's head in the sack.

'Good,' said the goat. 'Who knows, one day
It might prove useful in some way.
Let's go.' And so they kept on walking.
The ram was in no mood for talking.
His heart kept palpitating back

To what he carried in his sack.
But now the day was almost gone
And the black night was coming on,
And so – disheartened and dismayed –
He whimpered softly: 'I'm afraid.'

'Afraid of what?' 'Of wolves and things –
And beastly bats with wicked wings –
And being all alone at night
With neither food nor firelight
Nor all the farmyard beasts around,'
He said, and made a funny sound –
A sort of gurgle in his throat.
'You great big booby!' said the goat,
'Be quiet. Your depression's draining.
Now dry your face and quit complaining.
Why, isn't that a light out there?'
She pointed with her hoof to where
A distant campfire's golden gleam
Was half-reflected in a stream.
'That clearly is the place to go
If you're afraid of wolves, you know . . .
We'll be just fine.' And so they turned
To where the distant fire burned.

The timid ram controlled his fear
As they drew near and still more near –
And when at last they reached the cheering
Flame that lit the forest clearing,
Drenched with relief they looked around:
A great round tent stood on the ground,
And by the fire so high and hot,

Preparing porridge in a pot,
Complaining of their hunger-pangs,
Sat three huge wolves with yellow fangs.

'Hello,' the wolves said, 'Glad to meet you.
And gladder still, of course, to eat you.'
Towards the pair the trio padded
And with a grisly grimace added:
'You must forgive our etiquette.
Our porridge isn't ready yet.
It's still a bit too hot to serve.
We'll eat you first, as an hors d'oeuvre.'

At first the goat thought they should flee –
But then she turned, and casually
Said to her friend: 'Hey, Brother Ram,
Are you still hungry? I sure am.
Get that wolf's head out from your sack.
I'd like to have a sundown snack.'
The ram's jaw dropped, but in the end,
Under the sharp gaze of his friend,
He grasped the wolf's head tremblingly
And pulled it out for all to see.

The three great wolves were frightened witless.
Their eyes were glazed, their mouths were spitless.
They breathed a jerky, shallow breath
And shivered with the fear of death.
They stared from goat to ram, and then
Stared back from ram to goat again.   ~

'No, no!' the goat said to the ram,
'That was the wolf who ate the lamb.
Take out the bigger one who tried
To kill the sheep – before he died.'
So the ram put the wolf's head back
And pulled it once more from the sack,
And held it up for all to see.
'This one?' he mumbled fearfully.

The wolves turned green and almost died.
'I've changed my mind,' the goat replied.
'Take out the biggest one of all,
Who killed three oxen in their stall –
The one we slaughtered yesterday
And ate as wolf-liver pâté.
And, Brother Ram, don't tremble so.
It shows poor taste, as you should know,
To quiver with anticipation
Or to display overt elation
Merely because you've seen your meal.
Think how our friends the wolves must feel.
If they are frightened, they'll grow thinner
Before we've all sat down to dinner.'

So the ram put the wolf's head back
And pulled it once more from the sack.
At this the wolves, whose teeth were chattering,
Whose hearts were numb, whose nerves were shattering,
Looked at the head as if transfixed.
The first wolf said: 'I think I've mixed
Too little water with the oats.
Thick porridge isn't good for goats.

Dear guests, please stay here, and I'll go
Fetch water from the stream below.'
He gave a sort of strangled cough,
Tucked in his tail, and sidled off.

The second wolf sat for a minute,
Then murmured: 'Salt's what's lacking in it.
And what is porridge without salt?
It's like – well – whisky without malt –
Heh heh! – or piglets without trotters.
I'll get some from the friendly otters
Whose home is in the stream below.
Wait here – dear guests – I have to go—'
He gave a sort of strangled giggle
And squirmed off swiftly as a squiggle.

The third wolf said: 'Where are those two?
My dear dear friends, what shall I do?
I cannot have you waiting here
While chefs and waiters disappear.
I'll get them back at once. Please stay.
I'll go myself. I know the way.'
He gave a sort of strangled howl
And slunk off with a shifty scowl.

'Well,' said the goat, 'we've seen the last
Of our three hosts. Let's break our fast
With what's been cooking in the pot.
I'll bet my tail it's not too hot
Or saltless – or too thick for goats.'
And so they ladled down their throats
Delicious porridge spoon by spoon.

The ram swelled up like a balloon
And lay down on the ground, content.
The goat pulled him inside the tent –
And that was where they spent the night.
Indeed, as of the time I write,
They live there still, secure from harm,
Out of the reach of wolf or farm.
They eat wild strawberries and grass
And drink stream water, clear as glass.
They never argue, never fight.
They never have bad dreams at night.
With moderation and accord
They pass their days, serenely bored.

The Frog and the Nightingale

Once upon a time a frog
Croaked away in Bingle Bog.
Every night from dusk to dawn
He croaked awn and awn and awn.
Other creatures loathed his voice,
But, alas, they had no choice,
And the crass cacophony
Blared out from the sumac tree
At whose foot the frog each night
Minstrelled on till morning light.

Neither stones nor prayers nor sticks,
Insults or complaints or bricks
Stilled the frog's determination
To display his heart's elation.
But one night a nightingale
In the moonlight cold and pale
Perched upon the sumac tree
Casting forth her melody.
Dumbstruck sat the gaping frog,
And the whole admiring bog
Stared towards the sumac, rapt,
And, when she had ended, clapped.
Ducks had swum and herons waded
To her as she serenaded,
And a solitary loon

Wept beneath the summer moon.
Toads and teals and tiddlers, captured
By her voice, cheered on, enraptured:
'Bravo!' 'Too divine!' 'Encore!'
So the nightingale once more,
Quite unused to such applause,
Sang till dawn without a pause.

Next night when the nightingale
Shook her head and twitched her tail,
Closed an eye and fluffed a wing
And had cleared her throat to sing
She was startled by a croak.
'Sorry – was that you who spoke?'
She enquired when the frog
Hopped towards her from the bog.
'Yes,' the frog replied. 'You see,
I'm the frog who owns this tree.
In this bog I've long been known
For my splendid baritone
And, of course, I wield my pen
For *Bog Trumpet* now and then.'
'Did you . . . did you like my song?'
'Not too bad – but far too long.
The technique was fine, of course,
But it lacked a certain force.'
'Oh!' the nightingale confessed,
Greatly flattered and impressed
That a critic of such note
Had discussed her art and throat:
'I don't think the song's divine.
But – oh, well – at least it's mine.'

~

'That's not much to boast about,'
Said the heartless frog. 'Without
Proper training such as I
 – And few others – can supply,
You'll remain a mere beginner.
But with me you'll be a winner.'

'Dearest frog,' the nightingale
Breathed: 'This is a fairy tale –
And you're Mozart in disguise
Come to earth before my eyes.'
'Well, I charge a modest fee.'
'Oh!' 'But it won't hurt, you'll see.'

Now the nightingale, inspired,
Flushed with confidence, and fired
With both art and adoration,
Sang – and was a huge sensation.
Animals for miles around
Flocked towards the magic sound,
And the frog with great precision
Counted heads and charged admission.

Though next morning it was raining,
He began her vocal training.
'But I can't sing in this weather.'
'Come, my dear – we'll sing together.
Just put on your scarf and sash.
Koo-oh-ah! ko-ash! ko-ash!'
So the frog and nightingale
Journeyed up and down the scale
For six hours, till she was shivering
And her voice was hoarse and quivering.   ~

Though subdued and sleep-deprived,
In the night her throat revived,
And the sumac tree was bowed
With a breathless, titled crowd:
Owl of Sandwich, Duck of Kent,
Mallard and Milady Trent,
Martin Cardinal Mephisto,
And the Coot of Monte Cristo.
Ladies with tiaras glittering
In the interval sat twittering –
And the frog observed them glitter
With a joy both sweet and bitter.

Every day the frog who'd sold her
Songs for silver tried to scold her:
'You must practise even longer
Till your voice, like mine, grows stronger.
In the second song last night
You got nervous in mid-flight.
And, my dear, lay on more trills:
Audiences enjoy such frills.
You must make your public happier:
Give them something sharper, snappier.
We must aim for better billings.
You still owe me sixty shillings.'

Day by day the nightingale
Grew more sorrowful and pale.
Night on night her tired song
Zipped and trilled and bounced along,
Till the birds and beasts grew tired
At a voice so uninspired

And the ticket office gross
Crashed, and she grew more morose –
For her ears were now addicted
To applause quite unrestricted,
And to sing into the night
All alone gave no delight.

Now the frog puffed up with rage.
'Brainless bird – you're on the stage –
Use your wits, and follow fashion.
Puff your lungs out with your passion.'
Trembling, terrified to fail,
Blind with tears, the nightingale
Heard him out in silence, tried,
Puffed up, burst a vein, and died.

Said the frog: 'I tried to teach her,
But she was a stupid creature –
Far too nervous, far too tense,
Far too prone to influence.
Well, poor bird – she should have known
That your song must be your own.
That's why I sing with panache:
Koo-oh-ah! ko-ash! ko-ash!'
And the foghorn of the frog
Blared unrivalled through the bog.

The Elephant and the Tragopan

In Bingle Valley, broad and green,
Where neither hut nor field is seen,
Where bamboo, like a distant lawn,
Is gold at dusk and flushed at dawn,
Where rhododendron forests crown
The hills, and wander halfway down
In scarlet blossom, where each year
A dozen shy black bears appear,
Where a cold river, filmed with ice,
Sustains a minor paradise,
An elephant and tragopan
Discussed their fellow creature, man.

The tragopan last week had heard
The rumour from another bird
– Most probably a quail or sparrow:
Such birds have gossip in their marrow –
That man had hatched a crazy scheme
To mar their land and dam their stream,
To flood the earth on which they stood,
And cut the woods down for their wood.
The tragopan, good-natured pheasant,
A trifle shocked by this unpleasant
Even if quite unlikely news
Had scurried off to test the views
Of his urbane and patient friend,

The elephant, who in the end
Had swung his trunk from side to side
With gravitas, and thus replied:
'Who told you? Ah, the quail – oh well,
I rather doubt – but who can tell?
I would suggest we wait and see.
Now would you care to have some tea?'
'Gnau! gnau!' the tragopan agreed.
'That is exactly what I need.
And if you have a bamboo shoot
Or fresh oak-leaves or ginseng-root –
Something that's crunchy but not prickly . . .
I feel like biting something quickly.'
The elephant first brewed the tea
In silence, then said carefully:
'Now let me think what I can get you.
I fear this rumour has upset you.
Your breast looks redder than before.
Do ruffle down. Here, let me pour.'
He drew a lukewarm gallon up
His trunk, and poured his friend a cup.

A week passed, and the tragopan
One morning read the news and ran
In panic down the forest floor
To meet the elephant once more.
A cub-reporter bison calf
Who wrote for *Bingle Telegraph*
Had just confirmed the frightful fact
In language chilling and exact.
'Here, read it!' said the tragopan,
And so the elephant began:

'Bingle. 5th April. Saturday.
Reliable informants say
That the Great Bigshot Number One
Shri Padma Bhushan Gobardhun
And the Man-Council of this state,
Intending to alleviate
The water shortage in the town
Across our ridge and ten miles down,
Have spent three cartloads of rupees
So far upon consultants' fees –
Whose task is swiftly to appraise
Efficient, cheap, and speedy ways
To dam our stream, create a lake,
And blast a tunnel through to take
Sufficient water to supply
The houses that men occupy.'

'What do you think,' the tragopan
Burst out, 'about this wicked plan
To turn our valley blue and brown?
I will not take this lying down.
I'll cluck at them. I'll flap my wings.
I tell you, I will do such things –
What they are yet I do not know,
But, take my word, I mean to show
Those odious humans what I feel.
And the Great Partridge will reveal
– That Partridge, dwelling in the sky,
Who looks down on us from on high –
He will reveal to us the way –
So kneel with me and let us pray.'   ~

The elephant said, 'Let me think.
Before we pray, let's have a drink.
Some bamboo wine – perhaps some tea?'
'No, no,' the bird said angrily,
'I will not give in to distraction.
This isn't time for tea but action.'
The wattled horns upon his head
Stood upright in an angry red.
The elephant said nothing; he
Surveyed the landscape thoughtfully
And flapped his ears like a great fan
To cool the angry tragopan.

'It's infamous, I know,' he said,
'But we have got to use our head.
Praying may help us – who can tell? –
But they, of course, have gods as well.
I would endeavour to maintain
Our plans on a terrestrial plane.
What I suggest is we convoke
The Beastly Board of Forest Folk
For a full meeting to discuss
The worst that can occur to us.'
And so, that evening, all the creatures
– With tusks or gills or other features –
Met at the river's edge to plan
How they might outmanoeuvre man.
Gibbons and squirrels, snakes, wild dogs,
Deer and macaques, three types of frogs,
Porcupines, eagles, trout, wagtails,
Civet cats, sparrows, bears and quails,
Bloodsucking leeches, mild-eyed newts,

And leopards in their spotted suits –
Stated their stances, asked their questions,
And made their manifold suggestions.
Some predators drooled at the sight,
But did not act on appetite.
The leopards did not kill the deer.
The smaller birds evinced no fear.
Each eagle claw sat in its glove.
The mood was truce, if not quite love.
At meetings of the Beastly Board
Eating each other was outlawed.

The arguments grew sharp and heated.
Some views advanced, and some retreated.
Some feared to starve, and some to drown.
Some said they should attack the town.
The trout said they were unconcerned
If the whole bamboo forest burned
So long as they had space to swim.
The mynahs joked, the boars looked grim.
They talked for hours, and at the close
At last the elephant arose,
And with a modest trumpet-call
Drew the attention of them all:

'O Beasts of Bingle gathered round,
Though in our search for common ground
I would not dream of unanimity
I hope our views may reach proximity.
I speak to you as one whose clan
Has served and therefore studied man.
He is a creature mild and vicious,

Practical-minded and capricious,
Loving and brutal, sane and mad,
The good as puzzling as the bad.
The sticky centre of this mess
Is an uneasy selfishness.
He rips our flesh and tears our skin
For cloth without, for food within.
The leopard's spots are his to wear.
Our ivory unknots his hair.
The tragopan falls to his gun.
He shoots the flying fox for fun.
The black bear dances to his whim.
My own tame cousins slave for him.
Yet we who give him work and food
Have never earned his gratitude.
He grasps our substance as of right
To quench and spur his appetite,
Nor will he grant us truce or grace
To rest secure in any place.
Sometimes he worships us as Gods
Or sings of us at Eisteddfods,
Or fashions fables, myths, and stories
To celebrate our deeds and glories.
And yet, despite this fertile fuss,
When has he truly cared for us?
He sees the planet as his fief
Where every hair or drop or leaf
Or seed or blade or grain of sand
Is destined for his mouth or hand.
If he is thirsty, we must thirst –
For of all creatures, man comes first.
If he needs room, then we must fly;

And if he hungers, we must die.
   Think what will happen, when his scheme
To tame our valley and our stream
Begins to thrust its way across
These gentle slopes of fern and moss
With axe, explosive, and machine.
Since rhododendron logs burn green
They'll all be chopped for firewood –
Or logged and smuggled out for good.
As every bird and mammal knows,
When the road comes, the forest goes.
And let me say this to the trout –
The bamboo will be slashed, no doubt,
And what the tragopan and I
Delight to eat, will burn and die.
But what will happen to your stream?
Before the reservoir, your dream
Of endless space, can come about,
The soot and filth will snuff you out.
What tolls for us is your own bell.
And similarly let me tell
The leopards who may fancy here
A forestful of fleeing deer –
After your happy, passing slaughter,
You too will have to flee from water.
You will be homeless, like us all.
It is this fate we must forestall.
So let me say to every single
Endangered denizen of Bingle:
We must unite in fur and feather –
For we will live or die together.'   ~

All this made such enormous sense
That all except the rather dense
Grey peacock-pheasants burst out cheering.
The peacock-pheasants, after hearing
The riotous applause die down,
Asked, with an idiotic frown:
'But what is it we plan to do?'
A bison calf remarked: 'I knew
Those peacock-pheasants were half-witted.'
And everybody joshed and twitted
The silly birds till they were dumb.
'How typical! How troublesome!'
A monkey said: 'What awful taste!
How graceless and how brazen-faced,
When all of us are clapping paws,
To undermine our joint applause.'
Oddly, the elephant was the beast
Who of them all was put out least.
He flapped his ears and bowed his head.
'The pheasants have a point,' he said.

'Unfortunately,' he went on,
'The days of beastly strength are gone.
We don't have mankind on the run.
That's why he's done what he has done.
We can't, as someone here suggested,
Burn down the town. We'd be arrested.
Or maimed or shot or even eaten.
But I will not accept we're beaten.
Someone suggested that we flee
And set up our community
In some far valley where no man

Has ever trod – or ever can.
Sweet to the mind though it may seem,
This is, alas, an idle dream –
For nowhere lies beyond man's reach
To mar and burn and flood and leach.
A distant valley is indeed
No sanctuary from his greed.
Besides, the beasts already there
Will fight with us for food and air.
No, we must struggle for this land
Where we have stood and where we stand.
What I suggest is that we go
To the Great Bigshot down below
And show him how self-interest
And what his conscience says is best
Both tell him, "Let the valley be."
Who knows – perhaps he may agree,
If nothing else, to hear us out.
But we must take, without a doubt,
Firm data to support our prayer –
And in addition must prepare
Some other scheme by which he can
Ensure more water gets to man –
For, by the twitching of my trunk,
Without that we'll be truly sunk.'

And so it happened that a rally
Meandered forth from Bingle Valley
A few days later, up and down
The hills towards the human town.
With trumpet, cackle, grunt and hoot
They harmonized along their route,

And 'Long live Bingladesh' was heard
From snout of beast and beak of bird.
'Protect our spots,' the leopards growled;
While the wild dogs and gibbons howled:
'Redress our sad and sorry tale,
The tragedy of Bingle Vale.'
And there, red-breasted in the van,
Cluck-clucked the gallant tragopan –
Raised high upon the elephant's neck,
And guiding him by prod and peck.
The only absentees, the trout,
Were much relieved to slither out.
They asked: 'How can we wet our gills
Clambering up and down those hills?
The journey will be far too taxing;
We'd rather spend the time relaxing.
We'll guard the valley while you plead.'
'All right,' the other beasts agreed.

Meanwhile from fields and gates and doors
The villagers came out in scores
To see the cavalcade go by.
Some held their children shoulder-high
While others clutched a bow or gun
And dreamed of pork or venison –
But none had seen or even heard
Of such a horde of beast and bird,
And not a bullet or an arrow
Touched the least feather of a sparrow.
So stunned and stupefied were they,
They even cheered them on the way
Or joined them on the route to town –

Where the Great Bigshot with a frown
Said to his Ministers, 'Look here!
What is this thing that's drawing near?
What is this beastly ragtag army –
Have I gone blind? Or am I barmy?'

'Yes, yes, Sir—' said the Number Two.
'I mean, no, no, Sir – what to do?
They've not gone through the proper channels.
The Protocol Protection Panels
Have no idea who they are.
Nor does the Riffraff Registrar.
It's possible they don't exist.'
'Well,' said the Bigshot, getting pissed,
'Exist or not, they're getting near.
And you'll be Number Twelve, I fear,
Unless you find out what the fuss
Is all about, and tender us
Advice on what to say and do.
And think. And be. Now off with you.'
The Number Two was almost crying.
He rushed off with his shirt-tails flying,
Without a cummerbund or hat,
And flew back in a minute flat.
'Oh, Bigshot, Sir, thanks to your grace,
By which I'm here in second place,
Thanks to your wisdom and your power
Which grows in glory by the hour,
Thanks to the faith you've placed in me,
Which gives me strength to hear and see,
Thanks to—' 'Yes, yes,' the Bigshot said,
'Thanks to my power to cut you dead,

What is it you have come to learn?'
'Sir, Sir, they plan to overturn
Your orders, Sir, to dam up Bingle.
And, Sir, I saw some pressmen mingle
With the parade to interview
A clouded leopard and a shrew.
The beasts are all against your plan.
The worst of them's the tragopan.
His eyes are fierce, his breast is red.
He wears a wattle on his head.
He looks so angry I've a hunch
That he's the leader of the bunch.
And when I met them, they weren't far –
Oh Sir – oh no, Sir – here they are!'

For now a hoolock gibbon's paw
Was battering on the Bigshot's door
And animals from far and wide
Were crowding in on every side.
'Save Bingle Valley!' rose the cry;
'For Bingle let us do or die.'
'Wait!' screamed the Bigshot in a tizzy.
'Wait! Wait! You can't come in. I'm busy.
I'm the Great Bigshot Number One,
Shri Padma Bhushan Gobardhun.
I rule by popular anointment.
You have to meet me by appointment.'
'What nonsense!' cried the tragopan:
'You try to stop us if you can.'
The Bigshot sensed their resolution,
And turned from awe to elocution.
'Dear friends,' he said, 'regretfully,

The matter isn't up to me.
What the Man-Council has decreed
Is not for me to supersede.
It's true I, so to speak, presided.
But all – and none – of us decided.
That is the doctrine, don't you see,
Of joint responsibility.
But if next year in early fall
You fill, in seven copies, all
The forms that deal with such a case
And bring them over to my place
Together with the filing fees
And three translations in Chinese,
The Council, at my instigation,
May give them due consideration.
Meanwhile, my friends, since you are here
A little early in the year
– No fault of yours, of course, but still,
It's not the best of times – I will
Invite you to a mighty feast
Where every bird and every beast
Will sup on simply super food;
And later, if you're in the mood,
Please come to hear the speech I'm due
To give this evening at the zoo.'

At this pathetic tactless bribe
A sound rose from the beastly tribe
So threatening that the Bigshot trembled
And said to all who were assembled:
'My beastly comrades, bear with me.
You are upset, as I can see.

I meant the stadium, not the zoo.'
He gestured to his Number Two
Who scrawled a memo in his diary.
'Perhaps an innocent inquiry,'
The elephant said, 'may clear the air.
Please tell us all, were you aware,
Sir Bigshot, when you spoke just now,
That even if we did somehow
Fill out your forms and pay your fees,
Your cure would postdate our disease?
Before next fall our valley would
Have disappeared for ill or good.
The remedy that you suggest,
It might be thought, is not the best.'

A crafty look appeared upon
The Bigshot's face, and then was gone.
'Of course, my friends, it slipped my mind.
But then, these days, I often find
I have so many files to read,
So many seminars to lead,
So many meetings to attend,
So many talks, that in the end
A minor fact or two slips by.
But, elephant, both you and I
Appear to understand the world.'
And here the Bigshot's fingers curled
Around a little golden ring.
'This vast unwieldy gathering,
Dear Elephant, is not the place
Where we can reason, face to face,
About what can or should be done.

We should discuss this one on one.
To be quite frank, your deputation
Has not filled me with fond elation.
Tell them to leave; I'll close the door,
And we'll continue as before.'

Although the other beasts agreed,
The elephant declared: 'I'll need
My secretary and mahout
To help me sort this matter out.
Like all the rest, he's left the room,
But he can come back, I presume.
There's two of you and one of me –
So I expect that you'll agree.'
The Bigshot nodded: 'Call the man.'
Quick as a quack the tragopan
Opened the door and strutted in
To greet his buddy with a grin.
The Bigshot and his Number Two
Scowled as they murmured, 'How d'you do?'

Tea came; the Bigshot looked benign.
'Milk?' 'Thanks.' 'And sugar?' 'One is fine.'
'It's not too strong?' 'I like mine weak.'
At last the moment came to speak.
'You see, good beasts,' the Bigshot said,
'We need your water – or we're dead.
It's for the people that I act.
The town must drink, and that's a fact.
Believe me, all your agitation
Will only lead to worse frustration.
Go back, dear beasts, to Bingle now.

We'll relocate you all somehow
In quarters of a certain size.'
He yawned, and rolled his little eyes.

Immediately, the tragopan
Pulled out his papers, and began,
With fact and query and suggestion,
To give the Bigshot indigestion.
'You say the town is short of water,
Yet at the wedding of your daughter
The whole municipal supply
Was poured upon your lawns. Well, why?
And why is it that Minister's Hill
And Babu's Barrow drink their fill
Through every season, dry or wet,
When all the common people get
Is water on alternate days?
At least, that's what my data says,
And every figure has been checked.
So, Bigshot, wouldn't you expect
A radical redistribution
Would help provide a just solution?'

The Bigshot's placid face grew red.
He turned to Number Two and said
In a low voice: 'This agitator
Is dangerous. Deal with him later.'
Then, turning to the elephant,
He murmured sweetly, 'I'll be blunt.
Your friend's suggestion is quite charming,
But his naïveté's alarming.
Redistribute it night and day,

Redistribute it all away,
Ration each drop, and you'll still find
Demand will leave supply behind.'

The elephant first sipped his tea,
Then ate a biscuit leisuredly,
Then shook his head from side to side,
And, having cleared his trunk, replied:
'Well, even as regards supply,
I do not see the reason why
You do not use what lies to hand
Before you try to dam our land.
Even my short walk through this town
Shows me how everything's run down
During your long administration.
Your pipes cry out for renovation.
Your storage tanks corrode and leak;
The valves are loose, the washers weak.
I've seen the water gushing out
From every reservoir and spout.
Repair them: it will cost far less
Than driving us to homelessness
By blasting tunnels through our hills
And bloating your construction bills.
But that's just one of many things:
Plant trees; revive your wells and springs.
Guide from your roofs the monsoon rain
Into great tanks to use again.
Reduce your runoff and your waste
Rather than with unholy haste
Destroying beauty which, once gone,
The world will never look upon.'

The elephant, now overcome
With deep emotion, brushed a crumb
Of chocolate biscuit off his brow.

'Dear chap,' the Bigshot said, 'Somehow
I think you fail to comprehend
What really matters in the end.
The operative word is Votes,
And next to that comes Rupee-notes.
Your plans do not appeal to me
Because, dear chap, I fail to see
How they will help me gather either.'
He giggled, then continued: 'Neither
The charming cheques that generous firms
With whom the Council comes to terms
– Who wish to dam or log or clear
Or build – will come to me, I fear,
Nor votes from those who think my schemes
Will satisfy their thirsty dreams.
It's not just water that must funnel
Out of the hills through Bingle Tunnel.
Do animals have funds or votes –
Or anything but vocal throats?
Will you help me get re-elected?
You're speechless? Just as I suspected.
I've tried to talk things out with you.
Now I will tell you what to do:
Lift up your stupid trunk and sign
This waiver on the dotted line.
Give up all rights in Bingle Vale
For fur or feather, tusk or tail.
Sadly, since you're now in the know,

I can't afford to let you go.
Your friend will never leave this room.
The tragopan has found his tomb.
As for yourself, my Number Two
Will soon escort you to the zoo.
From this the other beasts will learn
Your lands are ours to slash and burn
And anyone defying man
Will be a second tragopan.'
He giggled with delight, and padded
His cheeks with air, and gently added:
'But if you go cahoots with me
I'll spare your friend and set you free.'
He stroked his ring. 'And I'll make sure
You'll be – let's say – provided for.'
Before you could say 'Pheasant stew'
The servile hands of Number Two
Grasped the bird's collar in a vice.
The elephant went cold as ice
To see his friend cry out in terror.
He would have signed the form in error
Had not the tragopan cried out:
'Don't sign. Gock, gock.' And at his shout
The Bigshot's son came running in
And struck the henchman on the chin.

While the foiled killer squealed and glared,
For a long time the Smallfry stared
With indignation at his father.
'Papa—' he said, 'I would much rather
Give up my place as Number Three
Than countenance such treachery.

Why can't we let the valley live?
Those who succeed us won't forgive
The Rape of Bingle. I recall,'
The Smallfry sighed, 'when I was small
You used to take me walking there
With Mama in the open air.
For me, a dusty city boy,
It was a dream of peace and joy.
Along safe paths we'd walk; a deer
Might unexpectedly appear
Among the bamboos and the moss
And raise its velvet ears and toss
Its startled head and bound away.
Once I saw leopard cubs at play
And heard the mother's warning cough
Before you quickly marched me off.
Until this day there's not a single
House or hut or field in Bingle.
How many worlds like this remain
To free our hearts from noise and pain?
And is this lovely fragile vision
To be destroyed by your decision?
And do you now propose to make
A tunnel, dam, and pleasure lake
With caravans and motorboats
And tourists at each other's throats,
Loudspeakers, shops, high-tension wires,
And ferris wheels and forest fires?
As the roads come, the trees will go.
Do villagers round Bingle know
What's going to happen to their lands?
Are they too eating from your hands?

I had gone snorkelling on the day
The Council met and signed away
The Bingle Bills. I know you signed –
But why can you not change your mind?
You talk of sacrifice and glory.
Your actions tell a different story.
Do you expect me to respect you –
Or decent folk not to detect you?
Where you have crept, must mankind crawl,
Feared, hated, and despised by all?
Don't sign, dear Elephant, don't sign.
Don't toe my wretched father's line.
Dear Tragopan, do not despair.
Don't yield the struggle in mid-air.
I'll help your cause. And as for you—'
(He turned towards the Number Two)
'This time your chin, next time your head—,'
Rubbing his fists, the Smallfry said.

The Number Two lay on the ground.
A snivelling, grovelling, snarling sound
Oozed from his throat. The Bigshot stood
As rigid as a block of wood.
He tried to speak; no words came out.
Then with an eerie strangled shout
He uttered: 'You malignant pup!
Is this the way I've brought you up?
Where did you learn your blubbery blabbering?
Your jelly-livered jungle-jabbering?
Your education's made you weak –
A no-good, nattering nature-freak
Who's snorkelled half his life away.

Who asked you to go off that day?
You've been brought up in privilege
With Coca-Cola in your fridge
And litchis in and out of season.
How dare you now descend to treason?
One day all this would have been yours –
These antlers and these heads of boars,
This office and these silver plates,
These luminous glass paperweights,
My voting bank, my Number Game,
My files, my fortune, and my fame.
I had a dream my only son
Would follow me as Number One.
I had been grooming you to be
A Bigger Bigshot after me.
You might have been a higher hero
And risen to be Number Zero –
But now, get out! You're in disgrace,'
He said, and struck the Smallfry's face.

The Smallfry, bleeding from the nose,
Fell, and the Number Two arose,
And slobbering over the Bigshot's hand
Called him the saviour of the land.
At this, the elephant got mad
And, putting down the pen he had
Clasped in his trunk to sign, instead
Poured the whole teapot on their head.
The water in a boiling arc
Splashed down upon its double-mark.
The Bigshot and his henchman howled.
The tragopan gock-gocked and scowled:

'You wanted water; here's your share.'
Then guards came in from everywhere –
And animals came in as well –
All was confusion and pell-mell
While news-reporters clicked and whirred
At limb of man and wing of bird.
The elephant stayed very still.
The tragopan rushed round – until,
Provoked by a pernicious peck,
The Bigshot wrung its little neck.

The tragopan collapsed and cried
'Gock, gock!' and rolled his eyes and died.
He died before he comprehended
His transient span on earth had ended –
Nor could he raise a plaintive cry
To the Great Partridge in the sky
Whose head is wrapped in golden gauze
To take his spirit in His claws.

What happened happened very fast.
The mêlée was put down at last.
The Smallfry cried out when he found
The pheasant stretched out on the ground.
The Bigshot too began repenting
When he saw everyone lamenting
The martyr's selfless sacrifice.
He had the body laid on ice,
Draped in the state flag, and arrayed
With chevron, scutcheon, and cockade –
And all the townsfolk came to scan
The features of the tragopan.

Four buglers played 'Abide with Me';
Four matrons wept on a settee;
Four brigadiers with visage grim
Threw cornflakes and puffed rice on him;
Four schoolgirls robbed the tragopan
Of feathers for a talisman;
And everyone stood round and kept
Long vigil while the hero slept.

A long, alas, a final sleep!
O, Elephant, long may you weep.
O, Elephant, long may you mourn.
This is a night that knows no dawn.
Ah! every Bingle eye is blurred
With sorrow for its hero-bird
And every Bingle heart in grief
Turns to its fellow for relief.
Alas for Bingle! Who will lead
The struggle in its hour of need?
Is it the grief-bowed elephant
Who now must bear the beastly brunt?
Or will the gallant martyr-bird
In death, if not in life, be heard?
Dare the egregious Bigshot mock
The cry, 'Save Bingle! Gock, gock, gock!'
And can a ghostly Tragopan
Help to attain a Bingle Ban?

For it undoubtedly was true
That suddenly the whole state knew
Of Bingle Valley and the trek
That ended in the fatal peck,

And panegyrics to the pheasant
In prose and verse were omnipresent.
Suggestions for a cenotaph
Appeared in *Bingle Telegraph*;
And several human papers too
Discussed the matter through and through.
The water problem in the state
Became a topic for debate.
The Bigshot, struggling with the flood,
Was splashed with editorial mud.
Then intellectuals began
To analyse the tragopan.
Was he a hothead or a martyr?
A compromiser or a tartar?
A balanced and strategic planner
Or an unthinking project-banner?
It seemed that nobody could tell.
And maybe that was just as well –
For mystery matched with eccentricity
Provides the grist for great publicity,
And myths of flexible dimension
Are apt to call forth less dissension.

This is a tale without a moral.
I hope the reader will not quarrel
About this minor missing link.
But if he likes them, he can think
Of five or seven that will do
As quasi-morals; here are two:
    The first is that you never know
Just when your luck may break, and so
You may as well work for your cause

Even without overt applause;
You might, in time, achieve your ends.
  The second is that you'll find friends
In the most unexpected places,
Hidden among unfriendly faces –
For Smallfry swim in every pond,
Even the Doldrums of Despond.

And so I'll end the story here.
What is to come is still unclear.
Whether the fates will smile or frown,
And Bingle Vale survive or drown,
I do not know and cannot say;
Indeed, perhaps, I never may.
I hope, of course, the beasts we've met
Will save their hidden valley, yet
The resolution of their plight
Is for the world, not me, to write.

Arion and
the Dolphin

—◆—

1994

A Libretto

For the Wild Dolphin, Fungie

Irish dolphin, swift and single,
Dwelling off the coast of Dingle,
Choosing now and then to mingle
    With the flipperless and glum,
Bringing wonder and elation
To our jaded human nation,
I present you this creation
    Of my fingers and my thumb.

Note on the first performance

Arion and the Dolphin was commissioned by English National Opera. The librettist was Vikram Seth and the composer Alec Roth.

The opera was first performed 14–19 June 1994 at the Drill Shed, HMS Drake, Plymouth, in a co-production between English National Opera; the Theatre Royal, Plymouth; Bournemouth Orchestras; and the Royal Navy. The performers included Richard Chew, *Arion*; Claire Bradshaw, *Dolphin*; Anthony Mee, *Periander*; and Jozic Koc, *Captain*. The chorus and children's chorus were recruited from the Plymouth area. The orchestra was the Bournemouth Sinfonietta; the conductor, Nicholas Kok; the producer, Rebecca Meitlis; the choreographer, Denni Sayers; and the designer, Henk Schut.

Further details of the opera, including a full technical specification, may be found in the composer's online catalogue at: www.alecroth.com

Cast of characters

Solo roles

Periander, Tyrant of Corinth	tenor
Arion, his young court musician	lyric baritone
Captain of the ship	bass-baritone
Dolphin	mezzo-soprano
1st Mutineer	baritone
2nd Mutineer	tenor
Messenger	boy or girl soprano
Sicilian sextet	soprano/mezzo/alto/ tenor/ baritone/bass
Master of Ceremonies	spoken role

Chorus

(Male Chorus, Female Chorus, Children's Chorus, Dancers):
Guards, Sailors, Sicilians, Dolphins, Fisherfolk, People of Corinth

The 9 scenes run into each other in a continuous action.
The arias and choral songs are indented in the text.

Scene 1

Corinth at night. A courtyard under the stars. Arion is asleep. His dreams are troubled and he wakes with a start.

PERIANDER *(shouting from offstage)*
Arion! Arion!

Arion gets up hurriedly, holding his lyre. Periander marches in with his guards.

PERIANDER
Arion! What's all this I hear about going to Sicily for some music festival?

ARION
Well—

PERIANDER
I won't have it.

ARION
But—

PERIANDER
Do you think I don't know what is going on behind my back?

ARION
I only thought—

PERIANDER
Don't interrupt! And don't deny it either.

ARION
But I didn't—

PERIANDER
You cannot go . . . and that is that.

Arion begins to strum the lyre.

PERIANDER
Arion,
Think of my court, of Corinth, and of me.

ARION
I do, my lord.
Yours is the only home that I have known
Since I was a boy, parentless and alone.
I do not gladly leave it empty of song.

PERIANDER
Good.

ARION
Sir, let me go to Sicily.
I'll be back before long.
I'll sing more freely when I'm free.

PERIANDER

What? Do you talk of tyranny?
　　Go! go!
I do not know why I should love you so.
I have two sons, one is a dolt, his brother
Hates me and flees me, claiming I killed his mother.
The rabble hate me, blood clings to my hands –
The blood of this, the blood of many lands.
My silent mentor used his stick to lop
The tallest stalks of corn from every crop;
So all of any weight or excellence
In Corinth have been killed or driven hence.
Do you not fear me, Periander, Tyrant of Corinth?

ARION

It is the dearest of my aims,
My lord, to quell such wild and unjust claims.
In Sicily, my lord, all men will know
Your greatness, for my songs will tell them so.
Let me take part, and let me spread your fame,
Lord Periander, when I sing your name.

PERIANDER

When you have gone long months across the sea,
And all the lyric fire that filled this hall
Has turned to air and ember, what of your
Fiery lyre, Arion of Lesbos, will my ears remember?
What of your voice will chafe my memory?

Go soon. Sing soon.
What is that harsh discord?
Your lyre is out of tune.

ARION

It is in tune, my lord.

PERIANDER

What?! Do you contradict me?
And if you go to Sicily,
Will your lyre be out of tune?
And if you sing my name,
Will your lyre be out of tune?
Go, go. But if you sing my name,
Be sure to win! Do you hear me?
If not . . . you'll die.

Periander dismisses Arion with an abrupt gesture and marches off
with his guards.

ARION *(looking up at the night sky)*
    Bright stars, bring comfort
    To those who dream.
    Bright stars, guide me to fame
    By land, by sea –
    So that my form and name
    May rest among you in the sky –
    Bright, constant stars,
    That I, like you,
    May never fade or die.
    And you, dark, restless sea
    Be gentle on my way
    From Greece to Sicily.

Scene 2

At Arion's invocation, the sea begins to swell, the Captain and the sailors appear, and the scene changes to shipboard.

CAPTAIN
>   Dark, restless sea,
>   Blue, green, grey, black –
>   Be gentle on our track
>   And grace my crew and me.
>>   Poseidon, bless my ship
>>   That we may rise and dip,
>>   Sailing with rapid clip
>   From Greece to Sicily.

SAILORS
>   Dark, restless sea,
>   Black, grey, blue, green –
>   Our decks are scrubbed and clean –
>   Our ropes run strong and free.
>>   Fair winds, fill out our sails –
>>   Bring us no gusts or gales –
>>   Keep us from sharks and whales
>   From Greece to Sicily.

Arion!
Let's hear you sing!
Sing for your supper!

ARION *and the* SAILORS

Dark, restless sea,
Blue, green, black, grey –
Be gentle on my way
From Greece to Sicily.
    May no storm shake the sky,
    Or seagulls wheel and cry,
    But dolphins dip and fly
Beside my ship and me.

CAPTAIN

Well, with a voice like that, I'm not surprised Periander did not want to let you go. How did your tune catch up with ours?

ARION

I care about time and timing, Captain: it's the heart of my music.

CAPTAIN

That's true for us as well. You'd make a good sailor. Perhaps I should set you to work.

ARION

I'd make a terrible sailor – ninety-nine oars pulling one way, and one in the other.

CAPTAIN (*drawing Arion aside, out of the hearing of the sailors*)
Those hands would grow callused too quickly anyway. You're best doing what you do, Arion. In your profession, if the risks are greater, so are the rewards.

ARION
What rewards?

CAPTAIN
Why? Aren't you rich? Hasn't your singing brought you
wealth?

ARION
In my own right, this lyre is all I have. And what risks?

CAPTAIN
Well, Periander has threatened you with death if you lose in
the Sicilian festival.

ARION
Periander—

CAPTAIN
He is an unhappy man.

ARION
Well, he certainly doesn't have much of a family life.

CAPTAIN
He is alone, and at a fearful height.

ARION
But many people are alone.
And you, Captain – do you have a family life? Or is your crew
your family?

CAPTAIN

My crew lead a hard life.
They care for silver, bronze, and when they get it, gold.
I care for them, perhaps they care for me.
I work them hard, they never mutiny.
I think I know their ways.
For more than half my nights and days
They are my family.

ARION

But what of land, of Corinth, towards which you often gaze?

CAPTAIN

You read my heart, Arion, through my eyes.

   I have a house on shore
   Not far from Corinth harbour, made of stone:
   A laurel bush, some flowers, olive trees;
   And there, when this good ship is on the seas,
   My wife and my three daughters live alone
   For many months, for years,
   In peacetime and in war.
   When I return, my wife is at the door.
   I wipe away her tears.
   I soothe her fears
   With gifts and practicalities.
   My daughters laugh to see me.
   I chase them and they flee me.
   The weeks fly by; then trade or battle draw
   Me once more down to shore
   To take sad leave of my sad wife and daughters
   And change untrembling land for trembling waters.

ARION
Have you no son to help you on the sea?

CAPTAIN *(giving Arion a conch-shell)*
Arion, keep this shell.
It is a gift from me,
So guard it well.
It will make music in your ear
Whenever you choose to hear
The ocean's surge, its rustling harmony.
Arion, keep this shell.
Be well, be well.
The days have passed in talk, and now I see
The distant citadel,
The crags of Sicily.

Scene 3

*As the ship approaches Sicily, or Sicily the ship, a group of Sicilians
– villagers and petty tradesmen – appears on shore, singing an
idiotic song.*

SICILIANS
  Si-ci-ly, Si-ci-ly,
  Such a pretty, gritty, witty co-un-tree.
  Si-ci-ly, Si-ci-ly,
  Won't you buy a little souvenir from me?

CAPTAIN
What is the meaning of this silly ditty?
Where's the official welcoming committee?

SICILIAN
Your boat arrived early. None of the officials is awake yet.

SICILIAN
Hangovers.

SICILIAN
Pre-festival festivities.

SICILIAN
So who've you got on board that's so important anyway?

CAPTAIN
The winner of your festival, for one.

SICILIAN
What do you mean? Who do you mean?

CAPTAIN
Arion – he'll teach you Sicilians how to sing.

SICILIAN
Arion!

SICILIAN
We've got good musicians too, you know. What do you think this is, a backwater?

CAPTAIN
No, no, far from it.

SICILIAN
Welcome, Arion of Corinth.

SICILIAN
Of Lesbos – he's from Lesbos.

SICILIAN
Nonsense. He's from Corinth – his patron is Coriander.

SICILIAN
Periander.

SICILIAN
The one who killed his wife?

SICILIAN
Or so they say.

CAPTAIN
He's here to represent Periander.

SICILIAN
Well, he'd better be good, then – or else he'll be for the chop.

SICILIAN
He's from Lesbos. Ask him. Go on, ask him.

SICILIAN
Ask him yourself.

SICILIAN
I don't need to. Welcome, Arion of Lesbos.

ARION (*singing beautifully*)
Thank you, citizens of Sicily.

The Sicilians are enchanted, and applaud him.

CAPTAIN
Arion, I can see you'll be well taken care of, after all. I must
go now. I'll return from Italy in a few days to take you home.
Till then—

ARION

But the competition – the festival – will you not be there? Will
you not hear me sing?

CAPTAIN

Some other time, my friend, some other time.
I'll hear you sing when I have leisure from my trade.
But now it's business before pleasure, I'm afraid.

ARION

Farewell.

Picks up his lyre, forgets the conch-shell.

CAPTAIN

Your shell. Don't forget your shell.

ARION

It is a gift from you,
I'll guard it well.

SICILIAN

He does have a nice voice.

SICILIAN

Let's take him off to have a good time in the town.

SICILIAN

Wine, women and song – off to the tavern with him.

SICILIAN

A proper booze-up!

ARION
Wonderful! A wonderful idea!

SICILIAN
But what about practising for the festival?

SICILIAN
It's in two days – just two days.

ARION
Oh – there'll be plenty of time to practise –
But now it's pleasure before business, I'm afraid.

Laughing, the Sicilians take Arion off to have a good time.

Scene 4

The festival. The Sicilians are having a good time, eating, drinking . . . and dancing.

DANCE INTERLUDE

MASTER OF CEREMONIES
And now, my lords, ladies and gentlemen, for such a distinguished and discriminating audience as yourselves, we present the singer of superb salutations to the royal ruler of cultured Corinth, the tender but tenacious Tyrant—

Laughter and jeers from the audience.

MASTER OF CEREMONIES
We present . . . the poet, composer, master of the lyre, discoverer of the tragic mode, lyricist of lugubrious lushness, fleetly flying on fluent feet, whose delightful daring with Dionysian dithyrambs has captured and enraptured the courts and colonies of Greece – here, to sing a song of praise to his munificent and magnificent patron, Periander – please welcome Arion of Lesbos!

Applause. Arion does not appear. General consternation.

SICILIAN
Where is he?

A Sicilian points out Arion, who has been sleeping off his revelry behind an olive tree. Arion wakes up with a start, struggles to his feet, and staggers towards the rostrum.

SICILIAN
He got drunk – he's been sleeping it off –

SICILIAN
That sleep will cost him his head.

SICILIAN
And he didn't practise at all!

SICILIAN
Too much wine and women, not enough song.

MASTER OF CEREMONIES
And now, ladies and gentlemen, Arion of Lesbos!

Arion strums his lyre (which is very out of tune) and attempts to sing, but all that comes out of his mouth is:

ARION *(to the tune of the silly Si-ci-ly song)*
Pe-ri-ander, Pe-ri-ander, such a pretty, gritty, witty . . .

Panicking at the thought of the future wrath of Periander, he fumbles for another tune:

ARION
Pe-ri-an-der . . . ooh!

His voice breaks, and he clutches his head in despair. The crowd grows restless.

MASTER OF CEREMONIES
Arion, according to the rules, two false starts is all you get.
Sing one last time, and then no more.

ARION
Oh gods! My art deserts me. Untrouble my heart – fill with
your inspiration my empty shell . . . the shell!

*Arion takes the shell the Captain gave him and puts it to his ear.
The crowd falls silent. Softly, he begins to sing. The words he sings
are fragmentary phrases, cries like 'Aaaaah', and nonsensical
syllables. The song builds in intensity, rising to an exciting climax.
The audience are inspired to join in, singing, dancing and stomping
around. Golden gifts are showered on Arion – a golden lyre, a golden
robe. An adoring girl touches him and gives him her golden chain.*

*Arion is delighted and beams at the pile of gold glittering in the
centre of the stage.*

SICILIANS
More! More! Another song!

MASTER OF CEREMONIES
Sing, Arion, sing once more! Stay with us in Sicily. Or at least
sing us one last song before you go.

ARION *(picking up his lyre, and singing in a quieter strain)*
    Dark restless sea,
    Black, green, grey, blue,
    Over whose waves I flew   ↗*

---

* a stanza break at the end of a page is marked by ~
  no stanza break at the end of a page is marked by ↗

To sing in Sicily,
    Accept my weight once more
    As gently as before.
    Bear me to Corinth shore
Alive, and safe and free.

Scene 5

The ship at sea. It is night. The stars shine above. The gold glitters below. Arion is on the afterdeck. He looks up at the stars, smiles, stretches and yawns, then falls asleep. The sailors emerge from the shadows and gather round Arion's treasure.

SAILORS *(in awe)*
Look at that – look at the gold –

IST MUTINEER
And all that for a song.

SAILOR
A single song.

IST MUTINEER
A single song
Gave him more than we earn our whole lives long.

CAPTAIN *(who has been watching, unseen)*
Enough of this—

IST MUTINEER
Tell me the reason why
We who bore him across the sea
Should not share in his fortune equally?

SAILORS
That's right – why not? –

2ND MUTINEER *(stepping forward)*
That's fair by me.
Without our help where would Arion be?
Without hard hands could soft hands strum the lyre?

SAILORS
Look at the gold dust glittering like fire.

2ND MUTINEER
Give us that gold –

1ST MUTINEER
– or we will mutiny.

CAPTAIN
You rogues – this gold has bent your brains.
He won it by his pains.

1ST MUTINEER
What pains? A single song?

SAILORS
A single song
Gave him more than we earn our whole lives long
With sinew and with sweat.

2ND MUTINEER
Captain – do not forget
You have a house, and we have huts and shacks.

This gold will help to paper up the cracks
Through which the wind knifes through
In hard midwinter, piercing us, not you.

SAILORS
But join with us, and you can share this fortune too.

CAPTAIN
I will not touch that gold for anything.

2ND MUTINEER
Here, Captain, here's a ring.

CAPTAIN
Not on your life—

2ND MUTINEER
If you don't like it, give it to your wife.

CAPTAIN (*flinging it away*)
Never!

1ST MUTINEER (*snatching a sword from the pile, and holding it to the Captain's throat*)
Captain, be reasonable. Do not die.
I'm sure your wife would wish you to comply.

MUTINEERS
Her golden-dusted dreams are all about you.
What would she do without you?
Let's take the gold
And stack it in the hold.

The Captain stays inside his room on board;
And when the gold is stored,
We'll deal with other things—

SAILOR
Listen – Arion sings –

Arion is heard singing in his sleep.

2ND MUTINEER
What of Arion?

IST MUTINEER
—Death.

CAPTAIN
No!

IST MUTINEER
Captain, save your breath.
Think of your family.

CAPTAIN
I cannot bear the pain
That they should wait for me and not see me again.

IST MUTINEER *(shouting to the sailors)*
Take the gold!

*Led by the mutineers, the sailors break open Arion's treasure and
start to divide it among themselves. They repeat the earlier words of
the mutineers to justify their actions.*

SAILORS
Gold . . . the glittering gold . . .

CAPTAIN
What shall I do?
What can I do?

 It's not the gods
  But our own hearts
   We need to fear.
  The evil starts
 Against all odds
  Not there but here.

Arion appears. A sudden silence.

ARION
Captain, you are ill. What's happening? You look pale.

CAPTAIN
Arion, you must die.

Arion laughs, then realizes that the Captain is serious.

ARION
Captain—

CAPTAIN
We much regret, Arion, that you must die.

ARION
What is my crime? Tell me the reason why.

CAPTAIN
You are too rich. Your prizes swell the hold.

ARION
Spare me my life. I'll give you all my gold.

CAPTAIN
When we reach Corinth gulf, the tides will shift;
You will retract your promise and your gift.
A forced gift is no gift—

ARION
– Here, take this shell.
Your gift once saved my life; it served me well.
May it remind you of our earlier trust
Before that love was buried by gold dust.

CAPTAIN
It's not my will. I have to mind my crew.

ARION
And seal my murder?

CAPTAIN
– What else can I do?

ARION
Let me sing one last song before I die.

Arion goes up onto the afterdeck; the sailors all gather round to hear him.

ARION

> I do not wish to die. I fear to die,
> To sink in the reflection of the sky,
> At such a fearful depth to be alone,
> To merge with shell and coral, slime and stone,
> By tentacles caressed, by green fronds curled,
> To drown myself in such a silent world.
>
> My voice was loved, myself I cannot tell.
> A hollow voice cried out from every shell.
> Those who gave friendship I least understand
> Who, when I needed love, let slip their hand.
> But so it was, and I am glad I leave
> No friends to mourn, no family to grieve.
>
> O world so beautiful, grey olive trees,
> Green laurel bushes, tempest-troubled seas,
> I shall not see you or the clouds at night
> Or the bright stars or sunset's golden light
> Or smell the hyacinth or hear the cry
> Of eagle or of wolf before I die.

His singing has an unsettling effect on the sailors. Some are deeply moved, others not. They start arguing. The scene becomes a riot. One sailor rushes to guard Arion with an oar or a sword, others attempt to charge him, only to be held off.

SAILORS

Spare his life . . . Stop up his mouth . . . Throw him overboard
. . . No! . . . Smash his lyre . . . Jump – and die. *(ad lib.)*

At the height of the clamour and chaos, Arion leaps off the ship into the waves.

Scene 6

A sea-change – a sudden silence – Arion is in the sea, sinking with his lyre – he is under the waves—

The stars disappear above, the moon disappears. The blackness is complete.

He is drowning and struggling and choking.

Dolphin sounds. Phosphorescence.

The beautiful swift trails of sea-beasts, including dolphins.

He is buoyed up by dolphins, danced and played with; and carried along (holding a fin, riding on a dolphin's back) at a wonderfully rapid rate.

Dolphin sounds: joyous.

Arion believes that this exhilarating experience is death.

ARION
> The dark forgetful river
> That bounds the dead for ever,
> Transport me to that shore,
> For I fear death no more.
>
> Death was not hard and slow
> But soft and swift. I go
> Calm to that under-land
> Now joy has seized my hand.

The dolphin sounds become clearer, and among the clicks, cries, bubbling noises and so on are heard a few broken words, at first incoherently, then with high but clear articulation.

DOLPHIN
Oh, no, no . . . no, no . . . *(clearer)* . . . musician—

ARION
Yes?

DOLPHIN
You are not . . .

ARION
I am not?

DOLPHIN
. . . are not dead.

ARION
Not what?

DOLPHIN
Dead. Not dead.

ARION
I am not dead? Why not?

DOLPHIN
Dolphin. Dolphin.

ARION
You are dolphins, yes, I see that . . .

DOLPHIN
Music. Music. We came to hear . . .

ARION
To hear me sing? On the boat?

DOLPHIN
On the boat. Then you leaped. And we saved you alive. Alive.
Alive.

ARION
Please don't repeat everything. It's hard enough to take it all
in once. You say I'm alive?

DOLPHIN (*delightedly*)
Alive. Alive. Alive.

ARION
I'm very grateful.
It's good of you.
Forgive me. I'm in shock.

DOLPHIN
Alive . . . you are alive . . .

ARION
And the ship?

DOLPHIN
Sailed on, sailed on. We took you away. They did not see.
They think you are dead. Your name, musician?

ARION
Arion.

DOLPHIN
Arion?

The dolphins sing the name's long vowels. They appear to like it.

ARION
You dolphins seem to be susceptible to music.

DOLPHIN
Very susceptible. Came to the ship. Lovely music.
Saved a musician. Arion. Excellent dolphins.

ARION
But aren't there evil dolphins too?

DOLPHIN
Evil?

ARION
Like the ones who tried to kidnap Dionysus the god of wine
and sell him into slavery?

DOLPHIN
Oh no, no, no – they were pirates, they were turned into
dolphins. Bad as men, as dolphins good.
   Their descendants are good dolphins, and proud of their
descent.

ARION *(aside)*
How smug.

DOLPHIN
Listen. A song.

DOLPHINS
    He turned himself into a lion of gold
    And round his head his golden eyes he rolled.
    Ivy entwined the ship, and flutes were heard.
    The oars, turned serpents, hissed each double word:
        Sleep, sleep,
        Leap, leap,
        Deep, deep.
    The babbling pirates, leaping overboard,
    Were smoothed to dolphins at a fluted chord.

A conch is heard.

ARION
The conch!

DOLPHIN
Listen!
That's the ship
From which you leaped.
We have overtaken it
And we will be in Corinth long before
The shell sounds on that shore.

ARION
The shell, the gifted shell
That once was mine may be their supper bell.

DOLPHIN

But now it's time for supper here as well.

ARION

Raw fish!

DOLPHIN

Would you like some prawns? We could manage that. And
sea-spinach. But not eels, I'm afraid. My aunt died of a surfeit
of lampreys, and we've never had them on the table since.
   Perhaps you'd like –

        A turbot,
        A burbot,
      A plate of plaice.
      A dab of dace.
   A ling, a lobster, and a loach.
   A roosterfish, a ray, a roach.
      A chub, a char,
      A grunt, a gar,
   Three pilchards and a pound of parr.

*There is a feeding dance as the dolphins catch and pass and share
and eat fish – more like play than supper.*

DOLPHINS

   Fish give us a sufficiency
      Beneath the sea
      As you can see.
   We eat with great efficiency
      Beneath the sea
      As you can see.   ~

Like other good cetaceans
We scatter good vibrations.
We harry herring happily
And swallow salmon snappily.

Our skins are smooth and rubbery,
Our bulky bodies blubbery.
We harry herring happily
And swallow salmon snappily.

With unspecific gravity
And sinusoidal suavity
We harry herring happily
And swallow salmon snappily.

With aquabatic levity
And aerobatic brevity
We harry herring happily
And swallow salmon snappily.

ARION
And doesn't anyone wish to eat you?

DOLPHIN
Certain sharks try to get at young dolphins. And some people
– in the Black Sea, mainly. They salt us and eat us later. And
fishermen don't like us on the whole. We eat their catch.
And they kill us for that. Or we swim with the shoals and get
caught in their nets.

ARION
That makes me doubly grateful that you saved me.

DOLPHIN
You're not the first man led by us to shore.
Why, there were plenty more.

*[ARION
Tell me about another.

DOLPHIN
   Icadius, Iapyx' Cretan brother,
   Shipwrecked, was guided by
   A dolphin to Delphi;
   And from that dolphin Delphi got its name:
   Apollo and the dolphin were the same.

   Or when Enalus saw his lover slung
   Into the sea to calm the waves he flung
   Himself into the waves that they might be
   United constantly.
   A dolphin saved him, and its mate his mate
   From their too-fluid fate.]

You need to learn about our life and lore.
As your after-dinner task
Forget the world you've left and bask
In the warm rhythms of our dolphin masque.

DOLPHINS *(The young dolphins perform a joyful dance for Arion.)*
   Round and round, round and round,
   Leaping up and plunging down,
   Fins and flippers flying free,   ⤔

---

*   This section of the original libretto has not been incorporated into the
    score.

We dolphins dart around the sea.
Round and round, round and round.

Clicking, we're clicking.
We're clicking as we hunt our prey.
We're clicking.
We're clicking as we find our way.
With great sophistication
And submarine location,
With our ultrasonic phonics we go snouting through the
    spray.

Clicking dance

Round and round . . . *&c.*

Whistling, we're whistling.
We're whistling to attract a mate.
We're whistling
We're whistling to communicate
The amatory yearning
That sets our insides churning
Round and round. Could this be love or was it something
    that I ate?

Whistling dance

Round and round . . . *&c.*

ARION
What joyful lives you dolphins lead
Both when you mate and when you feed.
Compare it to my own condition –
A poor, unhappy, flipperless musician.

DOLPHIN
Oh, no –
You interest us, we interest you.
And we can tell who's who.
And we like music too.
We have our ancient musical traditions.
That's why we are susceptible to musicians.
Perhaps we should sing together after supper.
You take the lower part, I'll take the upper.

*They sing a duet, the dolphin singing open vowels, Arion doing the
same as well as playing the lyre. Soon the voices of dolphin and
human are wonderfully intertwined.*

DOLPHIN
   I love Arion, and would like to be
   Bound to his voice and him eternally.

*The other dolphins leave one by one; Arion and the dolphin swim on
towards Corinth.*

ARION
   The days pass one by one.
   I feel my life has only just begun –
   And, for the first time, I am having fun!

ARION *and* DOLPHIN
   In air and water both, our voices part and blend,
   And I/you, who never sought a friend
   Have found one in the end.

Scene 7

Fisherfolk gather on the shore.

FISHERMAN
Look – look – in the gulf—

FISHERMAN
A dolphin and a young man with a lyre—

FISHERMAN
They'll get caught in our nets—

FISHERMAN
Save him—

FISHERMAN
No, no – they've swum under them—

FISHERMAN
It's Arion.

FISHERMAN
Arion!

FISHERMAN
Let's inform the court.

FISHERMAN
Let Periander know.

They go off to inform Periander.

ARION
　　Now, Dolphin, you must go,
　　My part is here above, and yours below –
　　I where the winds, you where the waters flow.
　　It must be so.

　　How sad I am that I must part
　　From the dolphin of my heart!

DOLPHIN
　　With you I will remain –
　　For if we part we'll never meet again
　　And I would die of loneliness and pain.
　　This I maintain.

Periander and his guards arrive. During this scene, the fisherfolk, quite delighted with the dolphin, prod it with their oars out of interest, and keep it apart. The dolphin is a little bewildered and frightened. Meanwhile, Periander draws Arion out of the water.

PERIANDER
Arion! Arion!

ARION
My lord, my friend the dolphin—

PERIANDER
What is this?
Arion, you're alive.
Did you win?

ARION
My lord . . .

PERIANDER
Get that dolphin away –
When did you return?
How did you fare in Sicily? What did you sing?
Where are your prizes?

ARION
My lord, the dolphin saved my life.

PERIANDER
What do you mean?
Don't speak in riddles.
Where's the ship? The Captain?

ARION
They saw my gold and forced me overboard.
The dolphin saved me, fed me, brought me here.
And now insists on staying on, my lord,
Unawed by fate, by foreignness, by fear.

PERIANDER
I see. Where are the Captain and the crew?
Speak, speak at once! How can I credit you?
I never heard of anything more strange

Than your strange history of chance and change.
Prove, prove your clever story if you can.
The Captain is a highly trusted man.

ARION

I trusted him, my lord – and half my grief
Is for my lost belief.
It is the bitter truth that I have told.
I won in Sicily. They stole my gold.

PERIANDER

Where is the ship? Where is the crew?
Where is my proof?

ARION

My lord, what shall I do?

PERIANDER

You say the dolphin wishes to remain.
How would you know? Explain at once. Explain!

ARION

We spoke, my lord—

PERIANDER

Spoke? Spoke? Spoke to that wretched fish?
Then let it speak again. It is my wish
The dolphin speak. Command it so to do
That I may hear this dolphin language too.
If the beast speaks, throw it a mackerel.
I, Periander, wait. Speak now! Speak well!
Speak! Speak!

The dolphin does not speak. Periander becomes more and more suspicious. Suddenly he turns to the guards and indicates Arion.

Arrest him. Take him away!

FISHERFOLK
But, my lord, what about the dolphin?

PERIANDER
Oh – do what you like with the dolphin—

The guards drag Arion off. The fisherfolk turn the dolphin into a sort of circus act. They force it through hoops, make it leap for dead fish, collect money for it.

FISHERFOLK
   Roll up, roll up, roll up, and see the dolphin play.
   Free for the under-fives. Half-price on Saturday.

Scene 8

Arion is asleep in his prison cell. He wakes. Through the bars he looks up at the night sky. The messenger enters.

MESSENGER
Arion of Lesbos, I am required by Periander, Tyrant of Corinth, to inform you that the dolphin is dead.

Arion starts. There is a look of horror on his face. The messenger continues:

> The dolphin wasted away
> From day to day . . .
> It glutted and it groaned.
> It squealed, it moaned.
> 'Arion . . . Arion . . .' all day long
> It seemed to say – a high, pathetic song.
> Into its misery the creature sank.
> Ringed by dead fish it stank.

Arion groans with misery.

PERIANDER *(who has been standing outside, listening)*
Ah, how I grieve
That I kept them apart. It is too late,
And I have earned his endless hate.

Periander enters the prison cell.

Arion – forgive me –
You did not feign that cry.
Forgive me that the dolphin had to die.
You are free. You are free. Open the prison gate.
The dolphin's tomb will be erected by the state.

Periander marches out. The guards remove the bars from around
Arion.

ARION *(who has taken in nothing of all this)*
    Alone am I, and sad that you are dead,
    That you are dead, not I –
    That you were kind to me and that led you to die.
    When all is done and said –
    When all is said and done,
    You were my friend, the only one.

Scene 9

The full chorus (everyone except the Captain and the sailors) enters in candle-lit procession. A tomb is built for the dolphin beneath a dark, starless sky.

CHORUS
Now the sun is setting
And the night is near,
Look down on our city,
Keep us safe from fear.

Till the hour of sunrise
Let our labours cease.
May our sleep be dreamless.
May we rest in peace –

Farmers in the mountains,
Sailors on the waves,
All who suffer sadness,
All who rest in graves.

May our sleep be dreamless.
May we rest in peace –

ARION
Day follows night, night day.
Try as I wish, I cannot keep away.

Night follows day, day night.
I watch myself mourn from a distant height.
I sing in my own voice, but in the end,
The voice is yours, my friend.
Why did you have to die?
Why? Why? Why? Why?
I ask, I ask, and there is no reply.

CHORUS

    Till the light of morning
    Let your mourning cease.
    May your sleep be dreamless.
    May you rest in peace.

*Arion sleeps, exhausted, behind the tomb. The distant sound of a
conch is heard. The Captain and sailors come up from the shore,
bearing flaming torches.*

PERIANDER

Welcome, Captain; home at last, I see.

CAPTAIN

Thanks to your lordship's prayers to the gods –
Though I have yet to see my home and wife—

PERIANDER

The gods, yes, yes; a happy voyage, I hope?

CAPTAIN

We carry merchandise from Italy –
Detailed in full, of course, at the customs house.

PERIANDER
Excellent, excellent. But where's Arion?

CAPTAIN
He won at the Sicilian festival.
All present praised him, and he gained great gifts –
But midway in our voyage came a ship
That claimed to go to Lesbos, and he too,
Longing to see his native coast once more,
Transferred his gold and sailed away from us.

PERIANDER
Why do you weep that he was fortunate?

CAPTAIN
I weep because I must.

PERIANDER
My gentle Captain –
Swear on your mother's womb that this is true.
Swear on the dolphin's tomb that this is true.
Swear that you do not lie.
Swear, that you may not die.
Swear, all of you.

CAPTAIN
What dolphin's tomb, my lord?

PERIANDER
This tomb that it has pleased the state
To raise. Swear. Swear. Why do you hesitate?

The sailors swear, placing their palms on the tomb. The Captain
cannot. Arion awakes. The sailors see him and are struck
dumb with horror. They tremble, and try to run, but are held
by the guards. The Captain turns around in amazement. Torn
between relief and shock, he moves towards Arion and says, with
unmistakable joy:

CAPTAIN
Arion –
Alive!
The gods be praised.

Arion turns away from him.

CAPTAIN
I have been thinking of you night and day.

Those nights and days
I have not slept
Upon the sea.
Your voice has crept
Through my heart's maze
To torture me.

SAILORS
It's not the gods
But our own hearts
We need to fear.
The evil starts
Against all odds
Not there but here.

PERIANDER
Take him away.

CAPTAIN
Tyrant, my ship is like your city.
I sacrificed, suppressing pity,
An innocent man. I was to blame.
You, Tyrant, would have done the same.

PERIANDER
I've heard enough.
Put him and all his ruffians to the sword.

ARION
Let them go, my lord.

PERIANDER
Arion, do not raise your voice.
They compassed death. I have no choice.

ARION
Defer their sentence for a day –
An hour, my lord – and hear me play.
Perhaps my words will draw your bitterness away.

PERIANDER
Play, then, Arion, and sing.
I, who have caused you grief, am listening.

*Arion turns to the Captain and in a gesture of reconciliation takes
the conch-shell once more and holds it to his ear. The sounds of the
sea are heard, and the cries of dolphins.*

CAPTAIN *and* SAILORS
Play, then, Arion, and sing.
We, who have caused you grief, are listening.

ARION
    I hear your voice sing out my name by night,
        By dawn, by evening light.

    I mourn for you, yet, Dolphin, to my shame,
        I never asked your name.

    Your element protected me, but mine
        For you proved far too fine.

    Dolphin, it was from your marine caress
        That I learned gentleness.

*

    May music bind the sky, the earth, the sea
        In tune, in harmony.

    Dark sea, protect all voyagers whose home
        Rests in your ring of foam.

    Warm earth, teach us to nourish, not destroy
        The souls that give us joy.

    Bright stars, engrave my dolphin and my lyre
        In the night sky with fire.

The northern constellations of Delphinus and Lyra appear in the night sky.

The
Rivered Earth

—◆—

2011

To Alec Roth and Philippe Honoré

Handwriting and calligraphy within by Vikram Seth
Pipal leaf motif reproduced by permission of Buddhapath.com

General Introduction

Some time ago, when I was 'between books', I took part in a project that resulted in several remarkable works of music – involving, from my pen, four very different libretti. Apart from the texts themselves, published here, each with its own brief introduction, I thought it might be of interest to write a more general account of this project, which was unusual in several senses: it was a collaboration between a writer, a composer and a violinist; it developed over four years, with a work produced each year; it took place with the encouragement and within the constraints of three festivals and, indeed, communities; the libretti touched upon three civilizations, Chinese, European and Indian; and much of the work – both literary and musical – was created in a house with rich literary and musical associations, a house on the River Nadder in Wiltshire.

The project was called 'Confluences', but because that name sounds a bit technical, I sought a more vivid title for this book and for the four libretti as a whole. The composer suggested 'the rivered earth', a phrase from the last of the libretti, suggestive perhaps of the beauty of our common planet. In fact, the two halves of the phrase encompass the four texts, since the first begins with the image of the moon reflected in a great river, and the last ends with the image of the blue earth spinning through time and space.

The composer Alec Roth, the violinist Philippe Honoré and I were standing in a red room with a large black piano, anticipating the arrival of the directors of the Salisbury and Chelsea festivals.

What we needed was a project for the coming year that would enthuse all three of us and would kindle the interest of the directors. But our various suggestions were all over the place – from unaccompanied choirs to the solo violin, from community choruses to chamber orchestras, from violin and piano sonatas to song-cycles, from pieces for instrumental ensembles to grand oratorios. What we were agreed upon was that crucial to the works would be Philippe's violin and Alec's composition and my words – and therefore the human voice, which has always been at the heart of Alec's music, even his instrumental music. But we could settle on none of the various alternatives.

About five minutes before our guests were due to arrive, I said, 'Let's ask for it all.'

'What do you mean?' said Philippe.

'I mean, let's suggest some sort of grand plan where each year we would undertake to create a new work and they would undertake to support its creation and performance. It's now summer 2005. So what about something for each of the four years from 2006 to 2009?'

'Four years?' said Alec. 'It's hard enough getting funding for one. Festival finances have always been in a precarious state. They stagger along from one year to the next: almost all their funding and fund-raising is on an annual basis.'

'Well, don't festivals ever commission composers or projects for more than a single year?'

'It's very rare. I can't think of an example of it, offhand.'

'So how come there's any continuity in what a festival offers from one year to another?'

'There isn't much. It's all a bit ad hoc. The moment the actual festival is over, they start thinking of what to do for the next. I suppose the overall vision of the director gives it some sort of continuity.'

'Haven't you ever had a commission for more than a single year?'

'No.'

'Well, let's ask for it. In fact, let's insist on it. And let's try to get a guarantee right from the beginning that they'll follow it through. I can't imagine anything more killing to any kind of long-term vision than the business of applying for a commission a year at a time and the uncertainty of whether it'll come through.'

'That's how it is in the real world.'

'I didn't know that. And some good ideas come out of ignorance. So let's give it a try.'

'There's nothing to be lost,' said Philippe. 'It would be fantastic to have a new piece to work on each year for the next four years.'

'They'll never agree,' said Alec.

An hour or so later we were looking at each other in amazement. Not only had Jo Metcalf Shore and Stewart Collins not blanched at the idea, they'd been intrigued. They had asked us to write up a proposal: ideas, forms, forces, venues, costs. But it was clear to them from the start that they'd have to get a third festival to join them to make it possible. Some time later they met Richard Hawley, who had recently been appointed director of the Lichfield Festival. Now that they had a troika, they set about trying to get funding. Eventually both the Arts Council and the PRS Foundation expressed their enthusiasm and guaranteed funding for three years, and the various festival boards signalled their approval – presumably assuming that funding for the fourth year would somehow work out.

But all this took quite some time – many months, in fact. By now Alec, Philippe and I were champing at the bit and had half given up hope. Indeed, by the time the confirmation of the project did come through, it was so late that I couldn't create a new work for the first year. I was in Delhi, Alec was in Durham – and there was hardly any time to consult, let alone write. In the event, we had to think of a different solution.

Yet we were all conscious of how unusual it was that our project existed at all. We dubbed it 'Confluences' to indicate the variety of ideas and geographies and forces that merged within it. The other reason for the name was that it implied a voyage downstream, with other tributaries (performers, influences, ideas, and so on) joining en route.

Our brief each year was to create a work of about twenty minutes for voice, violin and other forces. It would be given three performances over the course of a few weeks in summer – one at each of the three festivals: Salisbury, Chelsea and Lichfield, in that order. The first three years would touch upon China, Europe and India respectively; the theme for the fourth year was to be left open – to the suggestions of (among others) our audiences, to natural development from within the works themselves, and to any extraneous inspiration that might strike. The venues would be large local churches with good acoustics and lines of sight, as well as Lichfield and Salisbury cathedrals. The forces would range, depending on the year, from small ensembles to an orchestra to professional choirs to massed amateur choruses of men, women and children.

In fact, the works turned out to be between forty minutes and an hour long, and far richer and more complex than we had imagined. The first year produced a song-cycle for tenor, violin, harp and guitar, *Songs in Time of War*. The second year saw six pieces for unaccompanied professional chorus – *Shared*

Ground – interleaved with five pieces for unaccompanied violin – *Ponticelli* – something like a suite dovetailed into a motet, but composed so that they could also be performed separately. The third year produced an oratorio, *The Traveller*, for violin and tenor soloists, large amateur chorus (including children's choir) and string orchestra plus harp and percussion. For the final year, Alec created three separate but related works: a cycle of seven songs for tenor and piano called *Seven Elements*, a seven-movement sonata-like suite for violin and piano called the *Seven Elements Suite*, plus a short coda, *The Hermit on the Ice*, for all three performers.

Being indolent by nature, if there is one thing I hate, it is making an effort for nothing. It would be more than frustrating to write a halfway decent libretto only to find that the composer had made a botch of the music. Alec had set my poems in the past, as well as written an opera, *Arion and the Dolphin*, to a libretto of mine, so I was confident he would produce something good. But I could not have expected anything as magical as what emerged. The works he produced over these four years are profound, various, moving, imperishable. I am more privileged than I can say that my words provided him with some of the inspiration to create them. Let me leave a hostage to fortune and state that Alec Roth's works – and not just these but others – are among the finest ever created by an English composer. And part of the reason that they are not better known and more widely enjoyed is because Alec is so hopeless at self-promotion.

It was others who got hold of the BBC and told them of the reception and reviews the first year's première had received. Roger Wright of Radio 3 arranged for the final performance (in Lichfield Cathedral) to be recorded and broadcast, and this continued for the remaining three years. Thanks to sponsorship from an anonymous donor, the first of the works, *Songs in Time of War*, was recorded in 2008; the second, *Shared Ground*, was released in 2011.* (The performers are the same as at the festivals.) One hopes that CDs of the other works will follow. Indeed, because of the way the themes of the works, verbal and (in particular) musical, develop from year to year, echoing and reflecting what has gone before, it would be an enriching experience to hear the works performed one after another over the course of a day, or perhaps two evenings. The works form a family and, for all their differences, a close one.

The experience for me of creating these four texts, entirely in verse, was full of variety: a mixture of translation and original creation, drawing from a range of personal experience as well as the influence of others – and the consciousness that what I was writing had to be sung. One text was written many years ago – translations from Classical Chinese, a language monosyllabic in nature. One consisted of translations from Indian languages, which are far from monosyllabic, together with six original poems, three iambic, three trochaic, in a variety of line-lengths. For one I used another poet's forms as a template for my own inspiration. And for one I wrote eight poems in a variety of rhymed and unrhymed forms of my choosing. I talk about these in my brief introductions to the individual libretti.

Alec and I usually consulted closely at the beginning of this process before I went off to do my thing. But this was some-times quite frustrating for him. Once he sat in my house in Salisbury, cooling his heels for a week because I couldn't put myself in the right frame of mind to think about the project. We sat down and talked about it but didn't get anywhere. We

---

* SIGCD124 (*Songs in Time of War*); SIGCD270 (*Shared Ground*); signumrecords.com

then poured ourselves a glass of wine and went for a walk in the water-meadow past a bare oak tree, which was surrounded, owing to heavy rains, by a pool; we stood there, staring at what looked like the tree's roots but were actually its leafless branches reflected in the water. Some months later this image would lead to the poems of *Shared Ground*. The next year he wrote me a series of elaborate memoranda that helped me feel my way to my theme; and it was his strength of feeling for some verses of the Dhammapada that gave them such a prominent role in *The Traveller*. Even after I handed him the draft of a particular libretto, there were discussions, cullings, rearrangements, suggestions for amendment – and in one case even the request that I go back and produce something entirely different.

Words are all very well, but the success of a musical work lies in its music – and, on the whole, Alec's main task began after mine had ended – and Philippe's main task after Alec's. Before writing this introduction I talked to both of them in order to be able to cast some light on these later stages, and even occasionally on the actual process of composition, which strikes me as being as mysterious as that of writing. The consultation between them, the choice of the other performers, the involvement of the festivals and the local community, the programming for the first half of the concerts, the changes to the music made in the aftermath of actual performances: all these were essential aspects of the project, and because Philippe and Alec talk with great insight about them, I have set their thoughts down largely in their own words.

As a composer, Alec writes with particular venues in mind – their acoustic and visual and even dramatic possibilities. In the third year, our piece (based on India) was to be performed in Salisbury Cathedral. While we were still discussing possible themes for the libretto and before I had written a single word of it, Alec wrote me a note which he headed 'Memorandum 1 from AR to VS':

> I woke up this morning with an interesting sound in my head. Remember how the Advent Procession begins? Everyone stands up and faces West. All the lights are extinguished; it's pitch dark. Suddenly, quite high up a single candle flame appears. One by one other candles are lit from the first one and move out. In each aisle, North and South, a procession begins and the light spreads down the nave. Imagine this in sonic terms: darkness/silence; the sound of the solo violin; gradually its notes spread to other violins (or voices?); the sound, now a texture of overlapping harmonies, spreads out to envelop the whole building. This would be a powerfully dramatic beginning. Isn't there a verse in the Bhagavad Gita where Krishna says something like, 'I am the spark that brings life to all living things'? . . .

Similarly – and again this gives his music something almost indefinably personal – Alec writes with particular musicians in mind, not for, say, a general tenor or general violinist. He enjoyed this greatly over the course of the four years, because we were lucky to get wonderful performers. *Songs in Time of War* was sung by the tenor Mark Padmore with Philippe Honoré on the violin, Alison Nicholls on the harp and Morgan Szymanski on the guitar. *Shared Ground* was sung by the choir Ex Cathedra conducted by Jeffrey Skidmore, while *Ponticelli*, which interleaved its movements, was played by Philippe. In the third year, *The Traveller* was sung by Mark Padmore, together with large local choruses, including children's chorus. The solo violinist was Philippe and the orchestra was the Britten Sinfonia. In the final year, *Seven Elements* was sung by the tenor James Gilchrist with Rustem Hayroudinoff on the piano, the *Seven Elements Suite* was performed by Philippe and Rustem, and *The Hermit on the Ice* by all three.

Because Philippe was one of the three equal initiating partners in the project, and it was understood from the start that he would play a crucial role in the music, Alec wrote more for the violin over these four years than he could ever have imagined he would. I talked to Philippe about this.

VS: What was it like to have four years of Alec's music to play?

PH: I feel I was really lucky. You know what I think of Alec as a composer. Sometimes, as a musician, one works so hard in an orchestra or at sessions work, where you have no choice in what is being played, that there's a danger of getting a bit stale, even treating music as a humdrum profession. What can keep one's pleasure in music fresh is if one is able to play in smaller ensembles or to do solo work. And best of all, of course, is to work on something written specially for you, with your style and tastes and abilities in mind. So it was great to work with Alec's music – with a new piece every year. And of course frustrating sometimes.

VS: Frustrating?

PH: Well, I sometimes thought I didn't get enough of it! I was particularly frustrated in the first year, when we did *Songs in Time of War* sung by tenor, with a slightly unusual setting: violin as well as both harp and guitar – two plucked instruments similar in many ways – and no real bass instrument. The texture was very similar – though it actually worked really well. Talking of similar textures: there was pizzicato for the violin as well; in fact there's one number where I play pizzicato but the harp and guitar don't come in. Alec had also worked with me on various effects, and he used some of them. I especially remember what I call the pigeon noise – a sort of fluttering of feathers – it's a particular bowing effect. But anyway, it was an ensemble piece that year and the violin was not used as a main voice or a particularly important voice. It was merely another one.

VS: You did get that solo in 'The Old Cypress Tree' – that dance which Alec says is at the heart of things – a sort of reminder of when life was good and full of ordinary pleasures, before war destroyed it all. Though I admit you received it pretty late and it was sort of iffy whether it would be ready for the première. You got it one day before the performance, if I recall.

PH: That's right. So I don't know how well I played it in Salisbury. Chelsea was better, though, and Lichfield OK. Of course, Alec always made changes between performances; they were never exactly the same. He might change the voicing here or the pitch there – or tweak something else. Which was good in a way: it kept us on our toes.

VS: In the second year you got *Ponticelli* – the suite for solo violin whose movements were interleaved with those of *Shared Ground*. Alec dedicated it to you and – not to embarrass you – the reviewer in *The Times* said you played it magically.

PH: Well, the work itself was amazing. Of course when I practised it, I played it as a suite or partita, and it hangs together really well. In fact, it has the same number of movements –

five – as Bach's D Minor Partita, which ends with the Chaconne. Alec's piece too ends with a very rich and complex movement. There are common features with the Chaconne: not only melody but also chords, two voices, double-stops, etc. And unique features too, of course: that plucking while I'm playing arco, for example; very challenging. It's a tremendous addition to the solo violin repertoire.

Alec said he didn't want to echo the Chaconne too much, and I can't think of any direct references. But the way the variations in the last movement develop is similar to how the Chaconne develops – for example, with all that bariolage (is that a word in English? – we use it in French) across the strings.

You delivered your words very late that year, so Alec began composing the solo violin stuff quite early. I remember him coming to the Queen Elizabeth Hall, as the Royal Festival Hall was being refurbished, and our finding a dressing room at the back to talk things through between one of my rehearsals and a concert. We spent more than an hour discussing the music and I made various suggestions; but by then, of course, the piece was already quite advanced.

VS: Is there anything you're not quite happy with?

PH: I'm not too sure about the use of the mute in the first movement, now that I've listened to it on the recording for radio. In the crescendo, the mute prevents it from going beyond a certain volume of sound. But that's just an opinion.*

---

* Alec has subsequently made his instruction for this movement ('Flat Bridge') more flexible; it is now up to the violinist whether to use the wooden mute or not.

VS: Coming to the third year and *The Traveller* . . .

PH: Well, in the third year, Alec took a huge amount on and I felt he short-changed the violin. You gave him too many words, Vikram – and of course the words had to be sung and there was only so much space for the violin.

VS: Yes, I'm sorry. I didn't actually give him the words: I selected some texts and told him to cull them. But he greedily grabbed them all.

PH: Do you know, if there's one tune that I remember straight-away when I think of the project, it would be that theme in the solo violin meditation in year three, which appeared again in the violin suite in year four. Strange to think that it almost didn't exist. In fact, in Salisbury it didn't – when the work was premièred and reviewed.

VS: If it hadn't existed it would have been a tragedy. The reviewer in *The Times*, who came to the Salisbury performance, and who praised your playing of the Ysaÿe solo violin sonata – 'dispatched with fire and pluck' (nice pun there) – mentioned that he was disappointed that in the new work, you, as the supposed 'travel-ler', didn't have much to do on your own.

PH: I actually think that review made Alec decide to write something specifically for the violin – and, though he was very busy, compose it in time for Chelsea. I think he felt bad – but then went on to create something wonderful. [*Philippe pauses, then goes on:*] You know, I think, with Alec – though he has written a string quartet now, and instrumental works, and that nocturne for harp and violin that Alison and I played –

writing for the violin doesn't come naturally to him, and I don't think that that's what he wants to do first. He's very much in the voice and choral tradition. That's where he's at his most comfortable and of course singers love what he writes for them. And librettists too, I suppose, because the words are set so clearly. But it's a shame that he doesn't write more for strings because I think it would be fantastic. When he puts his mind to it, it really works. That Meditation was perfect. For me, of course, it was a great relief that I could say something individually for once instead of just being part of a big noise. And maybe the adrenalin brought about by the stress of its newness helped my playing! But it was also very good for the balance of the piece itself to have that reflection without words.

When he got around to writing it and sent me the score, I read it on my own at first. I then went to rehearse it with him; this was just two days before the Chelsea Festival. 'Oh God, why did you put me so high up there on the E string?' I asked him. He said – and this is typical of Alec, who composes for the sound of particular performers – 'Because when you play up there I find it beautiful and I wanted to use it.' Unfortunately I had – and still have – a wolf note on my violin that affects all the Cs and particularly the high ones. It was fine that year, but sometimes when I play that piece it drives me crazy. I know they say that only good violins have wolf notes, but . . .

VS: I can't understand how wolf notes can drive you crazy, Philippe, when you didn't seem to be distracted by the G-sharp hum from the fused fluorescent lighting in Salisbury Cathedral when you played the solo Ysaÿe.

PH: Hmm. Actually, it was very distracting before I began playing; but you just get on with it. Between movements it was a bit disturbing. But I love the Ysaÿe, and it was great to play it in that space, with some distance and resonance.

VS: In the fourth year you got plenty to do – with that violin and piano suite.

PH: Yes! But we had to fight for it. Alec wanted to write it for violin and guitar.

VS: I don't think Alec is in love with the piano. He thinks it a bit of a bully.

PH: Well, he writes well for it – in his own idiom – with an open texture. You know, it may be great to write for unusual combinations of instruments, but if you write for normal forces, like violin and piano, your pieces are much more likely to be repeated and heard. I really longed for something that I would be able to continue to play after the whole project was over.

VS: So we bullied poor Alec when he brought up the question of the guitar. I remember making it clear on the patio that day that I wasn't having it. My muse would go on strike.

PH: Perhaps there was a bit less novelty in the violin and piano piece of the fourth year than in the solo violin suite of the second year. But that was right in a way: themes from earlier years were brought in to weave things together, to give a sense of closure. The Meditation theme came in. So did the *Dies Irae* semiquavers and double-stops from the Ysaÿe. It gave me a lot of pleasure when I came to play it. In general, in an instrumental work by Alec, things always look a bit bare and almost unfinished on paper. There's no articulation, hardly any dynamic instructions – even less than in Bach! – not too many tempi indications either, and he writes in normal notation without the usual twenty-first-century markings. It looks easy but it's very deceptive. You have to explore it and understand it yourself. The moment I start to work on it, I begin to find things. The piece starts taking shape and grows richer and richer musically and emotionally, and this process never really stops.

A few weeks after I talked to Philippe, in the course of a conversation with Alec, I brought up the question of the violin. Had he ever played it?

AR: Not since I was at school and people begged me to stop. I tried the cello too, but not for long.

VS: So how do you write for strings? Especially something like the suite for unaccompanied violin that you produced in the second year?

AR: It's the same as when I compose for guitar – or any other instrument I don't play. The process goes something like this: I write a few sketches; then I take them to the performer, and we start playing around with them – and that's how I start learning about the instrument and what works well with it and what doesn't. The advantage of this initial ignorance is that you sometimes come across something that is quite original in conception, but which doesn't fall under the well-worn path of the fingers – doesn't sit, so to speak, and in some cases is physically impossible to play. When something like this happened, Philippe would say, 'I can't do it exactly like that but I could do it like this or like this,' and we found a way of adapting it to make it work. That was really satisfying for both of us because his ideas got into it. And over the four years, I've got better at writing for the violin and for strings in general.

Or else the inspiration might come more directly from hearing something he did. I remember asking him in a sort of workshop session to play the open strings bowed. The sonority he produced made a huge impression on me, and I began looking at the effect of an open string being played as a pulsed drone while the string below it or above it was being played melodically; and then moving up from one string to another in the same manner. I use that idea for the first movement of *Ponticelli*, the suite for solo violin. It's not like anything I've ever written before and I still think it's the best of the movements.

VS: I like the last movement best myself – it's got tremendous energy and compulsiveness.

AR [*laughing*]: Philippe was always looking for a challenge. So that's where I thought I'd keep him quiet with technical matters – but I was astonished by what he did. That last movement was full of all sorts of shenanigans: left-hand pizzicato as well as lots of right-hand pizz, multinote chords, harmonics, the lot. And he played it as if all that was no problem at all – and got to the heart of the music, to the dance of it.

VS: For me – and for Philippe too – one of the most beautiful moments of all was the Meditation by the violin towards the end of *The Traveller*. Which, of course, almost didn't get written.

AR [*looking slightly guilty*]: Er, yes, it wasn't there in the first performance, in Salisbury. Let me explain. I was writing the music in a very artificial order that year, not at all in the sequence of the libretto itself. I had to do all the children's choruses first – they needed a very long rehearsal time since they sang from memory. I gave them their parts just after Christmas, I think. Second, all the chorus work: the amateurs had to start learning it in the spring. Then, the solo voice for Mark Padmore. The orchestra next: a month before the première. Apart from this, there was the physical effort of producing all those parts. So with regard to the violin I rather lost my way. I saw the violin as 'the traveller', but the voices tended to dominate it whenever they appeared together because, well, they had the words. It was only after hearing the first performance that I realized that something was missing: a passage without words, an extended instrumental meditation, a fantasia for solo violin at the end of the last section. I thought, 'How on earth will I write it? It's just two weeks before Chelsea.' But as soon as I sat down, it came; and Philippe did his usual job of looking at it and playing it immediately and making it sound beautiful.

VS: To excuse you further, weren't you also burdened with conducting that year?

AR: Well, I had to be closely involved in the rehearsals any- way because of the intergenerational chorus – with ages ranging from eight to eighty! I had to be sure that everything was singable. The children were great – they sounded like real children, not choristers. And it was wonderful the way the communities got involved. In fact, in the case of Lichfield, they used the performance to establish a Festival Chorus, some- thing they hadn't had before. But the reason why I did the actual conducting – 'burdened' isn't how I'd put it; it was a pleasure too – was so that the festivals could afford four or five extra musicians for the orchestra. There were money problems that year because of the expense of an orchestra – and although the choruses were amateur, there were quite a lot of choir trainers and accompanists – and of course travel and administration costs. Even with regard to the use of Salisbury Cathedral, we kept wondering: could we manage it or couldn't we? But we had to assume we could; there was no other way to proceed, really.

VS: Since you've touched upon money and festivals, I should say that things for the most part ran smoothly on that front, even if there were some constraints and uncertainties. But the picture would not be complete if I didn't mention one unfortunate exception. The Chelsea Festival wound itself up at the end of year three, and a different organization called the Chelsea Arts Festival took its place. It was only with the greatest of persistence that Philippe received anything at all from them for that fourth year; they still owe him and the pianist more than half their fee. First they claimed that they hadn't received their invoices; then they claimed that they simply didn't have the money. It is painful to see musicians, who aren't rich by any means, being taken advantage of in this way. But, as Philippe says, when he thinks of the project, it is your music rather than this sorry business, isolated as it was, that comes overwhelmingly to mind.

AR: Well, that's one instance, involuntary in this case, of artists having to subsidize their own art. But the project did also benefit from the generosity of a great many people – such as friends of the festivals. And when the three-year guarantee of the funding agencies ran out, it was an anonymous donor who provided the commission fee for the fourth year.

VS: Continuing with the subject of festivals but moving from money matters to logistics, did you find having three performances in different places and on different dates a problem?

AR: In terms of logistics, perhaps – for example, finding dates when all the musicians were available – not just for the concerts, for the rehearsals as well. But in fact it was wonderful to have three performances. It made all the difference to the work. It's true, I could only compose with one venue in mind, and the other two festivals had to find something similar; but that wasn't a serious disadvantage. What was a huge advantage was the chance I got to listen to the music as it was actually being performed and to make changes for the next concert – sometimes just a bit of tweaking, but at other times, as with the violin meditation, a major change. And the performers became more comfortable with the music when they'd played it a couple of times. So by the time the third concert came around, it would still sound fresh, but you could tell they felt at home with it. In a way it's a pity that it's the first performance that gets reviewed! But at least the recording for radio was always done at the third performance, which of course was more polished; and besides, Lichfield Cathedral, particularly the Lady Chapel, has a very good acoustic.

VS: How did your works turn out to be so long – so much longer than the festivals had commissioned?

AR: I got carried away – and they didn't rein me in. Actually, the precedent was set by the first year; once that had turned out all right with the listeners and critics, the festivals weren't too concerned about limiting the length of the works in subsequent years.

VS: Well, why was the first year so long then?

AR: If you'd written me a short libretto, Vikram, twenty minutes' worth, so to speak, that's all I'd have written. But because you weren't given the time to write anything, I had to forage around for something from your work to inspire me. I chose your translations of Du Fu's poems, which turned out to be forty minutes long. So by writing nothing, you doubled the length of my work.

VS: Considering the length of your pieces, there was clearly no room for anything else in the second half of the concerts in which they were played. But what about the rest of the programming – the first half? From our point of view the new piece may have been at the centre of things, but for most of the audience, they were going to a concert which consisted of other things besides.

AR: The programming of a concert is very important – and I admit that in the first year, the first half was a bit ad hoc. *Songs in Time of War* had tenor, violin, guitar and harp – and there wasn't a lot we could choose from with those instruments. We had the Saint-Saëns *Fantaisie* for violin and harp, and Piazzolla's *Café 1930* for violin and guitar. And Mark Padmore sang Vaughan Williams's *Ten Blake Songs* with Gareth Hulse on oboe – though I hadn't used the oboe in my work. At one point, I did think of taking advantage of Gareth by having a few plaintive oboe notes sound offstage at the very end of my piece to represent the ghosts of the dead soldiers in the 'Ballad of the Army Carts'. But in the event, I didn't.

VS: The second year wasn't ad hoc in the least: all Bach and very symmetrical: a motet for double choir – *Singet dem Herrn ein neues Lied*, the Chaconne from the second partita for solo violin, another motet for double choir – *Komm, Jesu, komm*.

AR: I think it was the most successful year as far as programming went. *Shared Ground* and *Ponticelli* were basically inspired by Bach's motets and solo violin music. I really steeped myself in those works that year – I had never written for unaccompanied choir or solo violin before – and I can see a few direct influences here and there. For example, the repeated 'Komm' in *Komm, Jesu, komm* was reflected in my repeated setting of the word 'This' in the last of your poems. And the programme order of the first half established the interlocking of choir and solo violin which we further developed in the *Shared Ground/Ponticelli* sequence.

VS: The third year, when *The Traveller* was performed, the Britten Sinfonia played Britten's arrangement of the Purcell *Chacony in G*. And Mark Padmore sang Finzi's *Dies Natalis* with them. But the programming that year caused quite a few problems for Philippe, I remember. He had planned a Bach concerto, but because the festivals couldn't afford the expense a harpsichord would entail, that had to be dropped. Also, Richard Hawley at Lichfield, in retrospect quite rightly, though it was quite frustrating at the time, insisted on 'programming that made sense'. Philippe told me that he went back to thinking about solo Bach, then solo Bartók, and finally hit upon Ysaÿe, which was an inspired choice: the second solo violin sonata, with its *Dies Irae* theme in each movement. And that of course made perfect programming sense – *Dies Natalis*, the presence of the *Dies Irae*, and the stages of life and death in *The Traveller*.

AR: Which actually had an effect on my own music in the fourth year, when I incorporated the *Dies Irae* theme in the *Seven Elements Suite* for violin and piano.

VS: Coming to the fourth year then, apart from the *Seven Elements Suite*, you also wrote the *Seven Elements* song-cycle for tenor and piano and *The Hermit on the Ice* for all three. And the all-Schubert first half paralleled this: various songs with some link to each of the seven elements, then the A Major Violin Sonata and finally *The Shepherd on the Rock* in your arrangement for tenor, piano and violin (instead of Schubert's original clarinet).

AR: I learned a lot from doing that arrangement; it's quite a long piece. Getting it into James Gilchrist's range, preventing things from going off the lower range of the violin, and so on – I didn't adapt a lot, but there was a bit of fiddling and fudging, which I hope Schubert wasn't too worried about. The two halves of that programme influenced each other. The very idea for your poem 'The Hermit on the Ice' came from the title of Schubert's piece. And when I was setting the last two lines of your poem – 'The blue earth with its iron core / Spins on through time, spins on through space' – I decided to quote Schubert's lovely floating melody to the words 'und singen . . . und singen' in my violin and piano parts, as I imagined the earth singing Schubert as it spins away into the distance.

VS: We're talking in Salisbury now, in the Old Rectory in Bemerton where, in the early seventeenth century, the poet, musician and priest George Herbert lived and died; and this is where we had many of our earlier discussions about the project, including that crucial one in the red room. And when I've been in India or elsewhere, you've come and stayed here and kept the poetic and musical spirit of Herbert going – and indeed composed quite a lot of these works (as well as others) here. I know that the venue *for* which you compose is very important for your music. But what about the venue *in* which you compose?

AR: It has a huge effect on me. Take the Old Rectory, for example. I love Herbert's poetry. Also, as a teenager, when I had singing lessons, I sang some of Vaughan Williams's settings of Herbert, *Five Mystical Songs*, and I learned quite a lot from that about setting English texts to music. So for me, there was a particular atmosphere to the place where he'd lived. Besides, I loved the peace, the space, the greenery of it. And in practical terms, it was good to be able to spread my keyboard and computer and other equipment around in the red room and work on my music there – and the large table in the kitchen was invaluable when you weren't here and it was uncluttered, especially in the third year when I had all those parts to organize.

But it was in the second year that the sense of place was most critical. The libretto for *Shared Ground* consisted of your poems based on some of Herbert's own poetical forms, and you talk in those poems about your experience of living here. I knew the river that you talked about. I'd been with you when you saw the oak reflected in the flooded glade. It had an enormous effect on my setting of the poems. When you sent them to me from Delhi, I remember I found some of them difficult to set at first – but just being here, I'm sure, got me over some of those difficulties.

VS: Could you give an example or two of these difficulties?

AR: Well, the poem 'And' is so short – it's basically the shortest of the texts. The first time I started looking at the text, I thought, oh, there aren't enough words. I need some more. Then when I looked at it later, what caught my imagination were the words that begin the poem: 'And then I woke.' So what went before? The 'before', of course, was the sleep; the poet was sleeping and dreaming until the word 'And'. And so a lullaby rhythm came to me and a four-note gamelan ostinato. The music to the text itself is shorter than the music of the sleep that precedes it, and then the sleep just creeps back in again at the end of the setting. So I was able in a natural way to make a larger piece out of something quite short. What I used for the wordless sleep bit was the Western tuning equivalent of a Javanese pentatonic mode. Then when he wakes up, and I'm setting the words, I use the star mode. It's quite a sensuous piece.

VS: The star mode? What's the star mode?

AR: Oh, sorry, that's my private way of describing a particular mode I use a lot, which is built up of minor thirds and semitones alternately. I've used it pretty much in every year of 'Confluences'. I first discovered it when I was composing our opera *Arion and the Dolphin*, by piling up alternating fifths and semitones. Then it changed its fortunes and got squished, if you see what I mean.

VS: I think you've lost me, Alec. But to get back to how you disentangle difficulties when composing, I remember you telling me that you had great difficulty working on my poem 'Host', where I talk about the house itself and my sense of Herbert's presence.

AR: Well, I knew the house and its moods, 'Its stones, its trees, its air, / The stream, the small church, the dark rain'. But I just couldn't see, since it was such a personal statement, how I could get a choir to sing it in such a way that it would be intelligible emotionally – or even in terms of projecting the words clearly. Some time later, I happened to go up to London to hear Jeffrey Skidmore and Ex Cathedra (who were going to be our singers that year) perform a piece by Poulenc written around the time Paris was liberated: a most extraordinary work called *Figure Humaine*, set to poems by Paul Éluard. Hearing Poulenc's work inspired me to find a solution to the difficulty of setting your text. I have a solo voice from the choir singing your words as 'the guest', and the choir singing the words of the stones, trees, stream, etc. And the wonderful sonorities of the Poulenc led me to constitute my forces in the same way: to divide the singers into two choirs, each of six voices – soprano, mezzo-soprano, alto, tenor, baritone and bass.

But at the end of my setting, I felt I had left things somewhat up in the air with a single voice; I needed to anchor things, to bring them back to earth – and not just in musical terms. And that's why, immediately afterwards, I had the choir sing Herbert's short poem 'To My Successor', which is inscribed in stone above the porch of the Old Rectory – and which I would never have seen if I hadn't been staying there. I'm glad you let me interpolate it into the text.

VS: Well, it belonged. But I did refuse you permission to use your setting of Herbert's poem 'The Flower' at the very end of the libretto. I didn't want a text by me to close with someone else's words, however much I revered him. What gave you the idea of doing that?

AR: Well, let me go back a bit. You know that that year you gave me the poems for *Shared Ground* very late.

VS: I know. I know. I'm sorry. Muse failure.

AR: Well, I started working on other things. One, of course, was the solo violin pieces for *Ponticelli*. Then Judy* got me involved in the George Herbert hymn-tune project and I decided to set 'The Flower'. That's another thing that wouldn't have happened if I hadn't been here.

When I'd set it, the tune seemed too good to use only for the hymn, so I adapted it for the second movement of *Ponticelli*. Then, when I had finished both *Ponticelli* and the choral work *Shared Ground* with which it was interlocked, two thoughts struck me. First, it seemed a pity that the violin and the unaccompanied choir were never heard together, and I wondered if I could do something about that. Secondly, the final poem, 'This', is such a bleak poem. And I wanted there to be a sense of hope at the end.

VS: I didn't mind you adding hope, if that was your vision of things, but not with someone else's words!

AR: Yes, I accepted that. So I used the tune of 'The Flower', which I associated with hope, to create an epilogue or coda for

* Canon Judy Rees, a friend and neighbour, together with others from the George Herbert in Bemerton Group, encouraged composers to set a number of his poems as hymns, thus adding to the five for which we have well-known and often-sung settings. These nineteen new settings (including 'The Pulley', 'Easter' and 'Christmas') have now been published under the title *Another Music: Through the Year with George Herbert* by the Royal School of Church Music.

violin and choir, but with the choir singing wordlessly. It worked for the audience – and, at the time, for me. But I've been having serious second thoughts about it. I feel it's got to go. Even if the ending is bleak, it's right.

VS: Talking of words, I seem to remember you telling me that you wanted to compose the settings for my words first, and then use those tunes and textures as a source of inspiration for the solo violin pieces of *Ponticelli*. Because I was so late in giving you the words, you had to reverse the order and write the solo violin pieces first. How did that work?

AR: Well, there was a musical logic to what I said, but perhaps I was also just trying to hurry you along. Anyway, I couldn't sit around twiddling my thumbs, so I began work on the *Ponticelli*, the 'little bridges'. I got a lot of inspiration from the five bridges themselves.

VS: I should mention that when you told me about the five bridges in the water-meadow, I was a bit puzzled. I could see what you were referring to as the Arched Bridge and the Flat Bridge – which cross the two branches of the River Nadder – and the Rustic Bridge over the main ditch of the water-meadow – and, at a pinch, the Bridge of Sleepers, which is, well, a sort of half-bridge made of railway sleepers; but your Bridge of Sighs mystified me.

AR [*laughs*]: That was a great discovery. I was walking on the path that goes around the unwooded, open part of the water-meadow. It had just rained, and there was a sort of squelchy area. But I was helped to get across it by what seemed to be a log of wood under part of the path. And when I stepped on it, it made a sort of whooshing, sighing noise. Hence the name. I loved the noise. It only happened after rain. But now, a couple of years later, it doesn't do that any more. And the last time I tried to take that circuit, the swans were nesting there and they hissed me away.

VS: So the Bridge of Sighs has disappeared, perhaps for ever. And all that's left of it is your 'ponticello' of that name.

AR: That's right.

VS: So what did you use for ideas, since you didn't yet have the surrounding poems or their musical settings?

AR: The bridges themselves. For two of them it was the sounds they made – the watery moaning of the Bridge of Sighs, and in the case of the Bridge of Sleepers, the dull plonking noise the individual railway sleepers made when I prodded them with my umbrella – like a giant xylophone. The Rustic Bridge was made of narrow wooden planks, some of which had been replaced with bright new wood. The sequence of old and new wood made an interesting pattern, which I interpreted as musical intervals. The remaining two bridges also provided a visual stimulus in the form of their actual shapes. If you look at my scores you'll see that the opening bars of the music make an image of the Flat Bridge on the page, and the notation of the Arched Bridge music makes an arch shape.

VS: Really, Alec!

AR: Well, you pun quite a lot, so I don't see why I shouldn't – in a musical or a visual sense. Or verbally, for that matter, as with my violinistic title, *Ponticelli*. And, well, Herbert makes lots of puns too – serious puns for the most part – and writes some poems, such as 'Easter-Wings', in unusual shapes. You take your cue for your poem 'Oak' from that. And in fact, in my score of 'Oak', the choir begins by singing wordlessly, and the notation of the music on the page makes an hour-glass shape, mirroring the oak tree and its reflection in the pool below.

VS: Wordplay and shape-play! I'm not sure anyone will take us seriously if they find out how we amuse ourselves.

AR: They can judge the poems and the music on their own merits.

VS: Well, talking of punning, I'm very proud of that particularly puerile pun which came to me out of the blue – and which sums up our collaboration on the project.

AR: 'Seth wrote and Roth set'?

VS: That's the one! But to drift back into seriousness, here's a thought. A writer's book exists once it's written. And it's shared or received when it's read. I don't have to hear or see someone reading it for that to happen. And the process of reading is such a private one. I once came into a room where a friend of mine was reading one of my books, and he clicked his tongue impatiently and shooed me off. But the performance of music is different; it's a public act. And I don't know if a piece of music – or a play for that matter – could be said to be fully realized until it's been performed. I mention this because someone told me many years ago that she'd been at the dress rehearsal of *Arion and the Dolphin*, and she saw you sitting by yourself in tears and asked you if everything was all right. And you'd said, yes, everything was all right; it was just that you'd never really believed that you would hear and see it actually performed, and that that was why you were overcome. I cannot imagine what it must be like to hear your own music for the first time.

AR [*after a pause*]: You know, people assume composers can hear their music in their heads. Well, even if that's true in the abstract, it is the performers who really embody it and bring it to life – in a particular place at a particular time – and let us hear it with our real ears, not those of our minds. It's all the difference in the world. And the audience closes the circle – their attentiveness, their reactions, even the direction of their gaze. When *Songs in Time of War* was performed in Wilton Church, someone said that a veteran from the Second World War had broken down as he listened to 'Moonlit Night'. I was surprised at first, but they told me that he'd said it was exactly as it had been with him, separated as he had been from his wife by the war. To know that your music has moved someone so deeply, what could be a greater reward?

VS: That was the first year of 'Confluences'. I remember there was a long silence before the applause. But more important than the reception and the reviews was the freedom I felt it gave us for the rest of the life of the project. There would be, as you said, no Procrustean constraint on length. A trust had been established – which made everything in the years that followed much easier. Their attitude became, 'Go away and write and compose, we won't bother you.'

AR: Well, the festivals had taken a big risk with us. It was good to feel we hadn't let them down.

Songs in Time of War

烽火連三月

家書抵萬金

杜甫句 北京朴老

Introduction to

Songs In Time of War

In the first year of the project, by the time we got the go-ahead, I had no time to write anything new, so we decided to make use of something I already had in hand. Alec had earlier set to music some poems on the gardens of Suzhou that I had written while I was a student in China. Now he suggested that he set some translations from the Chinese poet Du Fu that I had done some years later.

I had turned to these poems at a strange time. In my twenties, I had lived in China for two years, studying at Nanjing University, doing research in economics and demography in nearby villages and travelling around the country whenever I got the chance to do so. I grew to love China – in a complex sort of way. In the middle of my time there I hitchhiked home to India via Tibet and wrote an account of this journey, *From Heaven Lake*.

In 1989, the brutal firings on Tiananmen Square took place. For months afterwards I could hardly bear to think of China or Chinese. Then, to my astonishment – for I was in the middle of writing *A Suitable Boy* – I began to translate poems from three of my favourite Chinese poets, Wang Wei, Li Bai and Du Fu.

These three great poets were contemporaries, and lived in the eighth century. Du Fu's poems are, to my mind, the most moving of all. He wrote most of the works presented here during a terrible rebellion in the Tang Dynasty, which caused vast devastation and famine. Du Fu was separated not only from the imperial court, where he was, for a while, an official, but also from his wife and family; he was later to discover that one of his sons had died of starvation.

The Chinese have always turned to their poets for solace in difficult times, so perhaps I should not have been surprised that something drew me back to them in 1989. In 2006, when we were looking for a text, the Iraq conflict was in its third year, and the waste and grief of war gave these poems, more than twelve centuries old, a new charge.

Alec declared my translations singable and arranged them in a different order to create a kind of narrative line, imagining Du Fu alone at night on the boat taking him on his final voyage along the River Yangtze, and reminiscing about family, friends, strangers, country, and the effect on all of them of the civil war. Alec wrote the work for tenor, violin, guitar and harp – to provide what he called an open texture, something less heavy than the piano, the traditional instrument for accompaniment.

We called the work *Songs in Time of War*. Its first performance took place in the beautiful Italianate church at Wilton near Salisbury, close to where Eisenhower, Churchill and others planned their strategy for D-Day during the Second World War.

Songs in Time of War

1. Thoughts while Travelling at Night

Light breeze on the fine grass.
I stand alone at the mast.

Stars lean on the vast wild plain.
Moon bobs in the Great River's spate.

Letters have brought no fame.
Office? Too old to obtain.

Drifting, what am I like?
A gull between earth and sky.

2. Grieving for the Young Prince

From Changan walls white-headed crows took flight
And cawed upon the Western Gate at night –
Then on officials' roofs they pecked and cawed
To warn them to escape the barbarian horde.
The gold whips broke, so hard were they applied.
The exhausted horses galloped till they died.
The court fled, panicked – those they could not find
Of the imperial line were left behind.

~ *

---

* a stanza break at the end of a page is marked by ~
  no stanza break at the end of a page is marked by ⁊

Below his waist, blue coral, glints of jade –
I see a young prince, weeping and afraid
By the cross-roads. Although he won't confess
His name to me he begs in his distress
To be my slave. Thorn scrub he's hidden in
For months has left no untorn shred of skin –
But the imperial nose betrays his birth:
The Dragon's seed is not the seed of earth.

Wolves, jackals roam the city. In the wild
The Dragon and his court remain exiled.
Take care, dear Prince. I daren't speak long with you,
But for your sake will pause a breath or two.

Last night the east wind's blood-stench stained the air
And camels filled the former capital's square.
The Shuofang veterans, bright in their array,
How bold they seemed once, how inane today.
I hear the Son of Heaven has abdicated,
And in the North the Khan, it is related,
And each of his brave warriors slashed his face
– So moved were they by the imperial grace –
And swore to wipe this great dishonour out.
But we must mind our words, with spies about.
Alas, poor Prince, be careful. May the power
Of the Five Tombs protect you hour by hour.

3. *The Visitor*

South and north of my house lies springtime water,
And only flocks of gulls come every day.
The flower path's unswept: no guests. The gate
Is open: you're the first to come this way.
The market's far: my food is nothing special.
The wine, because we're poor, is an old brew –
But if you wish I'll call my ancient neighbour
Across the fence to drink it with us two.

4. *A Fine Lady*

There is a lady, matchless in her beauty.
An empty valley's where she dwells, obscure.
Her family, she says, was once a good one.
She lives with grass and trees now, spent and poor.

When lately there was chaos in the heartlands
And at the rebels' hands her brothers died,
Their high rank failed them, as did her entreaties:
Their flesh and bones remained unsanctified.

The busy world, as fickle as a lamp-flame,
Hates what has had its day or is decayed.
The faithless man to whom she once was married
Keeps a new woman, beautiful as jade.

Those trees whose leaves curl up at night sense evening.
Without its mate a mandarin duck can't sleep.
He only sees the smile of his new woman.
How can he then hear his old woman weep?   ~

Among the mountains, spring-fed streams run clearly.
Leaving the mountains, they are soiled with dross.
Her maid has sold her pearls and is returning.
To mend the thatch they drag the vines across.

Her hands are often full of bitter cypress.
The flowers she picks don't go to grace her hair.
She rests against tall bamboo trees at nightfall.
The weather's cold and her blue sleeves threadbare.

5. *Dreaming of Li Bai*

The pain of death's farewells grows dim.
The pain of life's farewells stays new.
Since you were exiled to Jiangnan
– Plague land – I've had no news of you.

Proving how much you're in my thoughts,
Old friend, you've come into my dreams.
I thought you still were in the law's
Tight net – but you've grown wings, it seems.

I fear yours is no living soul.
How could it make this distant flight?
You came: the maple woods were green.
You left: the pass was black with night.

The sinking moonlight floods my room.
Still hoping for your face, I stare.
The water's deep, the waves are wide.
Watch out for water-dragons there.

6. Moonlit Night

In Fuzhou, far away, my wife is watching
The moon alone tonight, and my thoughts fill
With sadness for my children, who can't think
Of me here in Changan; they're too young still.
Her cloud-soft hair is moist with fragrant mist.
In the clear light her white arms sense the chill.
When will we feel the moonlight dry our tears,
Leaning together on our window-sill?

7. An Autumn Meditation

I've heard it said Changan is like a chessboard, where
Failure and grief is all these hundred years have brought.
Mansions of princes and high nobles have new lords.
New officers are capped and robed for camp and court.

North on the passes gold drums thunder. To the west
Horses and chariots rush dispatches and reports.
Dragon and fish are still, the autumn river's cold.
My ancient land and times of peace come to my thoughts.

8. The Old Cypress Tree at the Temple of Zhu-ge Liang

Before the temple stands an ancient cypress tree.
Its boughs are bronze, its roots like heavy boulders lie.
Its massive frosty girth of bark is washed by rain.
Its jet-black head rears up a mile to greet the sky.   ~

Princes and ministers have paid their debt to time.
The people love the tree as they did long ago.
The cloud's breath joins it to the long mists of Wu Gorge.
It shares the moon's chill with the high white peaks of snow.

Last year the road wound east, past my old home, near where
Both Zhu-ge Liang and his First Ruler shared one shrine.
There too great cypresses stretched over the ancient plain,
And through wrecked doors I glimpsed dim paintwork and
   design.

But this lone tree, spread wide, root-coiled to earth, has held
Its sky-high place round which fierce blasts of wind are hurled.
Nothing but Providence could keep it here so long.
Its straightness marks the work of what once made the world.

If a great hall collapsed, the oxen sent to drag
Rafters from this vast tree would turn round in dismay.
It needs no craftsman's skills, this wonder of the world.
Even if felled, who could haul such a load away?

Although its bitter heart is marred by swarms of ants,
Among its scented leaves bright phoenixes collect.
Men of high aims, who live obscure, do not despair.
The great are always paid in disuse and neglect.

9. *Spring Scene in Time of War*

The state lies ruined; hills and streams survive.
Spring in the city; grass and leaves now thrive.
Moved by the times the flowers shed their dew.
The birds seem startled; they hate parting too.

The steady beacon fires are three months old.
A word from home is worth a ton of gold.
I scratch my white hair, which has grown so thin
It soon won't let me stick my hatpin in.

10. *To Wei Ba, Who Has Lived Away from the Court*

Like stars that rise when the other has set,
For years we two friends have not met.
How rare it is then that tonight
We once more share the same lamplight.
Our youth has quickly slipped away
And both of us are turning grey.
Old friends have died, and with a start
We hear the sad news, sick at heart.
How could I, twenty years before,
Know that I'd be here at your door?
When last I left, so long ago,
You were unmarried. In a row
Suddenly now your children stand,
Welcome their father's friend, demand
To know his home, his town, his kin –
Till they're chased out to fetch wine in.
Spring chives are cut in the night rain
And steamed rice mixed with yellow grain.
To mark the occasion, we should drink
Ten cups of wine straight off, you think –
But even ten can't make me high,
So moved by your old love am I.
The mountains will divide our lives,
Each to his world, when day arrives.

11. *Ballad of the Army Carts*

Carts rattle and squeak,
Horses snort and neigh –
Bows and arrows at their waists, the conscripts march away.
Fathers, mothers, children, wives run to say goodbye.
The Xianyang Bridge in clouds of dust is hidden from the eye.
They tug at them and stamp their feet, weep, and obstruct
their way.
The weeping rises to the sky.
Along the road a passer-by
Questions the conscripts. They reply:

They mobilize us constantly. Sent northwards at fifteen
To guard the River, we were forced once more to volunteer,
Though we are forty now, to man the western front this year.
The headman tied our headcloths for us when we first left
here.
We came back white-haired – to be sent again to the frontier.
Those frontier posts could fill the sea with the blood of those
who've died,
But still the Martial Emperor's aims remain unsatisfied.
In county after county to the east, Sir, don't you know,
In village after village only thorns and brambles grow.
Even if there's a sturdy wife to wield the plough and hoe,
The borders of the fields have merged, you can't tell east
from west.
It's worse still for the men from Qin, as fighters they're
the best –
And so, like chickens or like dogs, they're driven to and fro.

Though you are kind enough to ask,
Dare we complain about our task?
Take, Sir, this winter. In Guanxi   ⨍

The troops have not yet been set free.
The district officers come to press
The land tax from us nonetheless.
But, Sir, how can we possibly pay?
Having a son's a curse today.
Far better to have daughters, get them married –
A son will lie lost in the grass, unburied.
Why, Sir, on distant Qinghai shore
The bleached ungathered bones lie year on year.
New ghosts complain, and those who died before
Weep in the wet grey sky and haunt the ear.

12. *Thoughts while Travelling at Night*

Light breeze on the fine grass.
I stand alone at the mast.

Stars lean on the vast wild plain.
Moon bobs in the Great River's spate.

Letters have brought no fame.
Office? Too old to obtain.

Drifting, what am I like?
A gull between earth and sky.

Shared Ground

Last night a storm raged round the bare oak tree.
A cold, sharp rain fell; wild in pace
The ice-fed air swirled free.
Now in this place
I see
No trace
Of wind or lee,
No grass, no earth — the space
Is a clear lake, deep as my knee.
I reach its edge and view, far down, my face.

I wade out to the bench, set down my wine,
My bread and cheese, and like some sage
Of old, sit down to dine.
I do not rage
Or pine
At age,
For youth once mine.
This pool, this plate, this page,
This tree whose roots are branch and tine
Hold me in its still hour-glass, its free eye.

Introduction to

Shared Ground

For the second year of the project I moved from China to Europe – from the Tang Dynasty to the Stuarts: to England, to Salisbury, to the very house where the idea for these works had been born, the house where the poet George Herbert had lived and died.

I first came across George Herbert's poetry in *The Albatross Book of Verse*, a popular anthology that had been given to my mother in Darjeeling on her eighteenth birthday; I requisitioned it and took it with me to my boarding school in Dehradun, where I dipped into it from time to time.

When I was seventeen or so, I came to England from India to do my A levels, supposedly in Physics and Mathematics. In the event, I did only one A level: in English. One of our set books was a collection of George Herbert's verse, edited by R. S. Thomas. I still have my copy of that slim volume, published by Faber, and well scored with my earnest and callow notations in red ballpen. I felt a great affinity for Herbert – for his clarity, his depth of feeling, his spiritual struggles (five of his poems are titled 'Affliction'), his delight in the pleasures of nature and music, his wit, his strange juxtapositions, his decorous colloquiality. Though I am neither Christian nor particularly religious, he has remained among my favourite poets.

When, more than three decades later, I heard that his house near Salisbury was on sale, I felt I had to visit it. I had no intention of buying it; I simply wanted to see the place where some of my best-loved poems had been conceived and written. I felt troubled, in fact, that in 1980 the church had sold his Rectory off. If they had to sell something to keep their finances in order, why not sell off a cathedral or two instead of the house of the greatest Anglican poet?

Herbert came from an aristocratic Welsh family; he was Public Orator at Cambridge and had a promising career as a diplomat or courtier ahead of him. Instead, he chose to be a parish priest. The humble parish of Bemerton near Salisbury was offered to him by Charles I 'if it be worth his acceptance'. Herbert found the house in a ramshackle condition, and when, in 1630, he became rector, repaired and expanded it at his own expense. It was to be his only parish; he died of consumption three years later at the age of thirty-nine.

I went down to see the house on an extremely rainy Sunday in June with Philippe and his mother, and immediately fell in love with it. Redone as it was by Herbert himself, it is spacious but not grand – a rectory, not a manor. The garden stretches down to the River Nadder and there is a water-meadow beyond. Though I could not really afford to, I made a bid for it. It struck me that had the house belonged to Donne or Milton or some more overtly forceful personality, I would not have been able to live there. I would either have turned into a ventriloquist's dummy or have ceased to write altogether. But Herbert, for all his depth and richness, is a clear writer and a quiet spirit. He might influence me but would not wish to wrest me from myself.

The Old Rectory faces the very small church of St Andrew's. This is where Herbert preached and from where he tended his small flock of about three hundred souls. One propitious shock I got on that first visit was to see a stained-glass window in the church portraying Herbert holding not a quill or scroll or book – or even, since he was an accomplished musician, a lute or viol – but a violin. In those days, Philippe and I were together, and I took this as a happy sign.

Despite many doubts and difficulties, I did, finally and somehow, manage to buy the house. At first, I used to imagine Herbert writing in his room, looking across towards the church porch – or walking across the fields to Salisbury Cathedral for evensong. After a while, I simply got used to the presence of my tactful host, who never tried to bully me into his philosophy or style. His presence and his poetry were kindly influences. It was not as if, by the nature of his argument, he directly tempered my turmoil; but that through his sense of sympathy and hard-earned stillness he made it more possible to live with it.

Perhaps it was because of this that I was unresistingly drawn into writing a few poems modelled on his verse forms. I was in Delhi at the time I wrote these – I recall street dogs barking late at night – rather than in the green shades of Bemerton: such are the vagaries of inspiration. Though I hope that the mood and spirit of these poems are my own, they are formally based on 'Paradise', 'Easter-Wings', 'Hope', 'Love (III)', 'Virtue' and 'Prayer (I)' – some of the loveliest of Herbert's poems. Since I was inhabiting Herbert's stanzas in both senses of the word, I called my poems *Shared Ground*.

Herbert was a serious poet but fond of wordplay. In 'Paradise', the rhyme-word of the first line in each tercet loses a letter in each succeeding line. In 'Easter-Wings', it appears from recent research (particularly by David West) that the original manu-script lines all ended with the letter E. In 'Prayer (I)', there is no main verb. I have kept to these features. In addition, and I am not quite sure why (except that it seems consonant with Herbert's spirit of simplicity), the poems of *Shared Ground* are all monosyllabic.

The unaccompanied choral settings of the poems alternated

with solo violin movements that Alec collectively called *Ponti-celli*. Thus the six pieces of *Shared Ground* were connected by five bridges.

It was the only time in the four years of our collaboration that I did not go to the first performance. I happened to be in Brazil and I decided, instead of returning to England, to go on to Peru. It was not just the attractions of Machu Picchu. These particular and personal poems sung to Alec's music would have overwhelmed me, and the ponticelli played by Philippe, now that we were no longer together, would have brought me to memories and thoughts that would have dyed my mind for days.

Shared Ground

1. *Lost*

Lost in a world of dust and spray,
We turn, we learn, we twist, we pray
For word or tune or touch or ray:

Some tune of hope, some word of grace,
Some ray of joy to guide our race,
Some touch of love to deuce our ace.

In vain the ace seeks out its twin.
The race is long, too short to win.
The tune is out, the word not in.

Our limbs, our hearts turn all to stone.
Our spring, our step lose aim and tone.
We are no more – and less than one.

There is no soul in which to blend,
No life to leave, no light to lend,
No shape, no chance, no drift, no end.

2. Oak

Last night a storm raged round the bare oak tree.
A cold, sharp rain fell; wild in pace
The ice-fed air swirled free.
Now in this place
I see
No trace
Of wind or lee,
No grass, no earth – the space
Is a clear lake, deep as my knee.
I reach its edge and view, far down, my face.

I wade out to the bench, set down my wine,
My bread and cheese, and like some sage
Of old, sit down to dine.
I do not rage
Or pine
At age,
For youth once mine.
This pool, this plate, this page,
This tree whose roots are branch and tine
Holds me in its still hour-glass, its free cage.

3. And

And then I woke. I tried, once more, to sleep,
But could not coax or keep
The thought of you, your laugh, your hands, your eyes,
Blanked by the sun's calm rise.

The dream was done; your voice was gone; the day
    That rose now, pink and grey,
Was there to work through, till the dark hours came,
    And you, your voice, your name.

4. Host

I heard it was for sale and thought I'd go
    To see the old house where
He lived three years, and died. How could I know
    Its stones, its trees, its air,
The stream, the small church, the dark rain would say:
    'You've come; you've seen; now stay.'

'A guest?' I asked. 'Yes, as you are on earth.'
    'The means?' '. . . will come, don't fear.'
'What of the risk?' 'Our lives are that from birth.'
    'His ghost?' 'His soul is here.'
'He'll change my style.' 'Well, but you could do worse
    Than rent his rooms of verse.'

Joy came, and grief; love came, and loss; three years –
    Tiles down; moles up; drought; flood.
Though far in time and faith, I share his tears,
    His hearth, his ground, his mud;
Yet my host stands just out of mind and sight,
    That I may sit and write.

4a. [Inscription by George Herbert*]

If thou chance for to find
A new house to thy mind
And built without thy cost
Be good to the poor
As God gives thee store
And then my labour's not lost.

* This inscription carved in stone is set into the north wall of the Old Rectory,
Bemerton, which was George Herbert's home from 1630 to his death in 1633 and
where he wrote much of his poetry.

5. Flash

Bright bird, whose swift blue wings gleam out
As on the stream you dip and rise,
You, as you scan for parr and trout,
        Flash past my eyes.

Bright trout, who glints in fin and scale,
Whose whim is grubs, whose dream is flies,
You, with one whisk of your quick tail,
        Flick past my eyes.

Bright stream, home to bright fish and birds,
A gold glow as the gold sun dies,
You too, too fast for these poor words,
        Flow past my eyes.

But such drab words, ah, sad to say,
When all that's bright has fled and gone,
Praised by dull folk, dressed all in grey,
        Live on and on.

6. This

Hearts-ease, hearts-bane; a balm that chafes one raw;
  The soul in splints; graph with no grid or gauge;
  A fort, a house on stilts, a hut of straw;
A tic, a weal, the flu, the plague, the rage;

Bug swept in through the net; moth with a sting;
  Two planes in fog jammed blind; a mailed kid glove;
  A dance on coals that makes us yelp and sing;
A rook or roc or swan or goose or dove.

A beast of light; a blaze to quench or stoke;
  Bread burst and burnt; sweet wind-fall; storm-cloud-milk;
  Hope raised and razed; skin-ploy; sleep-foil; steel-silk;
Hands held in lieu of breath; our genes' sick joke;
  The sea to drink or sink in; the gods' sty;
  What we must have or die; or have and die.

The Traveller

मैया मैं तो चंद खिलौना लैहौं।
जैसो लोटि धरनि पर मल्हौं तेरी गोद न ऐहौं॥
सुरभी को पय पान न करिहौं बेनी सिर न गुहैहौं।
ह्वैहौं पूत नंद बाबा को तेरो पूत न कहैहौं॥
आगे आउ बात पुनि मेरी बलदेवहिं न जनैहौं।
हलधर पाछ लावति कहति लपोटति नई दुलरिया दैहौं॥
तेरी तौ मेरी पुनि मैया अब हीं बिसाहन जैहौं।
सूरदास है कुटिल बरानी गीत दुमंगल गैहौं॥

Introduction to

The Traveller

The third year, 2008, coincided with the 750th anniversary of the consecration of Salisbury Cathedral; the work we created was to be first performed there. The forces were to be large: a festival chorus of local people (including a separate children's choir), a string orchestra (plus harp and percussion), solo male voice (tenor as usual) and of course solo violin.

I had ranged over China and Europe for the previous two years; the third year brought me home to India. I needed a theme at once grand and intimate – suited to the mood of the cathedral as night fell. Why not all human life?

With this modest thought in mind, I tried to look for a structure for the libretto. I found it finally in the mysterious hymn to creation in the Rig Veda. The hymn has seven verses. Within these seven pillars I nested six arches or zones: the stages of life and death. At Alec's suggestion, I called the piece *The Traveller*, to reflect our earthly journey.

To the four traditional stages of life in the Hindu scheme of things – childhood, youth, adulthood and old age – I added two more: those of the unborn and the dead. I searched for texts in various Indian languages – passages, both sacred and secular, that moved me and that suited these stages.

For example, the first Tamil text from the section on youth comes from an epic poem in which the husband of the heroine Kannagi is wrongly accused of stealing the Queen's ankle bracelet and is put to death. The first part of the extract is from the widowed Kannagi's accusatory lament, and the second from the Queen's premonition of the fall of the kingdom as a result of this injustice. The fury and courage of a young woman confronting the power of the state with the passion and rhetoric of raw grief was what forced this passage upon me. To Kannagi's incantatory speech I added the eerie, almost hallucinatory, vision of the prescient Queen.

I offered a preliminary choice of about twenty such passages to Alec in already existing translations and asked him to tell me which he wanted before I set about retranslating them myself. 'Oh, I want them all,' said Alec.

'But the piece will be an hour long,' I said.

'Well, then, they'll get more than they paid for. But I find all these passages inspiring. I've got to have them.'

So, pondering my tactical unwisdom, I got down to more work than I had bargained for.

The regular Hindi passages presented no serious linguistic problem. Hindi was my first language, and my grandmother insisted that I spoke no other for the first two and a half years of my life. The medieval Hindi of Kabir and the Brajbhasha of Surdas were familiar from literature studies at school as well as from songs. When I began translating the passages from Sanskrit, my long-forgotten schoolboy lessons in that language kicked in. This background helped a little with Pali as well. (There were problems, though, and choices to be made; in Pali, unlike in Sanskrit, the word *deep* is ambiguous, and the Buddha could have been telling his followers either to 'be to yourselves a lamp' or to 'be to yourselves an island'.) I had studied Urdu in order to understand the cultural world of the Muslim characters in *A Suitable Boy*, and had in fact already translated the two Urdu excerpts. When working on the Bengali poem, I was able to draw on the little Bengali that I had gained by osmosis from my mother, who speaks the language fluently. (I regretted, however, that there was no way in English to translate Ramprasad's wonderful pun on 'hope' and 'coming'.) For the texts from Tamil – a Dravidian language with an ancient literary tradition, utterly different from north Indian languages – I was forced to resort to a crib.

Apart from these translations, for each of the six stages of life I wrote a short poem of my own, each with the same number of syllables. The first three have a falling rhythm, and from poem to poem the lines get longer. The last three have a rising rhythm, and from poem to poem the lines get shorter.

My main reward for writing these libretti has always been the music. From the moment in the darkened cathedral that a small bell led into the first verse of the hymn to creation, I was held by the power of it.

> They say love is the reason why
> This soul of ours is bound with bone

could not have been more tenderly set. Nor could Kannagi's demand 'Is there a god?' have resonated with more indignation to the ancient roof and spire.

But the most memorable moment of all was absent; it did not yet exist. It was only created in time for the second performance, and it was wordless: when, towards the end, perhaps at the moment of death, the sound of the violin – 'the traveller', so to speak – wandered above the orchestra, gathering the threads of things that had gone before and weaving them into a meditation of unutterable loveliness, so that I was almost in a trance, only barely conscious that what I was hearing was being produced by human hands, and hands I knew, moving to and fro with one piece of wood against another, causing gentler elements to touch and vibrate and themselves set in motion the invisible, resonant air around.

The Traveller

1.1 Rig Veda 10.129 (Sanskrit, before 1000 BC*)
Creation Hymn Verse 1

There was no being or non-being then,
No world, no sky, no beyond.
What covered it? Where? Who sheltered it?
Was water there, unfathomably deep?

PART I: UNBORN

2. Dhammapada 1.1 (part), 11.146 (Pali, 4th century BC)

The mind precedes all states of being –
They are ruled by the mind,
They are made of the mind.

What is laughter, what is joy
When everything is burning?
Enclosed in darkness
Do you not seek a lamp?

* Several of these dates are uncertain

3. Six Ages: (1) Unborn (Vikram Seth)

Child of son, of daughter,
Tombed and wombed in water,
Flesh to bind and bound me,
Darkness all around me,
Neither seen nor seeing,
Being and not being,
In my world's cessation
Lies my re-creation.

4. Dhammapada 8.100–102 (Pali, 4th century BC)

Better than a thousand meaningless words
Is a single word that brings peace.

Better than a thousand meaningless verses
Is a single verse that brings peace.

And if one should recite a hundred verses,
All filled with meaningless words,
Better is a single word of truth
That brings peace.

Child of son, of daughter . . . &c. [repeat No. 3]

1.2 Rig Veda Creation Hymn Verse 2

There was no death, no immortality,
No sign of night or day.
Windless, that One breathed of its own accord.
Nothing else existed.

PART 2: CHILD

5. Children's Rhyme: Ram Ram Shah (Hindi)

Ram Ram Shah	Ram Ram Shah,
Alu ka rasa	Gravy made from spuds,
Mendaki ki chatni –	Chutney made from female frog –
Aa gaya nasha!	Drink it, and you're drunk!

6. Six Ages: (2) Child (Vikram Seth)

All these colours, named and nameless,
Beings, doings, aimed and aimless,
All these windows, walls and ceilings,
Moon and sun and words and feelings –
All these stars so high above me,
Bright with tears because they love me.

7. Krishna Wants the Moon (Surdas, Brajbhasha, 16th century)

'Mother, give me the moon with which to play
Or I won't come to your lap, but sulk on the ground all day. ⤴

I won't drink our cow Surabhi's milk or plait my hair.
I'll just be Papa's boy, and never yours – so there!'
'Listen, son, come closer to me – let's not tell your brother –
I'll get you a nice new bride!' says Krishna's smiling mother.
'Yes, Mother, yes, I swear by you, I'll marry right away.'
The poet adds: 'I'll pose as a guest and sing on that wedding-day.'

Ram Ram Shah . . . &c. [repeat No. 5]

8. *The Hope of Hope (Ramprasad, Bengali, 18th century)*

To come into this world: a hopeless call,
The hope of hope, that's all.
Like a deluded bee
Trapped on a painted lotus, who cannot struggle free,
So, Mother, am I, and you deluded me.
You called it sugar, while you fed me neem.
My sweet tooth, it would seem,
Has left me with this bitter mouth all day.
Saying to me, 'Let's play,'
Into this world you lured me, and I came.
But Mother, in your game
All happened as you willed
And nothing of my hope has been fulfilled.
Ramprasad says: On the world's scene
What had to be has been.
The evening now has come.
Pick up your child; go home.

All these colours, named and nameless . . . *&c. [repeat No. 6]*

1.3 Rig Veda Creation Hymn Verse 3

Darkness was covered by darkness in the beginning.
All this was indistinguishable water.
The germ of life, hidden by the void,
That One was brooded into being by heat.

PART 3: YOUTH

9. Dhammapada 18.251 (Pali, 4th century BC)

There is no fire like passion,
No grip like hate,
No snare like delusion,
No river like craving.

10. Shilappadikaram 19.51–59; 20.1–7 (Tamil, 7th century AD)

Are there women here, are there women
Who can bear such injustice to their husbands?
Are there women here? Are there such women?

Are there good men here, are there good men
Who nurture and protect their own children?
Are there good men here? Are there good men?

Is there a god here, is there a god
In this land where the power of the state kills an innocent man?
Is there a god here? Is there a god?   ~

Alas, I saw, I saw in a dream the sceptre and the parasol fall,
The bell by the palace gate toll by itself and resound.

Alas, I saw, I also saw the eight points of the compass waver
And darkness devour the sun.

Alas, I saw, I also saw a rainbow shine by night,
A glowing meteor fall by day. Alas!

11. Tirukkural 73; 1090; 1201 (Tamil, 4th century AD)

They say love is the reason why
This soul of ours is bound with bone.

When we drink wine, it gives us joy.
But with love, even the seeing is a joy.

With love, even the memory is sweet,
So love is sweeter than wine.

12. A couplet (Raheem, Hindi, 17th century)

Don't break the thread of love, Raheem has said.
What breaks won't join; if joined, it knots the thread.

13. Six Ages: (3) Youth (Vikram Seth)

Eyes sealed up with salt and heart charred through with fire,
All my charted days subverted by desire,
Who is this who weeps and who is this who's burning?
Who am I and why – and when am I returning?

1.4 Rig Veda Creation Hymn Verse 4

Desire came then in the beginning,
The first seed of mind.
Poets searching in their heart have found
The bond between being and non-being.

PART 4: ADULT

14. Six Ages: (4) Adult (Vikram Seth)

What can I build or do? What can I shape or form? –
From one and two make four, from cold and cold make warm?
What can I give the world? What can the world give me?
How can I render sight? How can I learn to see?

15. Bhagavad Gita 6.35 (Sanskrit, 2nd century BC to 2nd century AD)

Doubtless, O Arjuna,
The mind is hard to curb and restless;
But by practice and detachment
It can be held still.

What can I build or do? . . . *&c. [repeat No. 14]*

16. Bhagavad Gita 3.8; 18.23 (Sanskrit, 2nd century BC to 2nd century AD)

Perform the right action
For action is better than inaction:
Even the body's journey through life
Could not succeed without action.

The right action, performed without attachment,
Without passion, without hate,
Without desire for its fruits,
That action is called pure.

What can I build or do? . . . *&c. [repeat No. 14]*

17. Rise Traveller (from the Hymnbook of Gandhi's Ashram,
Hindi, 20th century)

Rise, traveller, the sky is light.
Why do you sleep? It is not night.
The sleeping lose, and sleep in vain.
The waking rise, and rise to gain.

Open your eyelids, you who nod.
O heedless one, pay heed to God.
Is this your way to show your love?
You sleep below, he wakes above.

Rise, traveller . . . *&c.*   ~

What you have done, that you must bear.
Where is the joy in sin then, where?
When on your head your sins lie deep,
Why do you clutch your head and weep?

Rise, traveller . . . &c.

Tomorrow's task, enact today,
Today's at once; do not delay.
When birds have robbed the standing grain
What use to wring your hands in vain?

Rise, traveller . . . &c.

1.5 Rig Veda Creation Hymn Verse 5

Their cord extended across.
What was above it? What beneath?
There were those with seed, those with powers –
Energy beneath, impulse above.

PART 5: OLD

18. Dhammapada 18.235 (Pali, 4th century BC)

You are now like a withered leaf.
The messengers of death are waiting.
You stand at the threshold of departure,
Yet have no provision for the journey.

19. Six Ages: (5) Old (Vikram Seth)

My eyes look back at me and say
Where were these wrinkles yesterday?
Where are the friends you used to know?
Where are the oats you used to sow?
Who is this stranger – foolish, wise –
Who stares at you with your own eyes?

20. Swollen with Pride (Kabir, Hindi, 15th century)

Swollen, swollen, swollen with pride, you wander.
On your ten months in the womb, why have you ceased to ponder?
Bees store honey, you store gold, but for all you gain here,
Once you're dead, they'll shout, 'Away! Don't let his ghost
    remain here.'
Your wife will follow to the door, your friends to your last station.
Then your soul's alone once more – no friend and no relation.
Burned, your body will turn to ash; buried, you'll lie rotten –
An unbaked water-swollen pot, you'll fall apart, forgotten.
Into the trap the parrot walks, lost in its own confusion.
Into the well of death falls Man, drunk with the world's delusion.

21. Mahaparinibbana Sutta, from D.xvi.2.25 and 2.26 (Pali, 5th century BC)

I have now grown old, Ananda, worn out, full of years,
approaching dusk. I am eighty years old. Just as an old cart is
kept going by makeshift repair, so too is it with my body.

Therefore, now, Ananda, be lamps to yourselves. Be a refuge
to yourselves. Seek no other refuge. Take the truth as a lamp.
Take the truth as a refuge. Seek no other refuge.

22. *From a Ghazal (Mir Taqi Mir, Urdu, 18th century)*

All my arrangements were in vain, no drug could cure my malady.
It was an ailment of my heart that made a final end of me.

My term of youth I passed in tears, in age I closed my eyes at last;
That is: I lay awake long nights till dawn and sleep came
  finally.

1.6 *Rig Veda Creation Hymn Verse 6*

Who really knows, who can declare
From where this creation came?
The gods themselves came later,
So who can tell from where it rose.

PART 6: DEAD

23. *Six Ages: (6) Dead (Vikram Seth)*

No breath to give or take,
No love to feel or make,
No thought or speech or deed,
No fear, no grief, no need,
No memory, no view,
No four, no three, no two,
No one, no entity
To be or cease to be.

24. Bhagavad Gita 2.11–2.17 (Sanskrit, 2nd century BC to 2nd century AD)

Though you speak words of wisdom,
You grieve for those for whom you should not grieve.
The truly wise grieve neither
For the dead nor for the living.

Never have I not existed,
Nor you, nor these kings,
Nor from this time on
Will we ever not exist.

The embodied self passes through
Childhood, youth, old age;
So does it pass into another body.
This does not perplex the wise.

Cold, heat, joy, sorrow
Come to us through the touch of matter.
What comes and goes is transient.
Arjuna, endure such things.

One whom these do not torment,
Who treats joy and sorrow alike
And is steadfast through all
Is fit for immortality.

What is not does not come to be.
What is does not cease to be.
Those who see the core of things
Know the truth about both these.

That which pervades this universe
Is indestructible.
No one can destroy
What cannot perish.

1.7 Rig Veda Creation Hymn Verse 7

Whence this whole creation has arisen,
Whether it was made or was not made,
He who surveys it from the highest heaven,
Only he knows; or perhaps he does not know.

EPILOGUE

Child of son, of daughter . . . *&c. [repeat No. 3]*

25. The Meeting Has Dispersed
(Munshi Amir Ahmad Minai, Urdu, 19th century)

The meeting has dispersed; the moths
  Bid farewell to the candle-light.
Departure's hour is on the sky.
  Only a few stars mark the night.

What has remained will not remain:
  They too will quickly disappear.
This is the world's way, although we,
  Lost to the world, lie sleeping here.

Seven Elements

Introduction to

Seven Elements

For the fourth and final year of the project, we reduced ourselves from the massed forces of the third year to just three performers: violin, tenor and piano. We agreed that there should be a song-cycle for tenor and piano; a suite or sonata for violin and piano; and a concluding piece for all three.

One year had related to China, one to Europe, one to India. But whereas these were zones of culture that I was familiar with, it was not at all clear to me what the theme for the fourth year should be. Various suggestions had been made by various listeners, as we'd hoped: why not try Australia, or Africa, or South America, or the oceans, or even outer space? But nothing seemed to click. I wanted the fourth year to be different somehow – and yet partake of something from the previous years, so that I could have in my text phrases and echoes of what had gone before. Since the first three years had dealt with various geographical spaces, perhaps the fourth could include the aspect of time. Then, I don't know quite how, the idea of the elements struck me, and I began working on a few poems based on these; but very slowly.

Shortly afterwards, I accepted an invitation from a literary festival in Milan: La Milanesiana. Its theme that year happened to be 'The Four Elements'. Alec's deadline was still some months off and I had been dawdling away. But my reading in Milan was due to take place much sooner than that, and this compelled me to write more and to waste my time less. (Not that I think wasting one's time is not a part of writing, but in my case it often seems to be the whole of it.) In due course, my seven poems were ready, all set to be translated into Italian.

But why seven – given only four elements? Well, apart from the four elements in the European tradition – earth, air, fire and water – in India there is a fifth element, a quintessence: space. And the five Classical Chinese elements overlap with these: they are fire, water, earth, metal and wood. By combining the elements of the three culture zones of the previous years, I had the subject for the concluding year. And somehow, through the elements, the oceans and nature and space and time were all included.

The effect of writing these seven poems about the elements was immediate and long-lasting. I began to see the world in sevens. The seven days of the week, the seven notes of the scale, the seven bright stars of the Great Bear, the seven animals that I have recently sculpted in different materials ranging from glass to plaster to wood to stone to steel to bronze to pewter. For some reason, the hotel in which we were housed in Milan had seven square black bottles of shampoo, conditioner, body lotion, hand cream, etc., with the labels Ira, Invidia, Superbia, and so on. This fed into my obsession, and I tried to connect the elements to the deadly sins. Of course, this sort of thing can drive you mad.

All seven poems were first recited in Milan, and published in an Italian newspaper. So, paradoxically, their first ever publication was in the form of a translation. I later showed them to Alec, and he seemed happy with them. He began setting them as his song-cycle. Parallel to these, he began writing his suite for violin and piano in seven movements, influenced both by the themes of the songs and by the music of the previous years.

The programming for the first half of the concert was planned to include seven Schubert songs loosely relating to the seven elements, followed by his entrancing 'The Shepherd on the Rock' in a transcription by Alec for tenor, piano and violin (in lieu of clarinet). So, by way of a parallel coda, I wrote an eighth poem which included all the seven elements and called it 'The Hermit on the Ice', to be set for the same performers.

Things seemed to be going along swimmingly and I was congratulating myself ón having finished my work on the entire project when I got a plaintive email from Alec.

One of the poems that had so pleased the Milanese audience did not please him at all. He liked the other six poems. But he couldn't do anything with 'Fire'.

'What's the matter with it?' I asked.

'Well, nothing really . . . I mean, everything.'

'So you don't like it?'

'Oh, I like it a lot . . .'

'Alec, you're talking in riddles.'

'It's just that it's a bit literary and, you know, indirect. The other poems I can work with.'

'And this one?'

'Fine as a poem, useless as a text.'

After a while he added, 'Couldn't you just go back and write something else?'

No, I said, I couldn't. This was the fruit of my inspiration. I couldn't go back to the muse and say, sorry, you've done your best and I've done my best, but my composer (who actually likes the poem) has nevertheless rejected our work. I was, in fact, quite annoyed. By now I had moved on and was working on other things. I couldn't revert to the elements just to appease a fussy composer.

But upon looking at the poems, I began to think that maybe Alec had a point. The other six poems – 'Earth', 'Air', 'Wood', 'Metal', 'Water' and 'Space' – related to their elements directly. In the case of 'Fire', however, I had worked much more metaphorically. I had used the sun and the moon as symbols of fire – and then used two characters to refer to these: one from Indian religious poetry, the infant Krishna; and the other from European drama, Oswald in Ibsen's *Ghosts*. This made things difficult for the audience – especially since everything was being sung. When reading a poem, you can slow down or even go back if you don't understand a reference, but you can't do the same when you're listening to a song. Alec was right; the poem wouldn't work.

But what could I do? Time was short, and I couldn't see how the same poet, within a couple of months, could write two completely different poems on the same subject and with the same title.

Eventually, as the deadline approached, Alec told me that the paradox was easily soluble. He suggested I go home and get drunk. This irresponsible advice worked. The muse – or maybe a different muse – re-emerged, not unwillingly, from the fumes of the wine, and the second poem, also called 'Fire', was born. I still don't know what to think of this particular poem, which is different from anything I have ever written. It sits in the middle of the libretto, and Alec has set it to some of his craziest music. But here, on the page opposite, is the rejected poem, which, though deprived of music, should not, I feel, be thereby deprived of existence.

Fire (1)

Mother, give me the moon.
I want it as my toy.
Mother, I want it soon
Or I'll be Papa's boy.
No, I won't plait my hair.
I won't go out to play.
I'll sulk on the ground all day.
I won't come to your lap – so there!
Nor will I drink this milk from Surabhi, our cow.
Mother, I want the moon – and I want it now.
Here in this bucket filled with water it scatters.
But that one there never shatters,
Cold in its silver fire,
Climbing higher and higher.
I now know, Mother,
You only love Balram, my brother,
Who loves to drive me wild.
He says you bought me, that I'm not your child.
No, don't sing me a tune.
Mother, give me the moon.
The moon, the moon.

Mother, give me the sun.
The horror, the horror has begun.
For ten years now my father has been dead.
This is his heritage, here in my sick head.
Who will rid me of my fear?
Regina would, her health and strength and cheer –
But she has gone and never will return.
Now everything will burn.

The orphanage has been consumed by fire.
My body is the wreckage of desire.
I burn, I burn away.
I'll lie like this for years, helpless and old and grey.
I didn't ask for life. I never sleep.
No, Mother, do not weep.
Help me to end my endless night.
The sunlight on the ice, this morning light.
I am cold. It is done.
Mother, give me the sun.
The sun, the sun.

Seven Elements

1. Earth

Here in this pot lies soil,
In which all things take birth.
The blind roots curve and coil
White in the sunless earth.
The soil slips over fire.
The great lands crack apart
And lava, pulsing higher,
Springs from earth's molten heart.

Here in this jar lies clay,
Dried clay, a whitened dust.
The moistened fingers play
To make it what they must.
The earth begins to reel,
Round, round, and near and far,
And on the potter's wheel
Is born another jar.

Here in this urn lies ash,
Dust uninfused with breath:
Burnt wood, burnt bone, burnt flesh,
The powdered clay of death.
The embers from the pyre
Sink on the rivered earth
And moistened into mire
Wait for a further birth.

2. Air

Air from your lips makes me vibrate,
Who am a tube of air,
And I make ripples where
Singing, singing,
I speak of joy and soothe the erratic pulse of hate.

Air from the sky slips past my arms
And buoys my tube of air
And thrusts me forward where
Winging, winging,
I soar above all earthly frenzies and alarms.

I am the stuff of death and birth,
Of wreck and of repair,
The unseen skin of air –
Clinging, clinging
To wrap and save for life the injured crust of earth.

3. Wood

A wooden bench. A wooden cuckoo-clock.
A pencil marks the surface of a pad.
Outside, a woodpecker goes pok-pok-pok.

A girl plays with a carved owl on a swing.
A log-pile lies beside a wooden bridge.
Listen: a bamboo flute begins to sing.

Some find the song too sad or too oblique.
I hear a wooden drumbeat sound from far.
The oak stirs in the wind; its branches creak.

~

The rains will come. The swing will rot and fray.
The logs will burn. The bench will crack and split.
The owl will break. The girl will move away.

The oak will die. The bridge will fall apart.
The cuckoo-clock and flute and drum will fade
But pok-pok-pok will echo in her heart.

As for myself, the nest is in my head.
The eggs are laid. The hatchlings will emerge
And pok-pok-pok will echo when I'm dead.

4. *Fire*

Fa-yaah
O fayah – fayah – fayaaah
Dizayaah
Hot hot hot
I'm burning a lot with dizayaah
O fayah fayah fayah
Hot as a filament wa-yah
Hot as prawn jamba-la-yah
I'm burning so hot
I'm baking a pot –
O hot hot hot as dizayaah
Fa-yaah! Fa-yaah!

All was born from me –
All your eyes can see.
Who gave life and birth
To sun and star and earth?

Who gave pulse and germ
To man and beast and worm?
Who is hot hot hot
When black space is not?
Who is bright bright bright
In this endless night?
Fa-yaah! Fa-yaah! Fa-yaah!

Fa-yaah
O fayah – fayah – fayaaah
Dizayaah
Hot hot hot
I'm burning a lot with dizayaah
O fayah fayah fayah
Hot as a funeral pa-yaah
Leaping up ha-yaah and ha-yaah –
I sizzle, I daze,
I fizzle, I blaze,
I scorch, I toast,
I smoulder, I roast,
I flare, I excite,
I flash, I ignite,
I rage, I lust,
I blaze, I combust,
Red, yellow, white,
I light up the night,
This endless night, with dizayaah,
O fa-yaah! Fa-yaah! Fa-yaah!

5. Metal

A steel tube on steel wheels upon steel rails.
A steel nib moves black fluid on the page.
Across from me sits a woman sadly looking
At the gold ring on her finger.
Around her neck is a gold chain with a cross.
She takes her mobile phone out of her bag
And taps its shining keys.

An aluminium tube thrust through the air.
Clunk goes my safety belt as I unclip it.
Near me tapping titanium keys
Sits a man in thought. From time to time he grips
The can of beer perched at the edge of his table.
He ignores the time on his screen and looks
At the platinum watch on his wrist, then out at the broad wings
That slice the sunset in two –

Cadmium red and orange, cadmium yellow and lemon.
Look, look, their tears fall down like mercury.
Trapped in their public and metallic zones,
On wheels, on wings, how can they shield their hearts
From the compulsive radium of love –
Or is it tarnished silver?

6. Water

The moon bobs in the river's spate.
The water's deep, the waves are wide.
Around my house lie springtime floods.
My friend and I drink tea inside.

Du Fu is singing at the mast.
Li Bai lies in his watery grave.
Far far away, on alien shores
The lashing breakers mourn and rave.

The hermit sits upon the ice.
The ice-bear moves from floe to floe
And from the hot spring newly bathed
Snow monkeys roll upon the snow.

The clouds disperse, the ropes thaw out.
Ice tinkles down from frozen sails.
The ocean churns and treasures rise:
Ambrosia and minke whales.

Slivers of ice brush past my face
As I swim in the icy bay.
A rumbling glacier calves a berg.
The watery sun shoots forth a ray.

The turbined vessel steams and steers
But cannot veer around the ice.
The beavers build but cannot dam
The stream that flows through Paradise.

Water destroys the unbaked pot.
Water is magicked into wine.

Water dissolves the fabled salt
And sinks the lover in the Rhine.

If only I were wine instead
Of water and my breath a cloud,
Of man's last disobedience and
This brittle world I'd sing aloud.

O water-being, drunk with gain,
Mere water are your brains and blood
And water are your flesh and tears
And water is the coming flood.

The ice-caps melt, the ports are drowned.
The current from the gulf is still.
The darkening planet drinks the sun
And cyclones swirl and whirl and kill.

Where are the islands of delight?
Where are the fields that now are dust?
Where is the crop of measured years?
I weep, I weep because I must.

The moon bobs in the river's spate.
The water's deep, the waves are wide.
Around my house lie springtime floods.
My friend and I drink tea inside.

My friend and I drink tea and wine.
Upon the pane our breath is steam.
Our tears flow down from grief and joy.
We dream and drink, we drink to dream.

7. Space

Space springs the stars apart.
Space fills the neutron's heart.
Air, water, earth, no less,
Are thin with emptiness.
We are such space-filled stuff,
How could we be enough
To be or touch or do,
To track black holes or view
Bright galaxies or trace
Dark matter spun through space?

To sense it, must we first
Return to space, dispersed? –
No soul in which to blend,
No life, no light to lend,
No breath to give or take,
No love to feel or make,
Stirless in zero space,
No entity, no place,
Ordained to retrogress
To shreds of nothingness.

THE HERMIT ON THE ICE

The hermit sits upon the ice.
The bluish light burns all around,
Immune to flame and sacrifice,
To breath and death and scent and sound.

The scent of pine, the river's roar
Are muted in his breath and pace.
The blue earth with its iron core
Spins on through time, spins on through space.

Note on Calligraphy by the Author

Songs in Time of War

The larger Chinese characters, to be read in vertical columns from right to left, are taken from Du Fu's poem 'Spring Scene in Time of War':

> The steady beacon fires are three months old.
> A word from home is worth a ton of gold.

Literally:

> beacon fire connect three month
> home letter worth 10,000 gold

The smaller characters – or colophon – without which the work would not be complete, state: 'Written by Xie Binlang at Autumn Waters Manor.'

Xie Binlang is my Chinese name, an emulation of Vikram Seth, with the surname first; Autumn Waters Manor is the name that was humorously given to the Old Rectory by my calligraphy teacher of many years, Zhao Yizhou, on his first visit there. It's a pun: the title of my favourite (and the most whimsical) chapter in Zhuangzi's philosophy is 'Autumn Waters'; and 'manor' has the same Chinese character as 'Zhuang'.

The style of the calligraphy is xing-cao or 'running cursive'.

The impression of the seal is red in the original work. The seal itself was carved by the late Zha Zhonglin.

Shared Ground

This is the handwritten poem 'Oak', which emulates the printed form of George Herbert's poem 'Easter-Wings'.

(In the first edition of 1633, and each subsequent edition, the poem has the shape of two hour-glasses. In the manuscript in the Dr Williams's Library in London, it has, far more aptly, given the words of the poem, the shape of two larks.)

The Traveller

These eight lines handwritten in Brajbhasha, a variant of Hindi, are the poem by Surdas, 'Krishna Wants the Moon'.

Seven Elements

This roundel is written in Arabic – which, like Chinese, represents one of the world's great calligraphic traditions. I studied Arabic calligraphy in the thuluth script for a few months with my teacher Nassar Mansour.

The numerals at the foot of the roundel indicate the year 1432, which in the Islamic calendar corresponds to 2011. In the image I have combined the words for the seven elements with seven bright stars in the night sky.

VS

Summer Requiem

2015

Summer Requiem

Since there is nothing left but this,
I shall watch the snakes as they twist across the plain.
They are independent of me like everything else.
Everyone I seek has a terror of intensity.
The liberated generation lives a restrained youth.
Stone by stone has been built across the mountain,
Yet people have broken their backs quietly gardening.
And whether the sheep escape or the radishes are blighted
Is all the same to me; I must forsake attachment.

The bells are ringing the tale of this city,
Gather and scatter, gather and scatter;
Down South, one sees the landscape flash green and white
'Showing no respect for space whatsoever';
In the nearby road, one shakes hands grimly.
Another is in 'a cocoon-like state' with anxiety,
Has eaten all my apricots, smiling, and now
I use my teeth as a nutcracker –
Only the stones are left, the nuts inside bitter.

Broken glass spangles the lawn;
Yesterday was revelry, so today we may not walk barefoot;
The shell of forgetfulness has broken sharply,   ⚡*

---

* a stanza break at the end of a page is marked by ~
no stanza break at the end of a page is marked by ⚡

The harmony warped in my hands.
Jaggedness and discontinuity, as if the pebbles
Smoothed by centuries were crushed again.
It is clear why men wish to live where linnets call
Or the green swell is in the havens dumb.
Birds are not desolate, impute how you may.

This garden was built for peace. But every day
Somewhere a lawnmower is grumbling busily,
Building chance events into a philosophy,
'Gather and scatter, gather and scatter'.
I have so carefully mapped the corners of my mind
That I am forever waking in a lost country.
Everything learnt has been trivial: on the evening road
I fumble to read the signpost with my fingers
Which claw so fiercely they're no use at all.

Returning to the wastes of expression,
I feel again dry ground, though sterile:
From the shining sea I was thrown back always
Into the harbours of regret.
I regretted my fingernails, my eyes . . .
The town bound knots, then tore the fibres open;
The ink ran out before there were things to say.
When the sky fell upon me in a blue shudder
I was left staring at the horizon.

Facts float like leaves
In my mind's calm river:
To have substance means to rot.
Cornflower and crocus have withered,
Acroclinium survives; it was always dry.

The cool of the evening brings relief to the sick fever –
Those loved eyes dead to me, those sighs stilled;
Late, late – even the rooks have flown home;
The hour of rust brings everything to a close.

Where the lock of longing was opened
There there will be a perpetual wound.
The steel cries out in grief, and there is no assuager;
Those who could have warmed are scattered,
And no one now can see the light in my window.
I stretch out my arms to the disbanded
But the flesh has pined away.
The crimson sun suspended on the dark spire
Can see me wander near the bridge.

Over the fields the pollen like last year,
The whistle of the train like – but, last year,
Last year I did not hear the whistle cry;
The sounds were a backdrop. Now with dead actors,
The canvas is all that remains of the history.
Bound and torn on the returning wheels, like pollen
Gathered and scattered, gathered and scattered,
What further pain can the future promise
To a wandering exile from heart to heart?

Memory is a poison; it has sickened my body.
The cleavage of attachment has frayed my mind.
Rabid and weary, autistic, spasmodic,
Exhaustion makes me dance like a puppet.
New gargoyles are carved, new stones cleaned;
Within ten weeks the old constructs are broken;
Magnolia and tulip rushed in and out of bloom;   ⨍

Rose and wistaria rush in and out of bloom;
Perpetual replacement is the only song of the world.

All striving lapsed, the reclaiming grass has covered
The brick and stone and earth and the steepest agony –
Invulnerable, cold, immune to pain;
The day sees me dreaming of sensitive hands
And of the dance of warmth across my skin.
The sun bursts through his disguise and sprinkles
Gold on the world; and the hours pass
In silent emblems of despair. Bee-filled hibiscus-filled
Summer songs underline winter.

The common air envelops the old beech.
Swinging from pain, the heart
Revels in its surroundings, and forgets; but they
Stun the air and blur my world, being absent.
In the summer's trap, one theme alone
Like the thin persistence of the flute
Upon the stifling air, attacks, attacks.
It sings that to be alive is a delicacy,
Clear filigreed glass in a vaulted hall.

The evening sun retreats along the lawn;
The broken diamonds shine on the lawn;
I stand by the city wall and hear the chimes
Collect and shower sound upon the city.
The words were here, engraved in earth and weed,
The words I read too late. I can remember
I stood two years ago, where now I watch
The summer turn to bitterness and fruit
And slow unsheltering of skeletal trees.

~

Between the chorus of the stars and of the birds
It released itself slowly, it turned away,
And next day under the misty wave
Of need it was unwetted. Thus atrophied
The love for lack of loving, the lovers through fear.
Now only the empty doors mark empty houses;
The rusted tracks lead to dead embankments,
The signals are always down, and whistles
Are forever smearing the air with grief.

The town is indifferent; a scrapyard claw,
It lifts and deposits elsewhere on the earth's grid.
The opened rose closes, and welcomes night,
And lets the seat of joy become a grave.
Mist lifts the cold plantations of the dew.
I recreate a hunger for the dead eyes
That tuned these discordant wires and made them sing,
Walking tranquillised in the mist, under
The serene and tender evening star.

Still day's death, across the fields
All swallows have flown.
The summer red sinks into the flowing dark.
From the field's corner fade the voices of the children.
Dark, as in some peace,
Twists the key of silence.
The beech proclaims power over the grasses.
Sombre thoughts become this hour,
Hour of red copper, rust, dark iron.

A Cryptic Reply

Abstractions have their place, the concrete too.
Opacity is nothing rare in you.
Prudence and love – that true link makes me smile.
A sea change may take long, or just a while.
The sun stays where it is, so does the sea.
It is the clouds and haze, the you, the me
(It's good that you imagine my concern)
That vary with the hours, burn off, or burn.

If friends are always elsewhere, never here,
Do more than just their features grow unclear?
I too will hope to look you up some day.
We each need love in our own time and way.
To ponder wholeness or to shape debris
Requires some sense of incoherency.
Since, with the tears, you sense a touch of peace,
Why hope that this or that or both should cease?

As for myself, the hope I had is gone,
And not much left in lieu to build upon.
Tale of two cities, three to be exact:
High on elation, short – I guess – on fact.
Great expectations – cue to shake my head –
Still, nothing I could wish I had not read.
My work continues, as it did before;
And sometimes I'm surprised I ask for more.

Late Light

At three the late light glides across
The last gold leaves on the black ground.
The snow is near, as is my loss:
The peaceful love I've never found.

Outside the great world's gifts and harms
There must be somewhere I can go
To rest within a lover's arms,
At ease with the impending snow.

Fellows' Garden

Despite the blights and doubts of love,
The windswept copper beech above,
Incognizant of what and why,
Tattered the puzzle of the sky.

When, snivelling on my grieving knees,
I'd feed the College tortoise peas,
The torpid glutton, on the whole,
Poured balm on my afflicted soul.

And from my unrequited heart
All Angst and Weltschmerz would depart
As spiteful mallets clicked away
A Christ Church twilight of croquet.

O mighty loves and griefs long gone,
Why won't your details linger on?
Why should it be that I recall
Beech, beast and mallet – and that's all?

Evening Across the Sky

Evening across the sky –
The glow dies in the west.
The last crows fly,
Cawing, each to its nest.
An early moon is here.
The stars appear.
Safe from all thought, all fear,
Now, heart, find rest.

Sleep dreamlessly.
Forget what chafed or held you fast.
Settle such quarrels with eternity;
The stars won't last.
The moon will die,
Earth, evening, you and I.
There are no fixtures in the sky
Free from the growing past.

Far from the City Tonight

Far from the city tonight, how bright are the stars –
How red is Betelgeuse, how red is Mars.
That such grand worlds should be mere points of light
Seen from our own seems less than strange tonight
When those worlds grand in their complexity
Known by their lesser names of you and me,
For all their flair and depth and hankerings
Hold less dimension in the scheme of things.

Can't

I find I simply can't get out of bed.
I shiver and procrastinate and stare.
I'll press the reset button in my head.

I hate my work but I am in the red.
I'd quit it all if I could live on air.
I find I simply can't get out of bed.

My joints have rusted and my brain is lead.
I drank too much last night, but now I swear
I'll press the reset button in my head.

My love has gone. What do I have instead? –
Hot-water bottle, God and teddy bear.
I find I simply can't get out of bed.

The dreams I dreamt have filled my soul with dread.
The world is mad, there's darkness everywhere.
I'll press the reset button in my head.

Who'll kiss my tears away or earn my bread?
Who'll reach the clothes hung on that distant chair?
I must, I simply must get out of bed
And press that reset button in my head.

What's in it?

I heard your name the other day
Mentioned by someone in a casual way.
She said she thought that you were looking great.
A waiter passed by with a plate.
She reached out for a sandwich, and your name
Went back from where it came.

But like a serious owlet I stood there,
Staring in mid-air.
I frowned, then followed her around
To hear, just once more, that sirenic sound –
Those consonants, those vowels – what a fool!
I show more circumspection as a rule.

I love you more than I can say.
Try as I do, it hasn't gone away.
I hoped it would once, and I hope so still.
Someday, I'm sure, it will.
No glimpse, no news, no name will stir me then.
But when? But when?

Caged

I lie awake at night, too tired to sleep,
Too fearful you should wake, too sad to weep.

I hear you breathe. I do not touch your face.
How do we live like this, caged in one space?

We two have lost each other, you and I.
Why could this not wait till our love could die?

Poor, pointless relic bent on staggering on
When courtesy and passion both have gone,

And all our energy, enhanced when paired,
And happiness, once multiplied when shared.

Light seeps out from the blind; what will it bring,
This day that could but will not change a thing? –

The litanies that bleed the heart before
It understands that it can bleed no more,

The bitter tone that taints our every speech,
The thoughts that we attribute each to each

As if we were not friends but manacled foes,
As if one sorrow were two private woes.   ~

What grew with time took time to disappear,
But now we see that there is little here.

We are ourselves; how much can we amend
Of our hard beings to appease a friend?

We cannot lose our ways, and cannot choose
To lose what then it would be peace to lose.

May love be ground away like all the rest
From those who are already dispossessed.

This Room

I love this room; this room means you to me.
The sun shines in, and sometimes music plays.
These books, this bed, this fan, that rug, these rays –
Predate and will outlast this ecstasy.
Wise to my heart, I'd rather not be free.
Let me meander on from heat to haze.
These things are everything, as are these days.
My aim will be the aim of things: to be.

Things to Say

I never look for things to say.
They find me and they crush my jaw.
They stop my mouth and mash my clay.
The slightest feather burns me raw.
They seek me where I cannot hide.
The air, the pollen and the leaf
Pursue me into omnicide
And pack my wordlessness in grief.

The Halfway Line

The scorpions in the bottle squirmed,
So mad with greed or zeal or hate,
That no one cared what thing he harmed:
Himself, his rival or his mate.

The bottle crashed, but each still stretched
His claws towards the halfway line
Marked on the broken glass, and retched
Out venom from an absent spine.

In Touch

If you can do so, read these words at night.
Lie down as if to sleep, turn off the light.

Now read me with your hands, as light as Braille.
My words may fail you, but your touch won't fail.

It will make true what now my heart can see –
You whom I don't know are in touch with me.

The cues of pain or grace are blind from birth,
Blind to the torque, blind to the tilt of earth.

Read out your words in lieu of mine, and I,
Far now, or dead, may ease them by and by.

Bright Darkness

My hands dissolve in water.
My body wastes away.
The air drifts past and through me
Each night and every day.

Bright darkness is my comfort,
Dark daylight is my friend,
And even I can't reckon
Where I subsist or end.

Not Now, Not Soon

Not now, not soon, but not too far,
May you not still be as you are,
Untouched by love for any being,
Unsearable, unstung, unseeing.
May you know love, and may it be
Returned to you as willingly.
If not, well, may you love in vain,
And know, if not that joy, this pain.

One Morning

One morning when the world was dark
My feet led me towards the park.
A blackbird sang an easy tune.
A contrail underlined the moon.
Dark horses crushed the plane leaves, white
With frost, then galloped out of sight,
And distant traffic, with a sound
Like muffled thunder, sped around.

Rose light enflamed the eastern sky.
A greyhound, masterless, loped by.
A poplar's black denuded crest
Thinned to reveal a magpie's nest.
On the red lake two snowy geese
Swam in a sarabande of peace,
And as I breathed the callous air
I lost the drift of my despair.

Parrots at Sunset

The parrots pair and nest
Now day is almost done.
Earth rises in the west
Against the reddened sun.

The hills assert their ranks –
Near, far and farther yet.
I give uncertain thanks
For the one world I'll get.

One sun, not two; one moon,
Not three. Four decades more,
I'd say, at most – and soon
I too, like those before

Who saw some rose-ringed pair
Of parrots court and nest,
Will, mixed with fire and air,
Disperse myself to rest.

The Yellow Leaves

The yellow leaves glint by; the branches merge and part;
 The clouds move past the window brightly.
What is this heaviness that won't unclench my heart,
 My work by day, my spirit nightly?

The year has months to go, the house is much the same,
 The universe is undiminished;
Nor is the darkness new, nor this ungiving game
 That waits till it or I am finished.

Day and Night

This was a day that came and went.
I don't know how the day was spent.
The sun rose up and reached its height.
The sun went down and it was night.
Somehow the hours that passed between
Dispersed as if they'd never been
Though I attended every one
Till both the day and I were done.

Sleepless, exhausted and perplexed,
Not knowing what is coming next,
I sense the stab of causeless fears,
The tedium of pointless tears.
Lonely, yet lacking will to find
One who could ease my limbs and mind,
I wait once more for faceless day
To blind the peaceless night away.

Late at Night

Late at night I lay awake,
Hearing in my spirit's ache
Voices I had eased away
In the bright forgiving day.

Through the hours of truth I heard
Like the driven fever-bird
Flinging out its cries of three
Every voice accusing me

Till I cried out in my fear:
Here I am, and you are here.
You can halt my heart, I know.
Do it then and let me go.

But the voices, soft somehow,
Whispered to my spirit now:
Live you must, for we must too
And we have no home but you.

Prayer for my Novel

Whatever force outside me moves my hand
And gives me strength to dream and understand,
Let me, by grace enlivened and by skill,
Enliven those who lived, and those who will.

The Shapes of Things

The shapes of things that are not here
Appear, disperse, and reappear:
A room, a face, a photograph,
A book, a letter or a laugh,
A turn of phrase or hand or mind,
Ungiven gifts you've left behind,
Each day recall themselves to me,
Altered into reality.

Things that are here and were before,
These too are altered at the core:
This pen, this bunch of keys, this chair,
The towel you used to dry your hair,
The song you sang whose words I knew
A year before I'd heard of you,
Even these hands, that felt your touch,
Though much the same, have altered much.

Red Rock
for Roger Howe

At Red Rock beach the waves come in.
The oystercatchers flap away.
The sun sinks into sand and skin
At four o'clock on Boxing Day.
    The bass thump of a volleyball
    Resounds below a skua's call.

The toddlers flap like little seals
Towards the magnet of the ocean,
Ignoring piteous appeals
From mothers bright with suntan lotion.
    I drink a bitter and a stout,
    Swim for a bit, and come back out.

The curved creek-current thrusts us through
Towards the sea, then back to shore.
To close the ring of gold and blue
We walk across the sand once more
    And float along the current's length,
    Resisting nothing but our strength.

And there – beyond the surf – a fin!
A curved back – and another – three!
Three dolphins ballet in the din
In bottle-nosed felicity.

How beautiful! They turn to greet us.
We love them, since they cannot eat us.

Ah, may it always be like this –
But '92's another year,
And an unkind antithesis
Lurks in a colder hemisphere.
      Advance, advance, Australia Fair –
      Next year I'll freeze, though God knows where.

In Shimla, fingernumbed and scowling,
In New York on a chilblained street,
In London with the north wind howling
Or vile Vienna in the sleet.
      Yet I'll be warm wherever I go
      If Red Rock burns beneath the snow.

Evening Scene from my Table

Evening is here, and I am here
At my baize table with a glass,
Now sipping my unfizzy beer,
Now looking out where on the grass

Two striped and crested hoopoes glean
Delicious insects one by one.
A barbet flies into the scene
Across the smoky city sun.

My friends have left, and I can see
No one, and no one will appear.
This must be happiness, to be
Sitting alone with birds and beer.

In a brief while the sun will go,
And grand unnerving bats will fly
Westward in clumped formations, slow
And dark across a darkened sky.

Haiku

through the winter night
sleep won't come and thoughts go round:
yowling cats on heat

finally at dawn
through my lids a sense of light,
in my mind a dream

i have lost the key,
now i'm flying, now i'm late,
now the dream lets go

safe in my razai
from the cold, i wonder how
i can hear this buzz

a mosquito's here –
out of season, out of tune,
homing in on blood

let me sleep in peace,
o mosquito, fact or dream,
till the crack of noon

then i'll get to work:
seven novels, seven plays,
seven children's tales

through the trees they sing
– sagging cables, unmaintained –
songs of speech and light

doors, bicycle bells,
sounds of cricket, car horns, dogs,
hawkers' cries and crows

sunset through the smoke
of the city to the west;
to the east a moon

full and gold and still;
by the wall the neighbour's guard
crouches by his fire

i too once was young
and these eyes that watch these hands
were not as they are

sometimes i recall
something of another face,
of another touch

just one room is left.
what may i put in it now
that there's not much time?

Tripping on a Bus

This is the schedule –
Give it away!
(Let it not stay.)
Give it to the lady –
The lady?
The lady who draws so beautifully
A face from Holbein,
Seated in the Greyhound bus depot
Waiting to go
To San Diego.
Give something to the lady.
(A smile, a cookie, a message . . .)

I see no lady.
An old woman, tired of despair,
Dreaming that tonight she will be happy
And put away sorrow for a year or two.
There will be sunflowers,
The scent of juniper, hay.
There will be coffee, the love of grandchildren.
Birthdays will be remembered . . .
She looks at the lovers with interest.

The sour conductor opens the gate.
Everyone is happy –
But look, the lovers are not happy –

They embrace, she is embracing him and crying.
He is saying something, she is not replying.
I think he is saying, 'Come back soon.'
(But she is not going to the moon.)
The lady looks perplexed and does not know
If this is the bus to San Diego.
The sour conductor's cheeks begin to glow –
'See, lady, see this sign – it says San Diego. S, A, N . . .'
The lady looks dignified. The lovers embrace again.

Not a word, not a word through the journey.
We look out the window:
A nuclear plant – two scoops of radioactive ice-cream –
Disneyland – where life is but a dream –
The crisp line of the sea . . .
I look at the lady.
O God! She too is crying,
As if a world were dying.
The sunset burns out with a terrible glow.
The bus pours on towards San Diego.

Tercets to Parsnip

Do not go screaming into that good pot.
Some like it tepid and some like it hot.
Some like your crossword and some like it not.

I've finished it. Would that I'd not begun.
Fine words were there, but when all's said and done,
They margarined a parsnip, buttered none.

The Infinite
translated from the Italian of Giacomo Leopardi

This lonely hill was always dear to me
And this hedge too, that keeps so large a part
Of the ultimate horizon from my view.
But as I sit and gaze, interminable
Spaces beyond it come to mind, unearthly
Silences, and deep, deep quiet – and for
A little while my heart lets go its fear.
And as I listen to the wind storm through
These branches, I compare its voice to that
Infinite silence; and eternity
Comes to my mind, all the dead ages, all
That lives and is, and all its noise. In this
Immensity my thoughts drown, and it is
Sweet to me to be shipwrecked in this sea.

To the Moon

translated from the Italian of Giacomo Leopardi

O gracious moon, I recall how last year
I came to this hill and watched you, full of pain,
And you hung there over that wood, just as
You do now and fill everything with light.
But nebulous and tremulous through the tears
That filled my eyes, your face appeared to me,
So troubled was my life; and is; nor has
It changed its style, beloved moon. And yet
It gives me pleasure to remember and
To count the stages of my sorrow. How
Pleasant it is, when one is young, and the path
Of hope is long and that of memory short,
To call to mind once more things from the past,
However sad, and though the pain endures.

Sonnet

translated from the French of Pierre de Ronsard

I can't love anyone who isn't you.
I don't know how to. No, my lady, no –
Venus herself could come to earth below
And not delight my heart the way you do.

So sweet, so gracious are these eyes I view,
A single glance from them is like a blow
That kills me, while the next one may bestow
Life where the first gave death – two worlds in two!

If I lived for five hundred thousand years,
Believe me, dearest love, and trust your ears:
I could love no one else – no one, nowhere.

I'd have to fashion other veins; my own
Are now so filled with love for you alone,
Nobody else could find a lodging there.

In a Small Garden in Venice

You and the girls will come back in a week
From your long Russian summer sojourn – and I,
Who haven't used it, will relinquish it.
Today I came to see if the plants were parched,
Sat at this wooden table, and claimed its peace.
I reach up to the trellis and taste a grape.
Which shall I crush with these too-restless fingers:
Rosemary, lavender – or that tomato leaf
Within whose shadow a gecko climbs the wall?
Domestic sounds are all I hear – a bottle,
Footsteps, a muted radio; the canal,
Its engine-gusts and thrum, is far away.
Few folk walk down the calle. This nest is green.
The sky is cobalt. Dull geraniums
Mark, but don't blare forth from the house beyond
That wall of yellow stucco and of stone.
The shutters are all shut and I'm alone.

Alone? Not quite. For in the small dark room
Just within doors with a table and narrow bed
– Cool, cool, a sanctum from this blaze of blue –
Two oval portraits, prints in black and white,
Lean on a shelf; one of them, Pushkin, who
Never stepped out of Russia in his life,
Let alone roamed around this town, but who
Belongs to you who know his works by heart

And, yes, to me, who, though I cannot read
A word of his by eye, know him by soul.
I wouldn't be here, were it not for him.
He gave me me. This morning, when I turned
The rabbit-key lent by your younger daughter,
I thought of visiting him, yet feared I'd lose
All that I had marked out to do today
By standing in a trance, held by his eyes,
His replicated, ageless paper eyes,
As once I stood five hours holding his book
In Stanford Bookstore, and forgot all else
– My economics lectures, food and drink,
Appointments, unpaid bills, the world, my friends,
Myself – what? – almost thirty years ago.
Translation though it was, though every Russian
– Yes, you included, when I met you first,
Before the concert in that cavernous room –
Shakes her head slowly when I mention this
In wistful sympathy ('What can they get
From Pushkin who can't understand our tongue?'),
Yet what I got, I got – and it got me
Out of myself, into myself, and made me
Set everything aside I'd set my thoughts on,
And grasp my time, live in his rooms and write
What even today puzzles me by its birth,
The Golden Gate, that sad and happy thing,
Child of my youth, my first wild fictive fling.

    The sun has edged itself across the table
Under the trellis. Now my mobile phone
Has turned too hot to touch, and now my head
Has turned too hot to think with, and I've come

Withindoors and am lying on the bed,
Limbs loose, hands slack. Pushkin looks down on me
As sleep and desperation melt my brain.
A clock ticks softly; on its face, IV
Instead of four I's, marks the hour of four.
My eyes begin to close, the sea to roar.

    Howling with fear, an Adriatic storm
Washes across the Black and Baltic Seas.
The Tiber teems with sharks; St Petersburg
Froths white with eels and monkfish, while a pike
Twelve metres long patrols the Grand Canal,
Capsizing gondolas and eating all
The honeymooning couples it can find.
I ply my small shikara filled with flowers
From shore to houseboat and to shore again,
Singing to ease the seas and the sad hearts
Of those who have lost friends to tooth and fin,
To eely turbulence and monkfish roil,
Casting chrysanthemums upon the waves
To calm the agony of single souls,
All those whose lovers are with them no more,
Till all is still on houseboat and on shore.

    And then I find myself alive once more
(Although I would have been content to end
Somewhere within that world) and since I am,
I wander out into the humid, green
And shadowless – now clouds obscure the sun –
Small garden where a gecko climbs a wall.
The lilies of the valley in the well,
That roundel filled with mud, are flowerless.   ⚘

Mosquitoes range at will, squat pigeons flap
Around me in the heavy air, the grapes
Look plump and green and sinister – and the steps
I hear beyond the wall, more frequent now
That it's the hour to go back home, speak out
Like a soft tattoo on an untuned drum:
Return to where you're loved, to the sound of a spoon
Against the wall of a pan, to a welcoming voice –
And I imagine someone pouring out
A glass of something under the trellised growth
To me and my companions, poets both.
Crushed grape within fused sand; they smile at me,
Nod at each other and drink silently.
The gecko does not speak and nor do they.
They have said all they came to earth to say.
Alone again, I toy with what they've left:
Fashioned from the lagoon, a common gift.
I turn the hourglass to re-sieve its sands,
A fragile monument half-built by hands.

Minterne: Four Poems

commissioned by Veronica Stewart for the Lady Digby to celebrate the 45th anniversary of the Summer Music Society of Dorset, set to music by Jonathan Dove and performed on 30 August 2007 in Minterne, Dorset by Patricia Rozario (soprano), Philippe Honoré (violin) and Steven Isserlis (cello)

1768; 2007

The roar
Of cannon shot
From shattered men-of-war,
The smoke, the screams of pain, the hot
Shudder of battle past, he turns to greet
The arts of peace for war, and for salt-water sweet:
Cascade and lake and stream and pool, not one straight line
– Even an oval cellar for his wine –
His sails furled up, his oaks and turf
Set down and, far from shore,
Of wind, not surf,
The roar.

Clear chords
And melody,
Still more than sails and swords
– Though born a daughter of the sea –
Give her delight – or both delight and pain,
Since music lives in each, and quickens each again.
Close on these walls rest snake and dove: an ancient tune
Entwining grief with joy, and night with noon.
All this she hears – and shares with love,
With words or without words,
Rich decades of
Clear chords.

Which Way?

Should I then say, can I then know
    Which way the wind should blow –
Across the grass, beyond the mulberry tree?
      For now I see
The sky in tatters – all the clouds awry
    And soon I will not see the sky.
    It will be closed, I will be dead
And all I wish to say will stay unsaid.

How could I know, when first I came,
    Nothing would be the same?
Where is the hedge, where is the hill beyond?
      No reed or frond,
No lake – a zone of mist, in which I stray,
    And soon I will have lost my way.
    Alone, I wander where I choose,
And soon there will not be a me to lose.

Rocking-Horse

Now there's something something Waterloo and something
   Tráfalgár
And it's far too sunny nowadays, too sunny, yes, by far –
And all I really want to do is ride a camel through
The Kalahari desert and across the Great Karoo.

Oh the confidence of houses with a rocking-horse or three,
Oh the ducks and coots that swim across a blue infinity,
Oh the dry-rot and the wet-rot and the loneliness of beams
And the empty Bath and Garter and the solid stuff of dreams.

Now the afternoon is burning and it must be half past three
And Mama is getting restless, but that doesn't bother me
And Papa is fighting France today unless he's fighting Spain
And I'm either three or thirty – which I'll never be again

And the day is past and passing and the afternoon is hot
And it's something something Waterloo unless, of course, it's
   not –
And it's tugging of the forelock or the foreskin to the squire
And the people down from London and the gentry of the
   shire   ~

And the music music music and the trees and trees and trees
And the duty to one's neighbours and the conquest of the
   seas
And this little nook of England and this heritage so rare
And the universe goes onwards and it doesn't really care

But it's ninety-six for seven and it's seventeen to three
And it's nine to four against us and it's getting late for tea
But the fig-tree has the oak-tree in an afternoon of fears
And the rocking-horse is sinking and the jockey is in tears

And the afternoon is fading and the tapestry is torn
And the universe is dying and the Aubusson is worn
But I love to sing regardless and I'll sing until I drop
But now the song is over and I don't know how to stop

So I'm something something singing in a something
   something song
And you're very very welcome to keep mum or sing along
But my baby brother's crying and the mercury is high
So until tomorrow afternoon I have to say goodbye.

The Tree of Many Names

One morning, one morning in May
As we strolled hand in hand beneath the tree
The sun rose. We could see
The fluttering doves emerge from out the mist.
There was no more to say.
We kissed.

One evening, one evening in May
As I strolled by myself beneath the tree
The moon rose. I could see
The handkerchiefs that shivered as they slept.
There was no more to say.
I wept.

One midnight, one midnight in May
As, old at last, I strolled beneath the tree
The starlight let me see
The trembling ghosts that wooed me as they cried.
There was no more to say.
I died.

***

Suzhou Canal on a June Night

I close my eyes to sense.
Above, a magpie cries.
Magnolias shed their scent.
The North wind soughs and sighs.

It brings the petals down
To graze against my hand.
The dialect of the town
Comes to me where I stand:

Softvoiced and liquid speech
Of quietcultured folk,
Two women's voices, each
Mellifluous. I stroke

The parapet of the bridge,
Held by the blind delight,
The sense of privilege
Of being here tonight.

The turning wind asserts
The foetid, useful noise
Of the canal. Late boats
Unload. With opened eyes

~

I see the boats swing through
Below me, and my gaze
Turns to the distant roofs,
To unrecovered days,

While in curved dark above
A half-obscured half-moon
Now jokes of endless love,
Now mourns for passing June.

The Forms Lie on the Table

The forms lie on the table, the paperclip removed.
The animal-cycle table is unfolded.
'What's your name?' I ask the staring boy.
The boy carefully spits on the floor, and smiles.

His grandfather puffs at his Double Happiness cigarette
And thinks of cement and lintels; he and his son
Are building a house, and forms are outside his ken
But he is polite and describes his expenditures.

The accountant's door faces panels of green
As yet untransplanted rice. Three women pass,
Bearing the harvested rape. The old man sighs
And says, 'My second brother was a pig.'

'That makes him 45 years old'; I fill the space
With a Bic pen. The boy looks at it
With wonderment at its transparency.
A picture of Lady White Snake looks down from the wall.

The abacus clicks, a chicken strays into the room.
The old man says that the Japanese burnt and killed.
The accountant mentions the Guomindang conscriptions.
The boy has heard this before and strokes his chin.   ~

A weasel runs along the embankment of the fields
And into the standing stalks. The golden goslings
Struggle into the pond. The oxen bolt
Towards the wheat despite the woman's curses.

And there beyond the trees the Great River flows
And flows onwards and onwards and its rippled gold
Pours itself onwards past the mulberry hills
And the investigators and investigated and the black tiles of
    roofs.

Dark

Now night.
The buses hum.
Cicadas –
It will not come,

The mood of night,
Of letting be,
Of letting darkness
Enter me.

The fear that oozed
Through sun and dust
Is moon-appeased.
I must

Not tremble for what died
Nor mourn for culm or grain
But case the root
For spring to quicken again.

For spring, for dawn
Against the stun of light.
Let it be. Let it grow.
Let there not be light.

A Winter Room

The sparrows bob from frosty twig to twig
Against an under-lit sky.
She sets down her cup and laughs.
When he asks why,
She says they remind her of something.
It would be too tedious to explain.
Nothing, no, she's not being secretive.
She laughs again.

How could he not be happy
Sitting here in this chair,
Hearing her laughter thaw the room,
He here, she there?
She gets up, goes to the sill.
He stirs his tea,
Sips, frowns, joins her at the window.
They watch the frozen tree.

Western Highlands

Across the loch, its surface malachite-pure,
The mist unravels from the farther shore.
I stumble upon a track in the faltering light.
Grey-veiled red deer pause in the stance of flight.

Full Circle

The circle from indifference
To new indifference
For you is perfect, but for me
The present still is tense
With rigid reminiscences that come
Unwished – of you, your home.

Gently I sift this great compacted
Stock of memories:
The house whose name evokes the wind
Through early-woken trees
Growing around and sheltering the lawn
With silhouettes of dawn;

How fine you looked, after hard mowing,
Resting in the clear shade;
And when, with the first touch of evening,
With casual skill you made
The hearth's full complement of log and coal
Blaze with a wild control;

The room of the two keyboards where,
Unwinding, we fed ourselves
On Bach; the files of bright-spined books
Ranged on its heavy shelves

Through which on spendthrift afternoons we browsed;
The warm and open house.

Last night when from that pitted roadway
I wandered as I dreamt,
The trees were bent, hostile, entangled,
Weeds massed and grass unkempt,
The house locked and the only key inside;
Ingress denied.

No Further War

We are the last generations; Surdas, Bach,
Rembrandt, Du Fu, all life, love, work and worth
Will end in the particular rain; no ark
Will screen its force, no prayer procure rebirth.
The government of nations is assigned
Sage, journeyman and lunatic by rota;
A couple of toxic madmen sting mankind
Each century; we won't escape the quota.
Dead planet of an unimportant star,
Beautiful earth, whose radiant creation
Became too radiant, no further war,
No suffering, frenzy or recrimination
Will litter your denatured crust or mar
Your deepening entropy with agitation.

Spring Morning

Wistaria tremble in the breeze.
As he hangs out his sheets, he hears
The medley of a mockingbird
Leap from a live-oak into his yard.
Two sparrows quarrel as they pass
To ruffle the sunned and shadowed grass,
Emerald with March rain, rich with weeds.
He thinks a little of his needs.

Sunday. He wraps a sourdough loaf
In foil and puts it in the stove.
No cat. No paper. No telephone.
His balance: that he is alone.
Light; work; a postcard from a friend.
He sees, as he breakfasts in a band
Of sun, pollen float through the door
Onto the breadcrumbs on the floor.

Meanwhile, cerulean days extend
Perturblessly without an end.
Wistaria or a sparrows' feud
Or ants adventuring through a wood
Of tall grass, let his heart be free
Of grand ferment. If eternity
Is long, he can link days to days.
The sun is generous; there are ways.

Cloud-Cancers

White on the sheet of night they fly,
Gulls, gliding on the ferry's smoke,
    While the waves lunge and lapse
    Along the delusive kelp-strung shore.

Here too the motion of the earth
Is palpable; here too he gives
    Himself to the place, the being,
    Changeable, that will not betray.

Cloud-cancers grip the derelict Bear.
There is no bitterness in his thoughts.
    He cannot believe, but prays
    To night, the earth, the moon, the waves,

This permanent and inconstant sea.
The great seals stare, while from the dark
    Gulls' yawp or sharp unsifted
    Echo of song exhausts his ears.

Old in his soul? The tapering mist,
Like unedged knowledge of love, sustains
    His heart till a new light,
    Slow to dawn, dawns in its time.

Index of Titles, First Lines and Last Lines

Eyes sealed up with salt and heart charred through with
  fire, 544

To make love with a stranger is the best.   152
To Manijeh   33
To shreds of nothingness.   570
To the Moon   615
To torture me.   462
To Wei Ba, Who Has Lived Away from the
    Court   173, 289, 513
To wrap and save for life the injured crust of earth.   564
To Yin Chuang   229
Tomatoes   28
Tourists   191
Tripping on a Bus   611
Two geese strut through the balustrade, where rust   95
Two years before an endless requiem.   216

Unclaimed   152
Uncomprehending day,   113

Voices   221
Voices in my head,   221

Wait for a further birth.   563
Waiting   136
Wake free from fear, half-free of sorrow.   203
Wake up! The smudge of dawn   40
Wake up, therefore, for me.   40
Walk   170
Was daylight still.   36
Watch out for water-dragons there.   288, 510
Water   568
We are the last generations. Surdas, Bach,   48
We are the last generations; Surdas, Bach,   636